D0831897

Topographies

Stephen Benz

Also by Stephen Benz

Guatemalan Journey
Green Dreams

Topographies

Stephen Benz

Etruscan Press

© 2018 by Stephen Benz
All rights reserved. Except for brief quotations in critical articles or reviews, no part of this book may be reproduced in any manner without prior written permission from the publisher:

Etruscan Press
Wilkes University
84 West South Street
Wilkes-Barre, PA 18766
(570) 408-4546

 Wilkes University

www.etruscanpress.org

Published 2019 by Etruscan Press
Printed in the United States of America
Cover design by Laurie Powers
Cover photo by James Going
Interior design and typesetting by Aaron Petrovich
The text of this book is set in Californian FB Text.

First Edition

17 18 19 20 5 4 3 2 1

Library of Congress Cataloging-in-Publication Data

Names: Benz, Stephen Connely, 1958- author.
Title: Topographies / Stephen Benz.
Description: First edition. | Wilkes-Barre, PA : Etruscan Press, 2018.
Identifiers: LCCN 2018005855 | ISBN 9780998750897
Subjects: LCSH: Benz, Stephen Connely, 1958---Travel. | Voyages and travels.
Classification: LCC G226.B46 A3 2018 | DDC 910.4--dc23
LC record available at https://lccn.loc.gov/2018005855

Please turn to the back of this book for a list of the sustaining funders of Etruscan Press.

This book is printed on recycled, acid-free paper.

To Autumn, Baylee, and Zoe:
May your journeys be full of wonder.

It behooves a man who wants to see wonders sometimes to go out of his way.
—Sir John Mandeville

We shall not cease from exploration
And the end of all our exploring
Will be to arrive where we started
And know the place for the first time.
—T. S. Eliot

Topographies

My thanks to the editors of the publications in which these essays first appeared, sometimes in different versions and with different titles:

Miami Herald Tropic Magazine: "A Lost Grave in the Everglades," "Open House at Trinity Site," "In Search of San Juan Hill," "Driving Lessons," "The Longest Road"
Briar Cliff Review: "Ash Hollow, Nebraska"
River Teeth: "A Grave on the High Plains"
South Florida Sun-Sentinel: "Ill-Fated"
Permafrost and Poydras Review: portions of "Forever West"
cream city review: "Unapproachable Evanston"
Superstition Review: "Liminal Wendover"
JMWW: "Land of the Lost"
Baltimore Review: "A Bolero in Havana"
Washington Post: "Our Mailman in Havana"
Borderlands: Texas Poetry Review: "Poetry in a Dangerous Time"

"The Paradox of Diego de Landa" originally appeared in Green Dreams (Lonely Planet)

I would also like to express my gratitude to my family, especially my parents, my brothers, my sister, and my children. They have been a source of inspiration and support.

My deepest gratitude and love goes to Jennifer Kepesh, who has shared in my travels and who every day helps me to find new reasons to love the world.

Topographies

Stephen Benz

Prelude: The Road Ahead

Highway signs and historical markers;
coyotes, salt flats, casinos, a gritty bazaar;
road songs and marketing slogans;
boleros and jukebox ballads;
empty churches, tenement flats,
blighted woods, a shuttered joss house;
Bible verses taken out of context;
Mayan codices in flames;
billboards aglow; oil jacks and dust devils;
baseball in the desert night; hardcore honky-tonk;
black ice in Texas, cactus blooms in Utah,
sagebrush as far as the eye can see;
Roosevelt Boulevard, Route 66, the Oregon Trail,
Donner Pass, Desolation Row;
train tracks crossing hinterlands;
a skiff drifting over a poisoned bay;
a convoy of westbound tractor-trailers;
diners in Casper, Grand Island, Elko, Socorro;
document checks and shakedowns;
suspicion of the stranger; atomic souvenirs;
senseless slaughter; the onset of winter storms;
no services next 100 miles;

Jack Kerouac in a truck stop reciting Thoreau;
two drunk women singing Landslide;
Stalin's ghost and gun smoke; dry lightning
and sandstorms; Rough Riders; an antelope grazing
at the corner of Rattlesnake and Uranium;
a jackalope on a plinth; "Today's top hits" fading
into "Golden Oldies 99;" tropical downpours;
cold mists; train whistles and typewriter clicks;
tumbleweeds and radioactive fallout;
Lenin, Emerson, Baudrillard, Wendover Will,
buffalo soldiers; the last passenger pigeon;
book-burning and bribery; smuggling and cannibalism;
terrorist hospitality; POWs painting rodeo scenes,
poets reciting on buses, peacekeepers pointing
Kalashnikovs; radio towers and royal palms,
western kitsch and neon lights; keno in the Rainforest;
Pushkin's verses, Parkman's laments,
Oppenheimer's musings; Dylan on the tape deck;
ghost towns and campgrounds and grain elevators;
filling stations and trading posts; border crossings,
pogroms, coal cars, dime westerns, freeway mirages,
false dawns; roadblocks, dead ends; columbine;
petrichor; a fragment of Jumbo's superstructure;
Air Moldova, Ferrocarriles de Cuba,
Kampgrounds of America, Greyhound buses;
patriotic bumper stickers, bogus business cards,
misleading maps, last-chance gas;
John Donne and the Bhagavad Gita,
prophecies of holocaust, doomsday scenarios;

rattle and hum, the king of the road,
a drifter's escape, the ghost of Tom Joad;
good roads, bad roads, hot winds, cold winds,
miles and miles and miles, no end in sight.

I

Reading the American Landscape

*. . . but I preferred reading the American landscape
as we went along. Every bump,
rise, and stretch in it mystified my longing.*

—Jack Kerouac, *On the Road*

A Lost Grave in the Everglades

To the starboard, Bradley Key hides behind its perimeter mangroves. This morning, the tangled growth of the key gives sanctuary to a tricolored heron, two great egrets, a flock of ibis, and a perched anhinga, its wings outspread to take in the breeze. Straight ahead, the placid waters of Florida Bay stretch to the Gulf of Mexico and Cape Sable, the very southern edge of the mainland, barely discernible in the tropical haze.

On this hot, humid morning we are paddling our canoe across the bay in pursuit of a skiff that once drifted over these waters, one hundred years before us.

To us—city dwellers—it's a beautiful morning on the bay. We don't notice the poisons leaking into these waters. We can't see the increased salinity destroying the fragile habitat, the mercury runoff killing fisheries. For the moment, the panorama before us looks too serene, too idyllic for us to worry about its impending destruction. Fish occasionally jump around the canoe. A few birds cruise overhead. The mangrove shore seems dense and unperturbed. For the sake of enjoying this apparent tranquility, we are willing to ignore the warning signs.

A century ago, that lone skiff we're chasing crossed cleaner waters. As it drifted slowly with the tide from the Ospreys toward Cape Sable, the skiff was probably surrounded by hundreds of hopping mullet and sea bass. Back then, the transparent sea sparkled, the bay bottom clearly visible from the boat, its marl bed magnified and shimmering. In contrast, the bay water today, though no more than three feet deep, is murky and brown, an opaque soup.

But even as the skiff drifted toward the cape over comparatively pristine waters, threats to the bay's environment had already appeared on the horizon, like a dark thunderhead in monsoon season. It was the height of the age of extinction, when humans believed that the biblical injunction granting "dominion over the earth" licensed them to exploit and, if they so desired, to extirpate species, no matter how wanton the motive.

Already hundreds of species had vanished as humans ventured into new territory and drove off the inhabitants. Some of the extinctions and near-extinctions were so spectacular they stunned the imagination. In North America alone, within the span of two generations—a mere fifty years—the continent's most populous mammal, the bison, had dwindled from a population of millions to a few thousand. The continent's most populous bird, the passenger pigeon, which not even one hundred years before had numbered in the *billions*, was reduced to a solitary caged wretch fading away in a Cincinnati zoo.

The same Buffalo Bill mentality that produced these ecological catastrophes was responsible for setting adrift the ghost skiff we are following across the now-polluted bay toward Cape Sable. On that hot July day in 1905, all nature seemed to shirk from the boat as it languished unmanned on the water, pulled toward shore by the tide, its dirty sail sagging in the still air. With the heat of the day, fish stopped jumping and sought the shady waters around mangrove roots. Birds retired to rookeries hidden in cypress swamps. On the mainland, panthers and deer withdrew to dense hardwood hammocks. Only a flock of turkey vultures kept active, circling overhead, studying the skiff. It was July 8, 1905, and the vultures were circling because in the boat's bilge water lay a corpse.

Some of the few residents of the coast—tomato farmers, fishermen, charcoal makers—looked up that day and saw the vultures. Curious, they rowed along the shore, found the skiff, now entangled in mangroves, and discovered the body lying in the hull. They knew the dead man—a resident of Flamingo named Guy Bradley. When they hauled him from the boat, they saw that he had been shot in the chest.

At the moment that Bradley's boat drifted ashore near Cape Sable, a fashionable woman was striding down Fifth Avenue in New York City wearing a white French straw hat with pink roses circling the brim and more than twenty aigrette plumes jutting erect from the back. By 1905, bird plumes had been a millinery fashion for more than thirty years, and during the first years of the new century, styles had become particularly extravagant. Indeed, on the day of Guy Bradley's murder, an entire aviary bobbed piecemeal down the sidewalks of Manhattan on women's heads—plumes, wings, tails, even whole stuffed specimens pinned to brims and crowns. In department store displays, window shoppers could gaze on the latest French import, a coral satin hat with green weeping "ospreys"—the industry's generic term for plumes from rare species.

The trend began in the 1870s, when stylish bonnets were trimmed with flowers, ribbons, lace, and bird plumes. At first, milliners used plumes readily available, such as peacock and pheasant. In the 1880s, however, bonnets fell out of favor, replaced by small felt or straw hats whose rolled brims could support long curled plumes. The most popular plumes, or "aigrettes," came from various species of wading birds, the most prized being "little snowies"—the curved, lacelike back plumes taken from the snowy egret. These plumes were softer, thicker, and fluffier than the plumes of other egrets and herons. This loveliest of aigrettes was considered de rigueur not only for hats but for evening coiffure as well.

In the 1880s, trimmings became still more intricate. Straining to produce something exotic, milliners added other bird parts to their creations. Almost every hat made had some part of a bird attached to it. At first wings were popular, then a bird's head or two. Eventually, whole birds were affixed to sealskin and velvet toques. A leading fashion magazine of the period, in announcing the coming fall fashions, named the birds to use: "The blackbird with pointed wing and tail feathers; hummingbirds in clusters of three and four; sea gulls of natural color and dwarfed copies of these." Such decorations were to be "placed on the back or brim of the hat with wings and tail pointing toward the front or back."

Then fashions became even more bizarre. By the middle of the 1880s, hats became wide in the brim and women walked around with stuffed birds, stuffed mice, even stuffed reptiles on their heads. A sophisticated milliner added real moss, twigs, leaves, and insects to the display. Any given woman on the street looked as if she had pilfered a diorama from the local museum of natural history.

Throughout the 1880s and 1890s, hats gained in height and width, their wide swooping brims and large crowns becoming ever more awkward, their trimmings ever more flamboyant. Huge fanciful chapeaux called "Gainsboroughs" became all the rage. The towering forms, trimmed with flowers, lace, ribbons, and feathers—always feathers—transformed a woman of modest height into a veritable giantess.

As a result of these trends, a new occupation emerged at the end of the century: a "trimmer" would hold lace, flowers, feathers, or wings in different places on a hat frame while the purchaser sat before a mirror approving or disapproving of the arrangement. A good trimmer knew that her client could never go wrong with a pretty display of cross aigrettes. Throughout all the vagaries, the little snowy plume remained the height of fashion; its pale opalescent white seemed the very symbol of purity.

But to obtain their precious plumes, women of fashion depended on a breed of men whose presence they would never have tolerated in polite society: the plume hunters— Florida crackers and Seminole Indians—who tramped through the trackless, mosquito-infested Everglades searching for the rookeries of herons and egrets. The best feathers were the nuptial plumes, grown in breeding season and displayed in courtship or in nest-side ceremonies when the males exchanged places with their mates over the eggs. These nuptial plumes descended from the shoulders to well beyond the end of the tail—startlingly beautiful when spread like a fan. The only way to obtain these plumes was to track down the nests deep in the Everglades, something only the hardiest backwoodsman could do.

The hunters did not concern themselves with beauty. To them, the plumes represented a fortune: thirty-eight dollars an ounce was the prevailing price in 1895, twice the value of gold. To get at this bonanza, the plume hunters were none too subtle in their methods. Egrets proved fairly easy to kill. They stayed at their nests and continued to provide for their young even when faced with obvious dangers. Big time plume dealers sent teams of forty to sixty hunters into the Everglades and the Ten Thousand Islands. Upon discovering a rookery, the plume hunters let loose a barrage. They would bring down hundreds of birds at once with their favorite weapon, the Flobert rifle.

To gather the plumes, they slit the skin off the birds' backs with a knife and peeled the feathers from the back and tail. Eyewitnesses claimed to have seen wounded birds skinned alive then tossed aside to die. Some hunters employed a ruse: they would tie a wounded bird to a plank, then prop it up in a marsh to attract the attention of other birds flying by. The decoys were left exposed until they died or were devoured by red ants.

* * *

Such a brutal occupation in such a remote wilderness attracted unusual characters. One of the swampland's eccentric residents, an old Frenchman named Alfred Lechevalier, traveled throughout the Ten Thousand Islands in search of the highest quality plumes. He had a side interest as well—the discovery of new specimens for science. More methodical than most hunters, the old Frenchman stripped the whole skin from a bird's body out to the first joint of the wing, then rubbed the skin with cornmeal and stretched it on small sticks to dry.

Lechevalier hired assistants to help him in his quest for perfect plumes. One of his assistants was a young man named Guy Bradley, whose skillful shooting and backwoods acumen made him a particularly proficient huntsman. Born in 1870, Bradley grew up in South Florida, mostly in Flamingo, a fishing village on Florida Bay. His father had been a postmaster on the east coast, renowned among residents as the man who would walk his route barefoot all the way from Lake Worth to Miami, a trek of some sixty miles. When Henry Flagler wanted to extend his railroad south to Cape Sable (he hoped to build a bridge from the cape to Key West), the elder Bradley hired on as a land agent and in exchange received free land in Flamingo. Deterred by marsh, muck, sawgrass, scrub palmetto, mudflats, lagoons, and several million mosquitoes, Flagler abandoned his project (not even the surveyors could penetrate the land; they sent Flagler a map with the vast area of the Everglades marked simply "Dangerous"). But the Bradleys stayed on in the hardscrabble village with its one dirt road, its rotting docks, and its spartan shacks. Young Guy Bradley worked on local tomato plantations and hunted plumes for Lechevalier.

Despite his knack for obtaining feathers, Bradley didn't much enjoy the work. He could see that the great flocks were disappearing. And he knew why: when he traveled up the coast to the newly incorporated town of Miami, he could see in the windows of Mr. Burdine's department store the *nature morte* hats from New York decorated with plumes and wings. Bradley realized that Florida had turned into a killing field for wading birds. During the 1870s and 1880s, as Bradley grew to manhood, Florida's abundant bird life had substantially diminished. Plumes were shipped north by the bale. In 1892, one agent alone shipped 130,000 dead birds from Florida. Ten years later, the count was 192,000.

Because the birds were hunted in nesting season, the toll was especially harsh. With the parents dead, eggs were left unprotected in the nest, easy prey for predators. Newly hatched birds starved to death. Entire rookeries were wiped out inside of five seasons. Visiting ornithologists, such as Princeton's W. E. D. Scott, were shocked by the sudden scarcity of birds that had once been too numerous to count. As a consequence, egret plumes became still more valuable, and the hunters became still more determined to shoot down every last bird.

During the years that Bradley tramped through the Everglades, growing ever more concerned about the vanishing bird life, small but increasingly vocal groups began to call for the protection of species headed for extinction. The movement started with the formation of the American Ornithologists Union (AOU) in 1883 at the American Museum of Natural History in New York. Among the AOU's first actions was a call for restraints on the unrestricted slaughter of birds. Three years later, the AOU established a Committee on the Protection of North American Birds. Estimating that five million North American birds were killed each year for fashion, the committee wrote a "model law" in the hopes that each state would use it as the basis for legislation protecting non-game birds and their eggs. That same year, George Grinnell, editor of *Forest and Stream*, formed the first Audubon Society. In an editorial announcing the new organization, Grinnell decried "the wearing of feathers as ornaments or trimming for dress." From the start, the killing of birds for fashion was the new conservation society's main cause. The first issue of *Audubon Magazine* (1887) contained a scathing attack on any woman who would wear "a charnel house of beaks and claws and bones and feathers and glass eyes upon her fatuous head."

Soon, however, Grinnell grew discouraged with the public's apathy. Abandoning the cause, he lamented, "Fashion decrees feathers; and feathers it is." Then in 1896, a high-society matron, Harriet Hemenway, resurrected the society. The new by-laws explained the society's goal: "to discourage the buying and wearing, for ornamental purposes, of the feathers of any wild birds."

This time the cause proved somewhat more popular, and by 1898 Audubon societies in fourteen states were organized to lobby for passage of the AOU's model law in their respective states. On the national level, Congress passed the Lacey Act in 1900, prohibiting the sale and shipment of millinery plumes. Under the Lacey Act, authorities seized huge quantities of plumes. One raid on a Baltimore warehouse yielded 26,000 bird skins. But the Lacey Act could not be applied to shipments from states that had no protective laws, and by 1900 the most important state, Florida, had yet to pass one.

The Florida legislature did finally pass such a law in 1901. Enacting a law was one thing; enforcing it was another. Because the legislature provided no means or money for the law's enforcement, the slaughter of birds continued unabated. In New York, William Dutcher, the president of the National Audubon Society, secured funds to support wardens in various trouble spots around the country. Finding a warden for South Florida was his top priority. Kirk Monroe, a resident of Miami active in Audubon causes, wrote to Dutcher recommending young Guy Bradley as "a strong fearless man fully alive to the value of bird protection." In May 1902, Bradley was hired as the Monroe County Game Warden for a monthly stipend of thirty-five dollars, paid by the Audubon Society.

Bradley was charged with protecting all birds in a vast region from the Keys to the Lee County line. Despite the enormity of the task, he undertook it with diligence and energy. He patrolled the waters of Florida Bay and the Everglades in his skiff, sometimes rowing, sometimes setting sail. He put up signs warning hunters of arrest, then tracked down violators and arrested those he caught in the act. It took courage and aplomb to arrest a gang of armed men. His success depended on a reputation for toughness and a deadly aim—the best shot in the Everglades, people said.

He couldn't patrol everywhere at once, however, so he resorted to tricks, such as moving the hunters' signs and altering their channel markers to lead them off course in the mangrove maze. Bradley also gathered information on dealers. He sent dummy letters to New York, posing as a hunter interested in bounty prices. His investigations provided evidence for punishing firms engaged in the purchase of illegal plumes.

But he could only do so much. Despite a network of spies hired to help him keep track of hunters, the killing went on. The Cuthbert Lake rookery, one of the last great breeding grounds, was discovered and shot out in 1904. "You could've walked right around the rookery on those birds' bodies— between four and five hundred of them," Bradley told the Audubon's secretary. He also let his employers know that his life was in danger.

Bradley had plenty of enemies. One in particular was a hunter named Walter Smith. Jealous that Bradley had gotten the warden's job over him and angry that Bradley had once arrested him, Smith told people in Key West and Flamingo that the warden was a marked man if he ever tried to assert his authority again.

On Saturday, July 8, 1905, Bradley saw a sail near the Oyster Keys. It was Smith and his sons, sailing past in plain view, a deliberate dare. Soon the hunters' guns sounded, and Bradley pushed his boat into the water. Smith could see him coming from two miles off. He had time to get away, but he waited. By the time Bradley came up, Smith's boys were bringing bird skins out to the boat. Minutes later, Bradley was dead in his skiff, and Smith set sail for Key West.

Smith maintained that Bradley fired first. He pointed to a bullet hole in his mast, and the only witnesses—Smith's sons—backed up his story. The Audubon Society paid for investigators to assist the prosecution. They demonstrated that Bradley's .32-caliber nickel-plated pistol had no powder marks, and that the cylinder was not under the hammer as it normally would be after firing. But there were no witnesses, and the grand jury refused to indict. Flamingo residents didn't need witnesses to find holes in Smith's story. They knew Guy Bradley, the best shot in Monroe County. If he had fired first, he sure as hell wouldn't have missed. They burned Smith's house to the ground.

When the story broke about the warden's death, it had an immediate impact on the nation's conscience. Donations to the Audubon Society increased. Some women's clubs forswore plumes and began calling the aigrette "the white badge of cruelty." A young family man was dead, thundered *Bird-Lore Magazine*, "and for what? That a few more plume birds might be secured to adorn heartless women's bonnets. Heretofore the price has been the life of the birds, now is added human blood." The cause had its martyr.

Bradley's name was invoked in the fight for even stricter laws. Sentiment for such laws was building, but not without a backlash. In Florida, the hired hunters kept at it, and in

1908 another warden, Columbus MacLeod, was killed in Charlotte Harbor. In New York, the millinery industry fought the laws to the end, calling them "most iniquitous and childish." The biggest battle occurred in the New York State Assembly. A law banning plume importation in New York would deal a serious blow to the traffic in feathers. Challenging the proposed law, the milliners first argued that egrets were not killed, that the plumes were simply gathered off the ground. But anyone could see the bales of dead birds unloaded at the docks in New York City. Next, the milliners argued that the herons and egrets were actually nasty birds, injurious to fish and natural resources, and undeserving of conservation. Finally, they tried a line that anti-conservationists have used ever since: twenty thousand workers would be thrown out of employment, they claimed, and investments of seventeen million dollars lost. But the Audubon Society made the stronger case, aided in part by the eloquence of a young state senator, Franklin Roosevelt. The New York Plumage Bill passed in 1910.

Still, fashions hadn't changed and milliners found ways to subvert the laws. The plume hunters in Florida now stuffed mattresses with feathers and smuggled them to Havana. The plumes traveled from there to Paris or London and then to New York. The milliners claimed the feathers were foreign and therefore exempt.

Finally, in 1913 a bill was introduced in Congress to ban the importation of plumes altogether. Again, the fight was bitter. James Reed of Missouri spoke for the exasperated milliners and anti-conservationists: "I really want to know why there should be any sympathy about a long-legged, long-necked bird that lives in swamps. Let humanity utilize this bird for the only purpose that evidently the Lord made it for, namely so that we could get aigrettes for the bonnets of our beautiful ladies."

But the Audubon Society, anticipating lobbying practices of later generations, turned to a new technology to persuade Congress. They showed a motion picture depicting a plume hunters' raid on a rookery. The graphic images of slaughter and skinning convinced Congress that egrets were indeed "bonnet martyrs." The bill passed. It had taken eight years, but at last Bradley's death meant something.

The snowy egrets reached their low point around 1910 when Audubon expeditions found only one remaining rookery in Florida and only 250 snowy egrets in the four southern states where breeding had been most common. In the decades to come, the population rebounded and the snowy egret was no longer endangered. Some argue that only a change in fashion in the 1920s saved the egret, that environmental legislation by itself could not have accomplished much. But it's ultimately a moot point: the legislation, however hollow, required enforcement, which led to Guy Bradley's death. That death led to more legislation, which in turn forced milliners to find new fashions and prompted people to rethink their fascination with feathers. Renowned naturalist Archie Carr put it best: "The spirit that accomplished that unprecedented feat was of unreckoned significance in the evolution of human concern for natural species." Guy Bradley, dead in his lonely grave on Cape Sable, had lived an obscure life. In death, he changed the world.

It is toward the cape and Bradley's grave that we have been headed, following in the wake of the warden's ghost skiff. Eight miles of paddling have brought us to a gritty beach just east of the cape. We jump ashore and walk along a ridge of broken bleached-white shells overlooking the sea. Somewhere along this beach, Bradley rests in his grave. The exact location of the gravesite is now uncertain. To be precise, the grave has been abandoned.

After Bradley's death, the Florida Audubon Society donated a gravestone with a plaque that read, "Guy M. Bradley, FAITHFUL UNTO DEATH, As Game Warden Of Monroe County He Gave His Life For The Cause To Which He Was Pledged." Over the years, the shifting sands of windy Cape Sable blew across the stone. Sometimes dunes covered it completely, and it would disappear until some caretaker came along to search for it and dig it out. Tropical storms sometimes altered the beach, and the grave ended up lost for long periods of time. After the creation of Everglades National Park, the Park Service decided to remove the plaque and display it in the Flamingo Visitors Center. The grave itself was abandoned to the blowing dunes. With some luck, park rangers told us, we might stumble across it.

But it is soon apparent we'll have no such luck. Beyond the shell ridge, the dunes are covered with tall weeds and entangled with creeping vines. We probe a few mounds and turn out only angry ant colonies. Hordes of mosquitoes make our time on shore a miserable experience. We stand by the canoe, pretending to feel in the wind that blows over us the spirit of the man whose bones are buried somewhere nearby. We'd like to say we sense his presence here. But it's no use. Something's wrong, and it's not just the vicious mosquitoes and horseflies (Bradley himself called them Cape Sable's sharpshooters). We look around and see that this isolated beach is dirty with litter. Styrofoam, plastic, aluminum—the jetsam of weekend boaters washed ashore. A container of motor oil turns in the surf, rainbow swirls oozing from its open top. We find a beer can with an old style pop-top; it must have been bobbing in these waters twenty years or more. We came here for inspiration. We leave depressed.

But just offshore, we stop paddling to watch a flock of white birds approach from the inland marshes. It would be fitting, we think, to see some snowy egrets fly over Bradley's grave, to see the bird with the all-white plumage, black legs, and startling yellow feet people have long likened to golden slippers. "Its delicate, ethereal quality," the Audubon guide says, "makes it unquestionably the most beautiful of our herons." It was this quality that John James Audubon himself captured in his breathtaking painting of the bird. But Audubon must have seen that the egret's delicate beauty would be its downfall. Though he painted in the 1850s, decades before the slaughter, Audubon hinted at things to come. We have to look closely to see it, there, in the lower right corner of Audubon's painting: the barely discernible figure of a hunter, lurking, approaching, gun at the ready.

The flock glides overhead: white ibises. During the canoe trip, we've also seen herons, pelicans, ospreys, even a bald eagle. But no snowy egrets. After 1910, they made a strong recovery, their numbers increasing until the 1950s. Then the population leveled off. Then it began to decline again—the result, environmentalists have speculated, of South Florida's profligate water management, urban expansion into the once pristine Everglades, and toxic runoff infiltrating the habitat.

The snowy egret is not endangered. Not yet. But its breeding grounds are threatened, and the ultimate devastation of its habitat may kill off the beautiful bird, once and for all. If so, Guy Bradley's act of sacrifice will be as isolated and forgotten as his grave.

Ash Hollow, Nebraska

The sun was just rising when I started across the ridge between the forks of the Platte, northbound on a county road for Ash Hollow State Park. Over the years, I have visited all of the highlights on the old Oregon Trail—the landmarks, the forts, the natural wonders. Of these sites, I find Ash Hollow one of the most intriguing, in part because it is relatively unknown, and in part because Ash Hollow represents the entire Oregon Trail experience condensed in one place.

In the 1840s, this twenty-mile stretch of Nebraska was a desolate, empty terrain that actually frightened some westbound emigrants. What little grass they found their cattle wouldn't eat. Water was scarce and undrinkable. They called this land and the vast surrounding region the Great American Desert. Those who weren't frightened by it were, at the least, dismayed. Francis Parkman noted that this desert "had not one picturesque or beautiful feature; nor had it any of the features of grandeur, other than its vast extent, its solitude, and its wildness." The ridge dividing the river—sandy, windy, and spotted with cacti—suggested to some of the pioneers "the roughest country the mind can conceive of," a country completely alien to them. They were approaching the true West.

When I crossed it 150 years later, the ridge was still striking for its vast extent and its solitude, but it was no longer wild. Over the years, irrigation had transformed the desert into farmland and the land was now fertile and green. Every so often I passed a house, its yard cluttered with threshing and plowing equipment. The bright sun, already hot, reflected off silver Quonset huts and storage bins. The transformation of this once desolate wasteland into a fertile and productive region still resonates as one of the West's most compelling parables, the kind Americans like to tell themselves as a reminder of the wonders they have worked on this once "useless land."

The county road brought me to Route 26, a highway angling northwest. Immediately the terrain became more rugged. Boulders jutted from the sandy soil. Crevasses and defiles fell away from the highway. The pioneers' fear of this landscape and the dislocation they felt when they encountered it epitomizes the paradox of the West. The idea of wide open space and ample acres for all lured the Americans westward, and yet these same open spaces disheartened many of them when they at last reached them. Battling wind and sand, discarding articles that weighed down their wagons, they hurried as best they could over places like this ridge, determined to get across and leave it forever behind them.

This first encounter with a quintessential western landscape gave them some idea of the rigors to come. Wagon wheels sank into deep sand and slowed their progress to a few miles a day. Grass and water were scarce, trees nonexistent.

Many journal writers among the pioneers marveled at this utter lack of trees—not a single one for hundreds of miles. Realizing this barren, desolate ridge was but the first of what would prove to be increasingly difficult passages, they quailed at the thought of the arduous journey ahead. They were still some two thousand miles from the west coast.

Pulling wagons over boulders and through the sand of this ridge, skirting the menacing crevasses, the pioneers got a glimpse of what those two thousand miles held in store for them. But the real lesson came when they reached the northern rim of the ridge and had to descend to the valley of the North Platte. On the main trail, this descent occurred at a place now called Windlass Hill, though the pioneers did not know it by that name. For them, it was the first real declivity they had encountered in their wagons; in effect, this was their first lesson in mountain driving.

Today, the hill doesn't seem all that remarkable. Route 26 drops down from the ridge in a series of smooth curves. In a matter of seconds, the highway brings you to the valley with hardly the need to brake. Unless you're looking for it, Windlass Hill seems inconsequential. But for the pioneers, the hill caused nightmares. Most had never seen a hill so steep, and none had taken a wagon down such a severe drop-off—about 800 feet of trail fell 235 feet from the brow of the hill to Ash Hollow below. To the journal writers among the emigrants, the view from atop this hill inspired exaggeration. Fanny Kelly wrote, "the eye is lost in space as it endeavors to penetrate its depths." Another traveler declared that "the road hangs a little past the perpendicular." Such hyperbole indicates the pioneers' inexperience with serious hills. To anyone reaching Ash Hollow from the west, this hill would be unremarkable, a mere bump compared to the soaring peaks and abrupt plunges of the western ranges. But in the mid-1800s, this first glimpse of mountain terrain took away the breath of westbound travelers.

Even a skilled geographical observer was prone to marvel at the sight from atop Windlass Hill. One of the best at describing the American West was Captain Howard Stansbury, whose 1849 exploratory journey for the Corps of Topographical Engineers is chronicled in *An Exploration and Survey of the Valley of the Great Salt Lake of Utah Including a Reconnaissance of a New Route Through the Rocky Mountains*. Stansbury's descriptions, like his titles, were long and thorough. A meticulous observer, Captain Stansbury carefully translated the West's most magnificent and awesome terrains into precise and exacting prose. The hill above Ash Hollow, for example, prompted this extended description:

> Before and below us was the North Fork of the Nebraska [Platte], winding its way through broken hills and green meadows; behind us the undulating prairie rising gently from the South Fork, over which we had just passed; on our right, the gradual convergence of the two valleys was distinctly perceptible, while immediately at our feet were the heads of Ash Creek, which fell off suddenly into deep precipitous chasms on either side, leaving only a high narrow ridge or backbone, which gradually

descended, until, towards its western termination, it fell off precipitately into the bottom of the creek . . . The descent is abrupt and precipitous. Immediately at your feet is the principal ravine, with sides four or five hundred feet in depth, clothed with cedar: into this numerous other ravines run, meeting it at different angles and so completely cutting up the earth that scarcely a foot of level ground could be seen. The whole surface consisted of merely narrow ridges, dividing the ravines from each other, and running up to so sharp a crest that it would be difficult for anything but a mountain goat to traverse their summits with impunity.

To the latter-day passer-by, speeding down from the ridge on the smooth highway, all this talk of precipitous chasms may seem overblown. But driving a station wagon is not the same as driving a covered wagon. To get down off of Windlass Hill, the pioneers had to lock wagon wheels, and in some cases lower the wagon by rope while all the men and teams of oxen held on at the top. In such circumstances, accidents occurred. Oxen slid and fell. Runaway wagons careened and crashed. Carts overturned and spilled out a family's belongings and pitched anyone foolish enough to be riding in the wagon headlong down the slope. In some cases, people attempting to keep control of beasts fell beneath the hooves. On one occasion, a skidding wagon wheel crushed a boy's head. Charles Scott, an emigrant of 1857, described his experience with the descent in his journal:

. . . a general runaway and smash up at Ash Hollow, a terrific scene. Horses dashing furiously with the pieces down hill and precipices, the noise, dust and confusion, the men shouting, halloing, and women screaming, made an impression on my memory, never to be effaced; 2 horses were killed and 7 disabled and unfit for service, in all about $25,000 damage done.

Just after the highway descended from ridge to valley, I came across a small gravel turnout that served as the parking lot for the Windlass Hill section of Ash Hollow State Historical Park. A marker briefly informed visitors of the place's historical significance. To one side of the empty lot stood a reconstructed sod house. An occasional truck churned past on the highway. It was still early morning, and I had the place to myself.

An asphalted trail led out of the parking lot and wound up the ridge to the peak of Windlass Hill. At the trailhead, a replica of a covered wagon's canvass top sheltered a couple of interpretive plaques and a horde of mosquitoes. Beyond the shelter, a few small pines, Christmas-tree size, dotted the landscape along with clumps of spiky yucca. A small sign with gold letters read "Oregon-California Trail."

Wagon ruts were still visible in the form of deep scars on the face of the hill. A century and a half of erosion from rain and snowmelt had deepened the ruts into gullies. Climbing the hill and looking straight down on the drop from up top, I had a better sense of what the pioneers confronted. After a long, hard, dry drive over the ridge, this descent was usually the last stretch for the day, with water and grass waiting below in the hollow. There it was, down below, tantalizingly close; but the huge obstacle of the hill kept it out of easy reach. Many pioneers reached this point at nightfall and had to negotiate the descent in darkness before they could make camp. I could see why those with no experience driving down hills would have dreaded the ordeal. But then exhaustion and fear are two of the exhilarations the traveler habitually seeks; maybe a few of the pioneers, thrilled to be experiencing the romance of a westward journey, got a rush from the challenge of the hill. Scott's account of the "runaway and smash up" he witnessed contains a hint of such a rush.

To the north, I could make out the winding line of the North Platte's bottomland and the patchwork of farms that now occupied it. To the west, the rolling hills ran on and on, too rocky and wrinkled for agriculture. The land bore no sign of human improvement save for a receding column of telephone poles. It was a cloudless morning, the sky deep blue directly overhead. Toward the horizons, however, a heavy agricultural haze obscured the view. High above, a couple of hawks circled on the constant winds. Jet contrails split the sky into quadrants. On this June day the wind was warm and pleasant, but that was not necessarily the norm in Nebraska at this time of year. Quite often, the pioneers experienced cool and even freezing temperatures at Ash Hollow. During the first week of June in 1846, about the time Francis Parkman and the Donner Party passed by, the overnight temperature dipped to freezing, and frost covered the campsites at dawn.

After passing the base of Windlass Hill, Route 26 winds into Ash Hollow itself, a three-mile long canyon cut through the hills by a creek, one of the Platte's tributaries (today, however, the creek's channel, altered by the construction of Route 26, no longer traverses the canyon in the same way that it did when the pioneers traveled through). The east side of the hollow is now a state park with a small museum interpreting local history and the Oregon Trail experience. A trail behind the museum leads to a cave where archaeologists have excavated a five-thousand-year-old campsite. Below the cave, at the foot of the hollow's limestone cliffs, a grassy lot surrounds a small unassuming pond. It doesn't look like much now, but to the pioneers this pond and its surrounding trees provided great relief. Here they found good water and shade after hundreds of miles on the treeless prairie with only brackish waters to slake their thirst. The pond's water was, according to Stansbury, "delightfully cold and refreshing . . . the best that has been met with since leaving the Missouri." For this reason, Ash Hollow developed a reputation as one of the better stops on the trail and proved, as one immigrant put it, "a delightful change from the monotony of the valley." Knowing that good water was available, the travelers looked forward to arriving at this oasis in the Great American Desert.

When I arrived there, the oasis was loud with the noise of a lawnmower. A young man in a bright red T-shirt that proclaimed the supremacy of the University of Nebraska football team drove the machine around and around the grassy lot. I sat down on the far side of the pond to look over the reading material I had picked up in the park's museum. One brochure promoted that evening's performance of the Ash Hollow Pageant, "a musical and dramatic presentation about the great human migration across the country." It was the winner of the Governor's Tourism Event of the Year, according to the brochure. A chuck wagon supper was scheduled to precede the performance.

The second brochure summarized the hollow's history. I was instructed to regard the blue limestone cliffs, which formed "the unusual geologic strata known as the Ash Hollow formation—a prime example of the Pliocene history of the Central Great Plains just prior to the Ice Age." I was sorry not to have a camera handy; it's not every day you come across a prime example of the Pliocene. Next, the brochure invited me to "visualize the vast encampments of white-masted prairie schooners that crowded this oasis during the height of the westward migration along the Oregon Trail." But I found visualization difficult that morning, what with the roar of the lawnmower and the clouds of mosquitoes that had decided to sample me.

I left the car in the museum parking lot and walked along Route 26 toward the North Platte. In the Ash Hollow cemetery, just off the highway, I came across the gravesite of Rachel Pattison, who had died during the trek west in 1849. A good many gravesites appear along the old trail, though most are now lost. Some thirty thousand people, or ten percent of the migration, died en route. Rachel's grave is particularly poignant because she was only eighteen when she died, a bride of two months. Her husband Nathan made this terse note in his diary: "Rachel taken sick in the morning, died in the night." Her father-in-law noted that she was buried "on the left side of the hollow as you go around the bluff up the river on the second bank." And with no more ceremony, the Pattisons continued their journey westward.

Rachel Pattison probably died of Asiatic cholera. Thousands did, especially during the Platte River stage of the journey, where crowded camps and polluted wells aided the spread of the disease. Asiatic cholera had first appeared in humid river ports such as New Orleans, then traveled up the Mississippi to the Missouri and the jumping-off towns of Independence and St. Joseph. The pioneers then carried it west with them across the plains, polluting the wells as they went. They had no idea what caused the illness. Few emigrants boiled water or washed regularly. Not knowing the cause made a terrible disease all the more frightening. Many journals recount cases similar to Rachel Pattison's: fine in the morning, dead by nightfall. The travelers knew that each day on the trail they ran the risk of being blindsided by death as they struggled along what one diarist called the "sickly course to the promised land." Another wrote, "We are not alone in the calamity, thousands are around us sharing the same fate. The sick and the dying are on the right and the left, in front and in the rear and in our midst."

Some diaries indicate that parties occasionally abandoned a living sufferer by the side of the road, their apparent callousness stemming from not only their dread of disease but also their haste to reach the west coast, especially during the gold rush. If a traveling party felt pangs of conscience, it might detail a couple of men to dig a grave and wait nervously with the victim, their horses saddled and ready to ride off as soon as he was dead and buried. Other entries record more compassionate occurrences, such as parties coming across the abandoned and tending to those who yet lived, burying those who had died. Many orphaned children and widows with children completed the overland journey in the care of altruistic strangers.

All along the Platte, in a landscape devoid of scenery, graves stood out, one of the few roadside distractions in the Great American Desert. Finding little else of note in the scenery, the diarists kept count of graves encountered and recorded the names of the dead wherever a poor cross or marker provided such information.

In some places, the emigrants came across clusters of graves. It could be a gruesome sight, too, because many bodies were buried without coffins, and wolves would dig up and devour the corpses. It was not uncommon to see gnawed limbs or bones scattered around the gravesites, a trail of mayhem following in the prairie schooners' wake. The prospect of a despoiled grave so troubled the parents of dead children, they would empty a metal or rawhide trunk and use it for a coffin.

The experience of death on the trail was intensified at Ash Hollow, where it was set against the backdrop of the place's distinctive beauty. Because the hollow was such a good campsite, wagon trains with sick travelers often laid up there while the victims recovered or succumbed. Thus, this one garden spot in the "Great American Desert" became one of the principal graveyards as well. By 1857, Arthur Menefee reported "a great many graves" in Ash Hollow. Most of these graves have vanished over time. Rachel Pattison's remains to represent all those that are now lost.

Indeed, much of the trail experience was intensified at Ash Hollow. The most significant aspects of the journey and of American expansion into the West were played out here. Illness and death—among the many trials and ordeals that the travelers encountered on their journey west—were part of that experience. The tenacity to overcome such ordeals lies at the heart of what school texts and the popular imagination consider the heroic, heaven-ordained mission of the pioneers.

Less often considered, but of greater long-term significance, perhaps, are the responses the emigrants had to the land in their initial encounter with it. These responses, ranging from admiration to hatred, from desire to fear, became the pattern for subsequent responses, a pattern that has lasted to our own time. The three-mile journey from the top of Windlass Hill to the Ash Hollow springs prompted all these reactions. The hill (and for that matter the hundred miles leading up to it) represented the fearsome land, a dangerous passage that had to be undertaken, a despised obstacle that had to be conquered. The hill was loathed because it threatened to prevent successful passage into the garden, the promised land, here represented by lush Ash

Hollow with its sweetwater spring. As much as the travelers abhorred the hill and feared its dangers, they delighted in the hollow and relished its much touted and much anticipated blessings. It was, in fact, a preview of the promised land of the west coast. In the same way that the successful passage of the dangerous hill brought one the reward of the hollow, successful passage of the dangerous deserts and mountain ranges would bring one the rewards of the bounteous life in California or Oregon. The fleeting exhilaration the emigrants felt as they camped and recuperated for the night in Ash Hollow presaged, they could presume, the joy they would feel when they reached the west coast and the dangerous two thousand miles of overland crossing were behind them.

The journals certainly express this exhilaration. Many travelers felt, as George Gibbs did in 1849, that the "scenery of Ash Hollow was a delightful change from the general monotony of the valley." The good water and abundant grass of the hollow provided much needed relief. The place was a veritable garden with chokecherry, gooseberry, currant, and raspberry bushes, and "an abundance of fragrant wild roses" and other wildflowers. The hollow teemed with life. The travelers saw buffalo, deer, antelope, and wolves. Swallows flitted from the cliffs, and the air was alive with doves, robins, goldfinches, sparrows, and bees. Eagles soared high above. The grasses sheltered crickets, grasshoppers, snakes, lizards, frogs, toads, and beetles. Especially in the early years of the emigration, the pioneers saw Ash Hollow as a wild and beautiful place—beautiful precisely because it was so wild. It luxuriated around them like a Thomas Cole or Frederic Church painting brought to life.

But as more and more emigrants rumbled through the hollow, the landscape began to change. Too many people were passing through it and availing themselves of its resources. Stansbury, following behind the huge 1849 gold rush migration, arrived in Ash Hollow on July 4—just two weeks after Rachel Pattison died—and noted the degradation of the place: "The traces of the great tide of emigration that had preceded us were plainly visible in remains of campfires, in blazed trees covered with innumerable names carved and written on them; but more than all in the total absence of herbage." Scholars estimate that between 1841 and 1860 somewhere between 250,000 and 300,000 people traveled west on the California and Oregon trails, and a great many of them passed through Ash Hollow. The effects of this human migration were in evidence almost from the beginning. Within a decade, the trees that gave Ash Hollow its distinctive beauty and its name had been largely cut down for firewood. In 1854 Sarah Sutton noted in her journal that the ash trees for which Ash Hollow was named had all but vanished. Just two years later, Helen Carpenter apparently saw no such trees and speculated that the place was so named "because the earth and dust look like ashes." In a few short years, in other words, the settlers had stripped the garden spot and left it denuded, the devastation so complete that Thaddeus S. Kenderine's 1858 description makes Ash Hollow sound more hellish than paradisiacal. Kenderine calls it "a valley of desolation . . . a bed of sand and gravel

. . . almost entirely destitute of vegetation and bounded on either side by gloomy, barren hills."

The treatment of Ash Hollow portended the destruction of the West in the decades to come. As more and more emigrants arrived to exploit the land, the environment suffered; resources were depleted and landscapes stripped. The pioneers showed little or no concern for those who might come after or for those who were already there. Rather, the emigrants responded to immediate needs and took what they wanted. The stripping of Ash Hollow was the first of many destructive acts, presaging a ruthless attitude toward nature that would culminate a few decades later with the senseless slaughter of millions of bison. Among westward-bound Americans, a predilection for exploitation of the land prevailed, even when the land was considered lovely and precious—perhaps *especially* when the land was considered lovely and precious.

Carefully observing this destruction, no doubt, were the people who had lived in and around Ash Hollow for generations: the Sioux and the Pawnee. Neither nomadic tribe had established a permanent village in the area, but Ash Hollow had been a favored campsite during buffalo hunts. The Pawnee frequently used the hollow as a wintering place. The Sioux and the Pawnee often clashed, and one of their major battles occurred in Ash Hollow in 1835. A few years later, early emigrants found evidence of the battle as they rode through, one emigrant noting a wasp nest occupying a skull. Some emigrants collected skulls and bones as souvenirs, only to discard them later on when the ruggedness of the trail forced them to lighten loads.

Although pioneers could meet up with American Indians anywhere on the trail, they rarely did, especially in the first five hundred miles of the journey. It was in the vicinity of Ash Hollow that first contact often occurred. In the 1840s, the emigrants might see Sioux war parties headed east for a clash with the Pawnee; or some small bands might ride up hoping to barter with the travelers. Occasionally, horses were stolen. But by and large the pioneers did not have problems with American Indians on this part of the trail—not to the extent anyway that Western movies and TV shows have suggested. Out and out attacks on the wagon trains, with painted braves swooping down from surrounding ridges to terrorize a small group of wagons hastily forming a circle for defense—that hardly ever happened, if at all. (And yet, today, just a few miles from Ash Hollow, tourist outfits offer reenactments of the trail experience for vacationers, including an Indian attack as a featured part of the package.) In fact, the Native Americans—even those of feared hunter-warrior tribes such as the Sioux and the Cheyenne—aided the emigrants more often than they harmed them. At different places along the trail, American Indians provided the emigrants with route information, assisted them in crossing rivers, and taught them about edible plants and roots in what seemed to the emigrants to be barren regions.

Trade was the most common kind of interaction, conducted usually according to the barter principle. The tribes didn't much like specie, but they prized a number of items that the emigrants carried—buttons, beads, mirrors, needles, thread, guns, ammunition, tobacco, coffee, sugar, beans, flour, bread, soap, fishhooks, knives, medicine, and blankets. American Indians especially liked articles of clothing, silk hats and vests being highly valued. In exchange, the pioneers got food to supplement their rather poor diets, including corn, peas, potatoes, pumpkins, onions, wheat, camas roots, and watermelon. The pioneers also traded for native horses, which were considered much superior to horses bred back east, at least for the purpose of plains travel. Likewise, pioneers discovered a great need for durable footwear that could withstand the rigors of a two thousand-mile walk (most emigrants walked alongside wagons rather than riding inside because the roads were just too bumpy). American Indian moccasins served the purpose well. Somewhere along the trail they also found the need to trade for buffalo robes, dressed skins (deer and elk), lariats, and ropes. For the most part, they traded just for what they needed; but now and then a pioneer made a deal to obtain a keepsake or a souvenir—not unlike their latter-day counterparts in station wagons stopping at kitschy trading posts along the tourist trails.

Despite these friendly interactions, conflict and hostility were inevitable as more and more emigrants crossed the plains and the game upon which the tribes depended began to disappear. Many emigrants, uneasy as they started west on the trail, expected the American Indians to cause problems. Suspicious, they brought out their guns whenever Native Americans approached and didn't hesitate to fire if they didn't like the look of things. Sometimes they were spooked by phantoms. In the middle of Kansas, the Graves party—who would later join the Donners—camped for the night on the open prairie. During the night, the guards thought they saw movement in the moonlight. Tyros on the trail, they immediately concluded that "savages" were moving in to massacre them. They raised the alarm, took up arms, and went out to meet the foe—which turned out to be nothing more than five-foot stalks of resin weed waving in the wind. The incident shows just how nervous the emigrants were about expected attacks. Several diarists recount similar episodes—nighttime shots fired in panic at the traveler's own horses and oxen and comrades. It was best to inform the guards before you stepped out into the prairie grass to relieve yourself under the moonlight.

Of course, pioneer nervousness had a lot to do with the baggage whites carried with them on the plains—namely, a callous attitude of cultural and racial superiority evinced by the total disregard that some of them had for the natives they encountered. Within a matter of years, this insensitivity soured the goodwill and mutually beneficial interaction that had marked early relationships. Along the Platte, problems arose when American Indians tried to exact tolls for crossing their lands. Some emigrant trains paid, but others regarded the demand for money as merely a more sophisticated form of begging. What's more, the travelers pointed out to each other, the country they were crossing rightfully belonged to the United States. In their view, the "red men" had no business trying to stop free traffic on the plains. As more and more Americans hit the trail, this belief became more and more entrenched. Wagon train captains, under the advice of guidebooks and mountain men, brandished weapons in response to the natives' demands and drove on, refusing to pay. Simple arrogance predicated on a firm belief in American Indian inferiority prompted whites into this confrontational stance. Farther on, in the Rockies, they would encounter mountain men and Mormons charging tolls for river crossings—much higher tolls than the American Indians were asking—and while the emigrants grumbled and sometimes argued, they generally paid the whites who extorted them. They did not immediately resort to their guns as they so often did in encounters with American Indians. Back on the plains, emboldened by their numbers—in the 1850s thousands were crossing at once in trains two and three miles long—the whites willingly instigated skirmishes with American Indians. In turn, the American Indians retaliated and began to attack the trains, stealing stock and occasionally killing an emigrant who had wandered a bit too far from the wagons. A century later, Hollywood created an entire industry out of exaggerating these incidents. Full-scale attacks never happened, and only a few isolated incidents ever justified use of the word massacre. But reports of massacres kept surfacing. In the 1850s version of Hollywood's fanciful revision of Western history, newspaper accounts frequently reported on attacks out west, reports that became increasingly sensational during the decade. Even though they consistently turned out to be false, newspapers loved to run accounts of brutal massacres—hundreds dying during midnight attacks, women raped by the score. No doubt they sold more newspapers this way. The false stories were forerunners of Hollywood's later mythmaking.

But American Indian retaliations were significant enough in the eyes of the emigrants to warrant military action. Their reports of attacks brought more soldiers out to the forts stationed along the trail. As trail traffic increased, the military responded to stories of American Indian attacks with retaliatory strikes. And before long, the Plains Wars broke out, hastened and made inevitable by the overland emigrations.

Throughout the West, the pattern repeated itself: early on, encounters were amicable enough, but with time relations between whites and natives deteriorated to the point of open warfare. In and around Ash Hollow, it happened the same way. By the mid-1850s, after a decade of trail traffic through Ash Hollow without incident, emigrants began to regard the hollow as a place of prime danger. Diarists called it "a favorite place of the Indians for an attack," noting that it was "an excellent place for ambuscades." The emigrants were wary not because of any precedent; in fact American Indians had never attacked wagon trains in the hollow. Rather, the pioneers feared reprisals for General Harney's 1855 attack on Little Thunder's tribe of the Brule Sioux in what is now called the Battle of Ash Hollow.

The events that culminated in the battle began the summer before and about one hundred miles away (in what is now Wyoming) with an incident known as the Grattan

Massacre. It was August 1854. Around one thousand Sioux had gathered at Bordeaux's Trading Post, eight miles east of Fort Laramie. They were awaiting distribution of their annuity—$50,000 in goods that the US government had promised to the Sioux in the Treaty of 1851. Signed at Fort Laramie, the treaty was supposed to ensure the safety of trail traffic, which had greatly increased since the discovery of gold in California. In 1854, delivery of the annuity had been delayed and the Sioux who had gathered at the trading post were somewhat disgruntled. They were also hungry.

A tragic and almost absurd chain of events ensued. First, a cow escaped from a Mormon wagon train. The stray wandered near the Sioux camp, where it was captured and butchered. The Mormon captains complained to the authorities at Fort Laramie. Upon learning of the complaint, the Sioux chiefs hastened to the fort and offered to pay for the cow. The offer was rejected. The guilty party must be punished, the authorities declared. A certain Lieutenant Grattan of the Sixth Infantry was detailed with a contingent of soldiers and two mounted cannons to arrest the cow thieves. Grattan was full of bluster and his interpreter was drunk; any chance of negotiation was doomed to failure. Grattan wasted no time in ordering the cannons to fire. Chief Conquering Bear was among those killed by the volley. The Sioux responded, and in short order Grattan and all twenty-eight men under his command were dead. The tribe then broke into storehouses and made off with their annuity.

Grattan's cannon fire inaugurated thirty-five years of warfare on the plains that included the Battle of the Little

Big Horn and culminated in the massacre at Wounded Knee. At the time, Grattan's impetuousness was disregarded; the Sioux were considered the aggressors and there were calls for retaliation and punishment. Before some sort of punitive expedition could be mounted, however, the Sioux struck again. A band of Spotted Tail's warriors attacked the Salt Lake mail stage near Laramie. Three whites died and some $10,000 worth of gold was stolen. It was clear to Americans on the frontier that a severe and uncompromising retaliation was necessary to punish these "savages thirsting for white blood."

Congress appropriated monies to fund a so-called "Sioux expedition." The man chosen to lead the expedition was General William S. Harney, a veteran of the Mexican-American War with a reputation for a severe, Puritanical sense of justice: Manifest Destiny's ideal avenging angel. Harney devised a plan of attack: he would send some troops up the Missouri to Fort Pierre and others up the Platte to Fort Laramie. Then, in a coordinated assault, the troops would attempt to pincer the Sioux somewhere in western Nebraska. The timing of the expedition was carefully plotted: by late summer the trail traffic would be finished for the season, leaving the field clear for the soldiers. Moreover, the Sioux, finished with their seasonal buffalo hunts, would be settling into camps along rivers. They would thus be easier to discover and attack.

Not everyone agreed with the need for or the desirability of revenge. The Superintendent of Indian Affairs at the time argued that the military was simply planning an indiscriminate "chastisement" of Indians rather than targeting the allegedly guilty parties. There was also the likelihood that brutal retaliations would provoke the Sioux into attacking pioneers traveling on the trails. For that matter, noted the federal government's Indian agent stationed on the Upper Platte, no emigrant trains had been bothered in 1855, the trail season following the Grattan Massacre. The agent argued that "the Sioux difficulties have been magnified by false and malicious reports."

The army wasn't in the mood to listen. It had suffered the insult of too many American Indian depredations—the raiding of mules and horses, the destruction of corrals, attacks on mail trains. The Grattan Massacre had removed all sense of restraint. The Sioux had to answer for their "crimes." "I shall not hesitate to attack any body of hostile Indians which I can overtake or chance to encounter," Harney declared. In short, he was fixing for a fight. How would he know a band was hostile? Simple. An order went out for all Sioux to report to Fort Laramie at the end of the hunts. Any band that remained at large would be by definition hostile.

Harney left Fort Leavenworth in Kansas on the third of August. Twenty days later, he reached Fort Kearney on the Platte. There he divided his troops for the planned pincer maneuver. With a force of six hundred soldiers, Harney advanced up the Platte for ten days. The soldiers' journals and the accounts of accompanying newspapermen tell of fog, mist, and thunderstorms. For entertainment, the men shot at bison. On September 2, scouts sighted a band of Sioux near Ash Hollow. The troops passed through the hollow and prepared for attack.

The American Indians standing in harm's way were members of Little Thunder's band of Southern Brule Sioux. They had recently finished with their buffalo hunt, and were encamped on Blue Water Creek, drying out their meat and engaging in routine chores. Whether or not the band harbored participants in either the Grattan Massacre or the mail train murders was unclear; in Harney's mind, however, the band was as good as guilty, for they were in blatant violation of the order to report to Fort Laramie. He was not about to wait for evidence, and he was not about to negotiate. "Having no doubt . . . of the real character and hostile intentions of the party in question," Harney advanced on the Indian camp. He sent no warnings.

When the American soldiers were spotted, three Sioux chiefs came out with a white flag to request a parley. Harney was not the sort to parley. He suspected a ruse—the white flag was likely a ploy to gain time. A parley would allow the women and children to break camp and escape, and on this day Harney had no intention of allowing anyone, including women and children, to escape. He ignored the white flag and ordered the advance to continue. A newspaper reporter following the troops wrote: "As we had come for war and not for peace we paid no attention to them."

Soon the troops opened fire. Equipped with newly issued long-range rifles, they were able to start shooting from a thousand yards off. It was a mismatch all the way. Five hundred soldiers attacked fewer than 250 Sioux, who were caught off guard. A cavalry force circled around the American Indian camp and ambushed anyone trying to flee up the creek. What followed was, as a participant put it, "a scene of carnage." Without an escape route, the Sioux tried to climb the hillside to hide behind rocks. Rifle fire brought down men, women, and children. The cavalry ran down others. In all, eighty-six Sioux—more than a third of the band—died, while seventy were captured. History calls this incident "the Battle of Ash Hollow," but the reports of participants and eyewitnesses describe something more like a hunt than a battle. "When the dragoons showed themselves then the fun commenced in reality," one newspaper correspondent wrote. "I never saw such a beautiful thing in my life." Harney himself reported that "there was much slaughter in the pursuit." Apparently, he was not concerned about being reprimanded for the massacre of fleeing women and children.

As it turned out, he had no reason for concern. President Franklin Pierce lauded Harney, and the press lionized him as a hero, even though there was no doubt women and children had died during the attack. One soldier described "women and children crying and moaning, horribly mangled by bullets." But most Americans agreed with a lieutenant who suggested that the Sioux were to blame, since the warriors had been hiding in the rocks alongside the innocent. To whites, it was American Indian cowardice that "caused the destruction of women and children."

While the pursuit was underway, Harney detailed some soldiers to burn the village. "A veritable mountain of Indian loot" contributed to the bonfire. As the day waned and darkness set in, the troops rounded up what survivors they could find. All captured men were killed. The women and children were taken back to the main camp on the North Platte. That night, a violent thunderstorm added to their misery. They were subsequently taken to Fort Kearney, where history loses track of them. Their fate after that point remains unknown.

I stopped in two convenience stores seeking directions to the battle site on Blue Water Creek. In both stores, the clerks had no idea about the location, and indeed had only vague notions of some long-ago battle. As it happened, however, a short way up Route 26 I came to a bridge over a small stream, and there was the inevitable historical marker. The sign noted that "a significant fight, commonly called the Battle of Ash Hollow, occurred at Blue Water Creek northwest of here."

That was all the help I was going to get in locating the site. County roads took me northwest of Ash Hollow. Pleasant green ranchland bordered Blue Water Creek, but it was private property and I didn't see much of the twenty-foot wide stream that drains the Sand Hills and meanders into the North Platte. I could, however, glimpse the rocky ledges and hillocks that rise up from the banks of the Blue Water. There, above the irrigation, the terrain was forbidding and desolate. I stopped the car and peered through binoculars at the steep cliffs, cut and scarred by erosion. In those rugged cuts, against the insurmountable cliffs, the Sioux had sought shelter from the barrage of gunfire.

A bend in the county road brought me close to the creek and gave me a long view of the sandy draw. I stopped the car again and thought about climbing through the barbed wire, going down to the water, taking some photos. But before I could get ten feet from the car, three huge hounds came bounding from the brush, howling and snarling bloody hell, forcing me to abandon further investigation.

A Grave on the High Plains

June 30 Alvah getting worse it's quite hopeless
complaining none. July 1 Alvah is rapidly sinking.
July 2 in the early morning hours Alvah died.
—journal of Pusey Graves, 1850

Wyoming is fertile ground for historical sites associated with the California and Oregon Trails. In the midst of a summer-long journey to retrace the old trails, I come upon one such site—the grave of a Gold Rush pioneer—just east of Glenrock. Located about two hundred yards off the latter-day interstate freeway that parallels long stretches of the trail, the gravesite proves to be a good place to pause and reflect upon the consequences of America's westward expansion.

For nineteenth-century Americans, westward was the direction of freedom—as Thoreau had famously posited—but the passage to freedom was fraught with danger. Tens of thousands died during the trek across the continent, and death came in many forms. Pioneers died from gunshot wounds and wagon accidents. They drowned at river crossings. They succumbed to cholera and typhoid and hunger. As they made their way west, trail travelers often passed the graves of those who had faltered along the way, the graves so numerous that, according to historian Merrill Mattes, "the trail to California took on the resemblance of an elongated cemetery."

Most of the graves are long gone. Wolves often dug up bodies soon after burial. Occasionally, American Indians desecrated graves to take the clothing. Time and the elements obliterated other graves, and eventually progress paved over all but a few of the remaining trailside burial sites.

But here outside Glenrock, Wyoming, there is an intact pioneer grave to contemplate, complete with the original headstone. The story of the pioneer's death is related on a nearby historical marker. Personally, I love these markers placed here and there along highways for the benefit of travelers who have the urge to stop and read a sign. Does anyone actually do this in our high-speed era? It takes a strong desire to break the inertia of an eighty-mile-per-hour cruise, to interrupt progress as it were, for the mere purpose of reading a brief text put up by the state historical society (or in this case the Oregon-California Trails Association) telling you in fifty or seventy-five or a hundred words that some obscure event in American history has consecrated this unlikely place. Why pause in the midst of pursuing your own inscrutable destiny just to learn about some forgotten episode?

My impression is that few people stop to read such signs nowadays. Windswept by the disturbed air of passing tractor-trailers and speeding cars, historical markers have a forlorn, abandoned feel to them. Most markers, it seems, are located along old two-lane highways, well off the beaten track. You find rather few along the interstate freeways— maybe at the odd scenic overlook, or at a rest area, where the marker is typically stuck somewhere off to the side, well away from the restrooms and vending machines that have prompted travelers to exit for a hurried pit stop.

Although the historical marker for the pioneer's grave is located just off Interstate 25, it is not easy to find. Along the freeway, no sign points to its whereabouts. Just getting to it takes some doing: You have to exit the freeway, make a sharp turn at the end of the off-ramp, and then backtrack a half-mile or so on a county road. As you approach, nothing announces the presence of the nondescript marker.

Hard as it is to find, this obscure grave does receive occasional visitors—trail buffs and readers of trail history who are drawn to the grave's poignant backstory. Here lies a man named Alvah H. Unthank, buried on July 2, 1850. As the marker explains, Unthank's name is found carved into Register Cliff, a sandstone wall some eighty miles away, just outside of present-day Guernsey, Wyoming. In the nineteenth century, numerous pioneers inscribed their names on the cliff wall, Unthank among them. You can imagine him chiseling away at the rock face, pausing now and then to wipe his brow, perhaps cracking a joke or sharing a witticism with his mates as he chisels, all of them laughing and admiring his handiwork and cheering him on. And so, brimming with optimism as he anticipated the wealth he would acquire in California, the young man, all of nineteen years old, inscribed his name boldly on the rock face for future travelers to see: *A. H. Unthank 1850.*

It was just about his last act on earth. Within days (perhaps even within hours) of chiseling his name, Unthank felt queasy with the early symptoms of cholera. Along the trail, thousands died of the dreaded disease. No one knew what caused it, but they knew its symptoms all too well: diarrhea, sore throat, vomiting, cramps, cold sweats. Unthank would have experienced all this before he succumbed. Just nine days after etching his name on Register Cliff, he died and was buried here, his grave now surrounded by weeds and a rusted metal fence.

Several hundred yards away across the North Platte River, a huge power plant overshadows Unthank's grave. Before setting out on this journey, I watched a few documentary films about the western trails. One of them paused at Unthank's grave to review the sad story. The filmmakers carefully constructed shots of the grave to show its isolation: lonely weeds bending in a harsh wind, a big, empty sky overhead, pronghorns and wild horses wandering the sage plains. Every signifier, including background music, suggested the profound loneliness of this remote grave, lost in the vast expanse of the West. The film did not show the slightest trace of modernity—neither the nearby power plant nor the freeway just up the embankment.

Yet when you are standing at Unthank's grave, you can't help but notice the billowing exhaust from the power plant. In the middle distance, mile-long trains bring hundreds of tons of coal to feed the generators. At night, the plant produces a glow that can be seen from a hundred miles away. Try as you might, you hear no hint of the haunting harmonica music that films about the West—whether documentaries or Hollywood Westerns—have so often chosen for a soundtrack. At Unthank's grave, freeway noise—the hum of high-speed traffic—provides the background music.

Why the elision of modernity in the documentary? Most likely, the filmmakers were striving for "authenticity," trying to create an appropriate nineteenth-century ambience. But I suspect the elision also has something to do with our need to believe that the old West, the pure and true West, is still out there waiting for us. And when instead we encounter the modernity that followed in the pioneers' wake—power plants, strip mines, hydroelectric dams, and bombing ranges—we, like the filmmakers, tend to shift our focus to vestiges and remnants and ghosts.

And here, amid all this, lies Alvah Unthank. The decades have passed and he—or his grave anyway—has watched the story unfold, a silent witness to the changes wrought upon the land. He has seen what the trail traffic, the railroads, and the freeways have brought. He has seen the bison disappear and the cattle arrive, the tribes dwindle and the settlers proliferate. He has seen cities emerge on the high plains and in the deserts. He has seen mines gouged in the earth, pits excavated, wells drilled, power plants erected.

Like those of us who have followed him, Unthank was probably enamored with the mythic West. Did he, as he lay dying, have an inkling of the myth's many convolutions? Do we, who have come after him chasing our own western myths, have a clue? Standing beside Unthank's trailside, freeway-side grave with a power plant view, I wonder what message he might have for those who stop to visit him.

A phrase comes to mind, a popular nineteenth-century expression that Unthank would have known: *seeing the elephant.* As various historians point out, this curious and complicated expression referenced both the "great adventure of going to California to dig up a golden fortune" (J. S. Holliday) and "all the deadly perils that threatened a westering emigrant" (Merrill Mattes). At the outset of the journey, trail travelers would speak exuberantly of "going to see the elephant." In this sense, the phrase indicated their initial high spirits as they anticipated the adventure ahead. But eventually, according to J. S. Holliday, "this special phrase, used by almost every Gold Rush diarist . . . took on poignant meaning." By the later stages of the venture, having met with hardships on the trails or in the gold fields, the westbound pioneers associated "the elephant" with the severe ordeals that they had encountered in the West. "Seeing the elephant" thus became an oblique way of expressing bitter disillusionment. Alvah Unthank had a closer brush with the elephant than he had expected. Too close, in fact: he did not survive the encounter.

In Unthank's time, the expression referred primarily to personal experience—all "the joys and sorrows, the hazards and heartaches of the covered wagon emigrants," as Merrill Mattes puts it. Contemplating Unthank's grave, taking in the power plant and the coal trains and the freeway noise, it seems to me that the now-outdated expression might aptly apply not only to the specific trail experiences of individual pioneers such as Unthank but also more generally to the national enterprise of westward expansion. This expansion, prompted by the region's wonders and the prospect of bounty and bonanza, was undertaken with zeal. According to the predominant narrative learned in American schools, the outcome was triumphant: great wealth extracted, deserts made to bloom, a wilderness tamed and turned productive, untapped power harnessed. The successful conquest of the West has long been a point of national pride, apparent evidence of a "Manifest Destiny"—one of the central themes of America's foundational myth. In this sense of the phrase— the high-spirited, zealous sense—America saw the elephant and experienced what Mattes calls "the wonder and the glory and the shivering thrill" of the western venture.

But inevitably, there was a downside to the enterprise's success, a downside often elided in the dominant narrative. Just as many pioneers experienced hardships—the severe ordeals and deadly perils that became associated with seeing the elephant—so too the national enterprise of westward expansion encountered mean realities. All too often, bonanzas turned into busts. Bounteous harvests gave way to crop failure when droughts hit and dust storms roiled. Depleted aquifers led to salinization of the soil, and man-made gardens reverted to wasteland. Newly encountered species numbering in the tens of millions were nearly extirpated, while newly encountered human cultures and languages—rich with unique and valuable wisdom—were brought to the brink of extinction and in some cases wiped out entirely. Marvels of nature were dammed, gouged, drilled, felled, plowed, burned. Land, water, and air were contaminated in the process. In this sense, too—the sense of disillusionment—America had seen the elephant.

Maybe this is the message one derives from a visit to Unthank's grave. I can imagine Alvah's spectral voice calling out to those of us who have stopped to read the historical marker and photograph his tombstone: "I saw the elephant. Look around—look with open eye—and you shall see it, too."

"Seeing the elephant" is now an obscure phrase, but it is related to other, more familiar expressions, motifs, and tropes that point to the American West as the locus of initial exuberance and subsequent disillusionment. *Across the great divide. California or bust. There's gold in them there hills. California dreaming.* Exuberant anticipation surely informs these expressions; but we know that disillusionment waits just down the road. This disillusionment is the upshot, the inevitable consequence of America's western dream, particularly the California dream. Joan Didion—herself a descendent of California pioneers—calls it "the golden dream," knowing full well that "dream" is sometimes a synonym for "delusion." Indeed, as Didion has repeatedly documented in her essays, the most compelling aspects of the golden dream may well be the most delusional. The multivalence of the elephant expression suggests as much: the pursuit of the dream is inherently convoluted—and ultimately delusional—in a region that has had so many contradictory impulses imposed upon it. And you can find tangible evidence of these impulses within sight of Unthank's grave: trail remnants, railroad tracks, freeways, fenced-in range, mining projects, energy production, pollution. These are the gritty details of Manifest Destiny—readily apparent, and yet so easy to overlook.

Leaving the gravesite, I merge back onto the freeway, rejoining the procession of RVs, tractor-trailers, and family sedans pushing hard for Casper and points west—all of us rushing on, chasing the dream, heedless of the landscape we cross and oblivious to the elephant looming in our path.

Ill-Fated

Most American history textbooks contain a sentence or two about the Donner Party. Having left the California Trail to attempt an unproven cutoff, the party's eighty people fell behind the main migration and ended up snowbound and starving in California's mountains, forced to resort to cannibalism in order to survive. The misfortune that beleaguered the Donner Party has turned their journey into a well-known cautionary tale in American history, a tale with all the lurid appeal of tabloid news. Textbooks and roadside historical markers find the story irresistible, never failing, of course, to mention the broken taboo for which the party is infamous.

I, too, find the story irresistible. As an inveterate traveler, I hold in special esteem any hard-luck travel story, and the trek of the Donner Party is the quintessential hard-luck story. One summer, I felt compelled to go west and retrace their route.

Such was my purpose in following the trail. But what about the members of the Donner Party? What were their reasons for going west? It's hard to say for sure, especially since an overland journey to California in 1846 was a rather risky proposition. The trail across the "Great American

Desert" and over the Rocky Mountains was sketchy at best in the years before the Gold Rush of 1849. True, the renowned trailblazer John Charles Frémont had just tentatively mapped the route and declared it viable for wagon travel; but the trail still harbored a host of unknowns from weather to terrain to the presence of American Indians. And only a handful of forts represented civilization from Independence, Missouri to Sacramento.

Nevertheless, thousands hit the trail in 1846 for somewhat obscure reasons. Certainly some sought a better life, particularly those stung by the panic of 1839 and its after-effects. Others just felt the need for more room and looked west, as their ancestors had done, to a wide-open and seemingly empty land. But the case of the Donner brothers, leaders of the ill-fated party, is harder to figure. They were, for one thing, on the elderly side: George Donner was sixty-two in 1846, his brother Jacob, sixty-five. Moreover, both were successful landowners with no apparent economic motivation for leaving their prosperous Illinois farms and striking out across two thousand difficult miles for an uncertain future in a land that did not yet belong to the United States. They had money and prominence in the community. God was in heaven and all was right with the world. And yet they decided to ditch it all and head west across what was then called "Indian Territory" on the maps.

Apparently, the main attraction for the Donners—as for so many pioneers since—was California, or better, the idea of California. In 1846, it was still Mexican territory, a sparsely populated and unknown wilderness. Accurate maps did not yet exist. Only a handful of Americans had even seen California. But already an aura was developing around the place, a set of wondrous images coalescing about the magical name. Legend held that it was a veritable Garden of Eden where anything and everything grew, where winter was unknown, and where people suffered no illnesses. The Donners must have seen the notices in newspapers and broadsheets describing this fanciful paradise—hearsay and rumor for the most part, but convincing enough to entice even established, well-to-do men of property to sell all and set out for the unknown.

So off they went. The Donner brothers left Springfield, Illinois with their large families—sixteen people all told—in April 1846. The family of James Reed, another prominent and wealthy citizen of Springfield, joined them. Reed brought along his mother-in-law, some seventy years old and in poor health. She survived the bumps and jolts of wagon travel for a little over a month before she died. Reed buried her beneath a tree in Kansas. In hindsight, she was the lucky one.

To join the Donner Party on the worst part of their journey, take Interstate 80 and head west. The urban blight of the rust belt soon gives way to suburban sprawl. Then come the rolling hills of the Midwest, then the vast expanse of prairie, or what used to be prairie before it was plowed under. You cross the Mississippi River and then the Missouri, picking up speed as the population dwindles with the rainfall and the road ahead empties. Beyond the 100th meridian lies True West, a land with too little rain for profitable agriculture and a lingering aura of lawlessness. Ranchland replaces the farm belt. The tidy burgs of Middle America yield to tank towns and unincorporated hamlets. Cattle roam the vast fenced-in tracts, while pronghorns and prairie dogs prevail in the open range. Coyotes prowl everywhere. The road leaves Nebraska and enters Wyoming. The Medicine Bow Mountains rise up to the south, the Laramies to the north, your first glimpse of the Rockies. Interstate 80 pushes hard across southern Wyoming into the basin of the Great Divide and the badlands of the Red Desert—a treeless land with brick red soil, wild horses, oil and gas wells, red-tailed hawks, and sage. Here, the freeway traverses the longest stretch of unfenced land in the lower forty-eight, bringing you closer to that elusive promise of unbridled freedom that the American West so tantalizingly represents.

After Rock Springs, Interstate 80 crosses the Green River and heads for the southwest corner of Wyoming. A short detour off the freeway leads to Fort Bridger, and it is there— there on the banks of Black's Fork with the snow-capped Uinta Mountains to the south—that you overtake the legendary Donner Party—the luckless members of the worst overland journey in the history of westward expansion, Manifest Destiny's ill-fated outcasts.

From Independence, Missouri to the Continental Divide at South Pass, Wyoming—half the journey—the Donners and the Reeds were no different from the hundreds of other pioneers making their way west in 1846. For the most part, the first thousand miles passed with little difficulty and without significant incident. In fact, in a letter home, Tamsen Donner—George's wife—wrote, "We are now on the Platte, two hundred miles from Fort Laramie. Our journey so far has been pleasant, the roads have been good and food plentiful. Indeed, if I do not experience something far worse than I have yet done, I shall say the trouble is all in getting started."

According to the Donner Party legend, the group's one distinguishing feature was the Reed family's double-decker wagon, a huge vehicle outfitted with steps, spring seats, and a sheet iron stove for warmth on chilly mountain mornings. Dubbed the "prairie palace car," the wagon was comfortable but cumbersome, and its necessarily slow pace caused the party—already late in starting—to fall behind much of the year's migration. Little historical evidence exists for the "prairie palace car," but there's no doubt that the Donners and Reeds were advancing more slowly across the continent than the other pioneers. By July 20th, paused on Little Sandy Creek in western Wyoming, the families had become concerned about their pace. They had taken two months to cover the first half of the journey, with the most difficult miles yet to come. They knew they must reach the Sierra Nevada Mountains before the onset of winter storms— storms that could begin as early as October.

With these concerns in mind, the Donners and Reeds became interested in rumors of a new, quicker route to California. As they traveled west, they heard talk of this new possibility, a shortcut to California that would save hundreds of miles and several weeks' time over the proven route.

Hitherto, pioneers to California had traveled north from Fort Bridger to Fort Hall in Idaho. They then passed down through northern Nevada to the Humboldt River. The new trail proposed to cut directly west across Utah and eastern Nevada to reach the Humboldt. While crossing Wyoming that July of 1846, the California-bound travelers considered this new possibility. They discussed and debated. Many were chary of striking out across unblazed territory. Others were swayed by the thought of saving time, especially as the season wore on and they faced the prospect of snow in the California mountains.

When they reached South Pass, the pioneers learned that the shortcut's promoter, a young man named Lansford Hastings, was promising to meet interested parties at Fort Bridger. Just twenty-seven years old, Hastings had somewhat grandiose visions about emancipating California from Mexican hegemony and establishing an independent republic. He foresaw himself as president of this new nation of California, but for this to happen he needed Americans to come in abundant numbers. At the time, Oregon was still the preferred destination on the Pacific coast. It was certainly easier to get to, following a well-traveled trail. In contrast, the California trail was less direct, less traveled, and less certain. Hastings wanted to change all that by promoting an easier route, and he had determined that the easier route must go by way of the Salt Lake and its neighboring desert.

He based this determination on his own scanty experience and the word of roaming mountain men. In 1842, Hastings himself had gone west and gathered information for his book, *The Emigrants Guide to Oregon and California* (1845). Late in 1845 he met John Charles Frémont, the renowned trailblazer, in Sacramento. Fresh off one of his long journeys across the unmapped Great Basin, Frémont shared what he knew. More convinced than ever that destiny favored him and his route, Hastings left California eastbound in April 1846 to test the route and intercept California-bound pioneers. Hastings sent ahead an open letter to all emigrants claiming the cutoff would save some three hundred miles over the existing road. He promised to lead interested pioneers to California via the shortcut.

Cautious pioneers doubted Hastings's claims and decided to keep to the original trail. James Reed and George Donner—eager to reduce the number of miles their plodding caravan must travel—argued in favor of the new route. About sixty other emigrants agreed with them. At a campsite on the Little Sandy River (near present-day Farson, Wyoming), the newly formed group elected George Donner as their captain. A few days later, now known as the Donner Party, the travelers arrived at Fort Bridger and the trailhead for the Hastings Cutoff to California.

Today, Fort Bridger is a state historic site and souvenir shop where visitors can stroll through houses, stables, and stores reconstructed to look as they did when the US Army occupied the site in the late 1800s. The staff takes this reconstruction a step further, dressing in costumes of the time period and offering demonstrations of what they call "living history." Beyond the visitor center, the state's park service has built a facsimile of Jim Bridger's original fort, which predated the military facility by several decades. It was this "fort"—really more of a trading post—that the Donners came to in 1846. The log structure is now a gift concession selling mountain man articles: flasks, animal horns, chaps, boots, moccasins, knives, muskets.

At Fort Bridger, the Donner Party learned, to their consternation, that Lansford Hastings had already left for California with a contingent of pioneers. It was still possible to follow a trail out of Fort Bridger that would lead them back to the main California route, but after three days of resting and repairing, the Donner Party decided to pursue Hastings. This was their fateful decision: now there would be no turning back and no hope of assistance anywhere between Fort Bridger and California. Among those joining the Donners and Reeds, the party now included a Chicago businessman, an English cutler, a carriage maker from Illinois, a widow from Tennessee, several German and Irish families, and an elderly Belgian immigrant. Only half of them would survive to see their destination, Sacramento.

Leaving Fort Bridger, I could have driven Interstate 80 into Echo Canyon, Utah, an easy seventy-five mile drive at freeway speeds. But in the interests of authenticity, I followed an approximation of the more serpentine route followed by the Donner Party. Armed with directions from one of the Fort Bridger rangers, I proceeded on a succession of state and county roads through wild and isolated land. The scenery—not to mention the gravel surface—became increasingly rugged: canyons, steep hills, mineral-colored rivers, foaming springs. But it was the kind of scenery rarely seen from the freeway, so I pushed on, following ambiguous maps, crossing the fast-running Bear River, until I came to Yellow Creek and a dirt track that led past a strange rock formation called The Needles. At some point, I crossed into Utah, and then, just when I was beginning to wonder if I had become lost, I spotted the glimmer of truck traffic crawling along a distant ridge: Interstate 80.

But the dirt track dead-ended at a barbed wire fence paralleling the freeway. So I had to backtrack and try several rutted paths until I found one that rattled over a cattle guard and accessed a paved frontage road. It took me six somewhat arduous hours to reach this point out of Fort Bridger. For the Donner Party, the same route took six days.

Eventually, I came to the Utah Welcome Center in Echo Canyon, a beautiful place of high red cliffs and deep shadows. I climbed a small bluff above the picnic tables to an overlook of the canyon, the Weber River, the old railroad, and the new freeway. In pioneer times, the canyon walls produced remarkable echoes as the wagons rattled through, but with the constant whine and roar of freeway traffic, the canyon's signature sounds have been consigned to the past.

As the Donner Party came out of Echo Canyon, following the Weber River, they encountered their first bit of bad news. Stuck in the top of a bush, a note from Hastings informed anyone following his trail that the Weber River canyon had proven too difficult for wagons. Another route should be taken. Disconcerted and angry, the party rested for four days debating what to do. James Reed rode ahead on horseback to find Hastings and the advanced parties, catching up with them on the shores of the Great Salt Lake. Hastings rode with Reed to the top of a mountain and pointed out what he thought would make for a better route through the difficult Wasatch Range. Reed returned to the camp, marking trees as he went so that the party could find its way through the maze of canyons and forests.

The next thirty-six miles were a hellish ordeal. The Donner Party had to cut its own trail, hacking through tangled, thorny undergrowth and chopping down a seemingly endless thicket of aspen, willow, and alder trees. Their wagons broke down trying to negotiate the boulders in and around the creeks. The men collapsed under the strain of the backbreaking work. It took twenty-one days to hack through the canyons up and over the many folds and ridges of the Wasatch. Twenty-one days to advance thirty-six miles.

Today State Road 65 follows this arduous trail. I stopped at a place now called Mormon Flats, located a few miles off SR 65 down a rough, narrow road. Here, at some springs, the Donner Party rested for four nights and three days; or, rather, the animals rested while the men continued to hack out a trail through the Wasatch Range. Equipped with axes that needed constant sharpening, they had to cut down aspen trees and chop through oak chaparral. They had to cut low enough for the axles and the oxen's bellies to clear, and they had to cut wide enough for the wagons to pass through. When one of Reed's axles broke despite these efforts, he and some of the men had to spend a night fashioning a replacement. The crew had to clear away boulders. They had to move felled trees from the path. They did all this for eight torturous miles up to the pass at Big Mountain, and then for another sixteen miles down the other side through Emigration Canyon. And they did the work on minimal rations, with little sleep. It's hard to imagine the toil this required, the exhaustion, the sense of futility that must have overwhelmed them at every stroke of the ax. At what point did the Donner families wonder why they had given up prosperous lives in Illinois for this uncertainty, this excruciating travail?

The setting certainly belies the torments the Donner Party suffered. In summertime, wildflowers crop up in open patches, dazzling the senses with their colors and fragrance. The abundance of wildflowers made me think of Tamsen Donner, who was something of an amateur botanist, according to the record. Back in Illinois, as a schoolteacher she collected samples of wildflowers. She may well have done the same on the westward journey wherever she could. The prairies of Kansas and Nebraska offered up some interesting specimens, but the badlands of Wyoming yielded precious few. Mrs. Donner had seen mostly sagebrush for weeks before the party started over the Wasatch Range. Imagine her pleasure in finding such variety in the mountains, a pleasure that may have quelled for the moment some of the fears she harbored as the party left the main trail to attempt the unknown cutoff.

Along the Donner trail through the Wasatch, there are daisies, phloxes, poppies, wild roses, gentians, and

Indian paintbrush in shades of yellow, white, pink, blue, and vermilion. There are lavender thistles, too, along with blossoming cacti, nettles, and clover. Swaths of color. Swirls of color. Shimmering streams of color. The wildflowers of the Wasatch Mountains surely must have solaced Tamsen Donner in her worry and fear. I imagined her collecting samples of them in between camp duties and the care of her children. While the men continued their assault on the mountain, she took stock of the flowers and fought her premonitions about where the uncertain trail was taking them.

Once they reached the pass at Big Mountain, the Donner Party faced an even meaner task in descending. Keeping control of the wagons was a constant concern. Nowadays, State Road 65 hairpins down the mountain, crisscrossing the pioneer trail's more direct—and more dangerous—descent. A turn onto Emigrant Canyon Road leads to the outskirts of Salt Lake City. A roadside historical marker identifies the place where the Donners, exhausted by continuous trail-cutting, finally gave up following the creek and double-teamed their wagons to haul them over the canyon's north ridge. Up above, a condominium tower now dominates the ridge.

Founded in 1847, Salt Lake City did not exist when the Donner Party finally made it out of the mountains and onto the open plain. They must have been relieved to reach flat land, even though it was a strange, barren land bordering a lake saltier than the ocean. Just a year later, Brigham Young would see the same valley and confidently declare, "This is the place." But to the Donner Party, the valley did not seem so inviting. They wanted nothing more than to hurry across it toward their own concept of a promised land, California. Interstate 80 now follows in their footsteps, squeezing through the narrow strip of land between the northern spur of the Oquirrh Range and the Salt Lake shore.

But while the freeway cuts a direct path toward the Nevada border, the Donners were forced to zigzag westward, constantly searching for water. One member of the party, a consumptive named Luke Halloran, died near here. At present-day Grantsville (twenty miles down the Tooele Valley on State Road 138), the party found several good wells, and today's traveler can find a night's rest in the Donner Motel. Grantsville also boasts the Donner-Reed Memorial Museum, home to a collection of artifacts recovered from the Great Salt Lake Desert—items cast off when the pioneers attempted to lighten their loads during the difficult passage. Of particular interest are some extra-large wagon wheel hubs, supposedly from James Reed's "prairie palace car."

The Stansbury Mountains separate Tooele Valley from Skull Valley. To bypass the mountains, the Donner trail and the modern highway head northwest out of Grantsvillle and past a cement plant toward the tip of the Stansbury Range. This is Timpie Point, where the freeway, the old Lincoln Highway, the Western Pacific Railroad, power lines, pipelines, cables, and the vaguest trace of the Donner trail all squeeze between the range and the lake.

Salt flats spread from the lake down into Skull Valley. Scrub brush and stands of gray, unkempt saltbushes are the predominant vegetation. A rarely used road heads south down Skull Valley, with a barren range close on the left. To the right, a vast sagebrush basin extends toward the western range that encloses the valley. The road passes an abandoned ranch house and some dry springs, then pushes on to a ghost town near where the party found some clear springs—the last good grass and water before the desert crossing.

It was here that the party found another shredded note. Hastings had left a message for them affixed to a board, but only a few tatters remained and the words were inscrutable. Tamsen Donner found some pieces caught in sage bushes and managed to figure out the gist: "two days and two nights of hard driving cross desert reach water." It was not a propitious message. They had been led to expect a desert crossing of forty miles. Now the shredded note seemed to indicate that it would be twice that.

The Donner trail crosses Skull Valley, a rough track cutting through sage in a serpentine course. No car can negotiate this terrain. Lacking four-wheel drive, I was forced to return to I-80, where a historical marker at a scenic viewpoint read, "For the next 40 miles you will be crossing the Great Salt Lake Desert. The ill-fated Donner Party lost valuable time because of the soft muddy flats. Don't let it happen to you! Drive carefully and stay on the highway." From Springfield, Illinois all the way to California, there are dozens of historical markers devoted to the Donner Party. A good many of those markers use the epithet "ill-fated" to describe the Donners.

Over and over again, you read the same words on markers, in history books, in museum signage: *the ill-fated Donner Party*, their whole story neatly summarized in that one epithet. An ill fate seemingly dogged them every step of the way.

For many miles, the freeway is bordered by the eerie white expanse of the Great Salt Lake Desert. Just the sight of it blanches the imagination. The Donner Party's crossing of this desert presented them with yet another horrific ordeal. The wagons sank into soft sand and muck. Everyone, including children, was forced to walk—a hike of seventy-five miles over four days and nights. Oxen were lost, wagons abandoned. In the glare of the sun, the blinding white surface of the desert produced visions—weird reflections that appeared to be giant men riding parallel to the pioneers. Thirst distorted their perceptions. The children were given lumps of sugar. The adults chewed flattened bullets. At night, the desert was bitter cold. Days were brutally hot.

The remnant of their trail runs somewhere to the north of today's freeway, angling across the white shimmer of the desert toward the Silver Island Mountains on the Nevada border. Here, it is not possible to follow in their footsteps. A large portion of the salt flats is now on land belonging to the air force, which uses it for a hazardous waste dump.

Just beyond the Bonneville Speedway, however, at the western edge of the desert, determined trail buffs can follow a rugged dirt road thirty miles north to some springs at the base of beautiful Pilot Peak. The springs gave the pioneers and their remaining oxen life-saving water. They camped here for several days, recovering from the disaster of the desert crossing. The men trekked back into the desert to retrieve some of the supplies on the abandoned wagons and search for missing oxen. But they had little time to devote to lost causes: already snow was apparent on the summit of Pilot Peak. Even as the Donners were suffering from heat exhaustion, their real problem was the looming winter.

I arrived at Wendover in the evening just as the neon lights of the town's casinos began to glow in the desert night. Perched on the edge of the salt flats, Wendover straddles the Utah-Nevada border, but all the action is on the Nevada side. I crossed the state line and parked at the Red Garter Casino. Just about the only place to park in Wendover is at one of the seven casinos. In fact, just about the only place to eat, sleep, or drink in Wendover is at one or another of the casinos. A border town, Wendover exists solely to draw Utah residents to attractions legal in Nevada but not in Utah. It's a timeless never-never land, where people drink beer at seven in the morning and eat pancakes at midnight. The slot machines keep up a constant jangling of computerized beeps, bongs, and whistles. The casinos do their best to deny reality, especially the reality of the desert just beyond the mirrored walls. One casino offers a "Rainforest Buffet" in a restaurant decorated with plastic palms, silk jungle flowers, and neon lianas. A fountain splashes and pre-recorded parrots squawk from speakers implanted in the ceiling. Diners play keno from their booths while they await their meals. The desert that nearly did in the Donner Party seems a thousand miles away.

* * *

West of Wendover, the land is austere and beautiful, with long vistas of mountain ranges and valleys that reveal exactly what the Donner Party saw as they followed Hastings's barely discernible trail. The first of September found them still six hundred miles from Sacramento. The nights were growing colder. Their food supplies were rapidly dwindling. Since many of their cattle and oxen had perished in the Utah desert, the Donners were forced to consolidate items into fewer wagons. By this point, everyone—men, women, children, the elderly—had to walk full time.

After leaving the springs at Pilot Peak they headed for an obvious pass over another mountain range. Interstate 80 crosses the same pass at Silver Zone Summit. After this pass, the Donner Party broke southwest toward a low point in the looming Pequop Range. The interstate veers northwest toward a much higher summit in the same range. But the highway engineers had the advantage of knowing what lies ahead: by taking the higher, northern pass, the modern road bypasses the huge East Humboldt Range and the Ruby Mountains on the other side of the Pequops. The Donners took what appeared to be the easier route, but ended up running smack into the higher ranges beyond the Pequops.

As I came down from Silver Zone Summit and exited onto a frontage road, I needed to make my own decision: follow the Donner trail or keep to the freeway? To the south, there was nothing but a few rutted Bureau of Land Management roads paralleling abandoned rail lines. A good fifty miles of wasteland lay in that direction. Alternatively,

I could continue on the smooth freeway for thirty miles to Wells, Nevada—no metropolis, to be sure, but at least a place that offered the prospect of a drink and a meal. At the cattle guard between paved road and dirt track, I stared into the long, isolated valley for a good five minutes. Then, reluctantly, I nudged forward into the ruts.

I was now in the very heart of America's largest desert, the Great Basin Desert, covering some 200,000 square miles. Most of the desert lies within Nevada's borders. The Sierra Nevada Mountains, three hundred miles west, effectively block the moisture-laden winds off the Pacific Ocean, leaving fewer than ten inches a year for the Great Basin. It is a bleak place with austere mountain ranges, dry lake basins, salt-encrusted playas, vast sandy stretches, alkaline sinks, and sagebrush-covered plains. It's sometimes called Basin and Range country, and that pretty much describes one's experience in crossing it: range then basin then range then basin, on and on. Few trees, little water. A barren terrain where geologic forces are continually stretching the earth's crust, a process millions of years old.

At ten miles per hour, that terrain seems especially tedious and vast. For hours under a blazing sun, the car labors over the washboard track, lurching into and over gullies, scraping against silver-green sagebrush. A veneer of dust coats the glass and distorts your view. You pass a railroad junction; a sign indicates that this was the town of Shafter, but only one concrete foundation, home to mating lizards, remains of Shafter's former glory. The track traverses the valley and climbs to a pass. From the summit you can see yet another valley and another mountain range. During the rough descents, the car scrapes bottom frequently, leaving you seriously worried about the wisdom of the venture.

Fortunately for me, a paved highway appeared. Route 93 leads straight to the snow-capped Ruby Mountains, the highest in Nevada. At the base of the range, the road turns to gravel—rough, but not too bad—and heads south, just as the Donner Party did when they found no pass their wagons could negotiate. For three long, desperate days they bore to the south, knowing that it was west they wanted to go and that each mile to the south further delayed their arrival in California.

The road runs past a beautiful, hidden part of Nevada, the Ruby Lake National Wildlife Refuge. This freshwater bulrush marsh, an oddity in the Great Basin Desert, provides a rest area for migratory birds, including trumpeter swans, canvasback and redhead ducks, cranes, herons, egrets, and falcons. A causeway takes bird watchers into the marsh, though the refuge is so isolated few make the journey. For the Donner Party, the marshes provided a small measure of comfort—at least they had water and good grass for the oxen—as they worked their way along the eastern slope of the Rubies. But once the party rounded the southern spur of the range, they had to turn north again across a dry land. Sixty more miles in the wrong direction, still getting no closer to California.

The map promised me a paved road somewhere near a town called Jiggs. I found the paved road all right, but Jiggs was nothing more than a bar and a post office. Still, it was the closest thing to civilization I had seen in two hundred miles. I stopped for a cold beer. Inside the dim, well-antlered bar, the barmaid was watching *Wheel of Fortune*. Without a word, she handed me a bottle, then settled back onto her stool, enthralled with the show and oblivious to my presence. She continually prompted the contestants by suggesting solutions to the puzzle, and when I returned to the car outside, I could hear her shouting, "M, M, M" to the television.

In need of a break after two hundred miles of wilderness, I came into Elko to rest for a few days. It was night when I arrived and checked in to a dingy flophouse, the "Louis," on the far west end of town.

In the light of day, I learned that Elko is the home of Marty's Gun World, Al and Marge's Mining Supply, Brenda's Flowers, and a Wedding Chapel. I went for breakfast in the coffee shop of the Commercial Casino. The casino lobby is famous for its stuffed polar bear, the "Legendary White King," supposedly the largest polar bear ever caught. The bear occupies a glass display case. A placard says that White King "spends it's [sic] life on polar ice in the Artic [sic] region." But the text doesn't explain how he ended up in Nevada. And why use the present tense for something so obviously dead? Presumably it had been quite a while since White King had spent any time on polar ice.

In the coffee shop, I took a stool at the counter. Behind me, two elderly folks in a booth discussed their gambling successes and failures loud enough for all to hear. She was losing heavily, it seemed, and he was berating her. "I told you, stop drawing to fill straights," he said. "It ain't gonna happen. Play for pairs and three-of-a-kind and you might— repeat *might*—come out ahead."

Just west of Elko, the Donner Party met up with the Humboldt River and the main line of the California Trail. They had finally finished with the accursed Hastings Cutoff. Near today's freeway, a historical marker indicates the spot and mentions the Donner Party—still "ill-fated" wherever they turn up. They reached the Humboldt River on the last day of September, seventy-three days after they had made the fateful decision to try the supposed shortcut. The party had fallen several weeks behind the rest of the pioneers on the trail. Depleted and demoralized, they struggled westward. Death stalked them. Somewhere along the Humboldt, James Reed got in a fight with a muleteer named Snyder and killed him. Reed was banished from the party and forced to ride alone on a horse to Sacramento. Some of the families ran out of food and had to beg from those who still had supplies. But by this point no one had much of anything, and sharing did not seem prudent. One frail, elderly man fell behind the group. No one volunteered to go back and find him. He was left to die in the desert.

The Humboldt is one of America's most vital rivers, historically, and one of the strangest. It winds its way around mountain ranges until it dies out, drying up in a sink. Its water is warm and unpleasant to taste. At times it is scarcely more than a series of half-stagnant pools. But without the Humboldt's guidance and its water, the journey to California's goldfields would have been a much more difficult proposition.

The main trail followed the Humboldt to the river's vanishing point east of what is now Reno. Every thoroughfare since has done the same: the railroad, the Lincoln Highway, Interstate 80. In every Nevada town along the way, you can see the whole history of ground transportation in the West: down by the river, a few decrepit, boarded-up buildings clustered around the old depot and the railroad tracks; a bit to the north, a Main Street of casinos, brothels, and marriage parlors on what used to be US 40; further north still, gas stations, hotels, and fast-food franchises lining the exit ramps on the interstate. Carlin, Battle Mountain, Winnemucca, Lovelock—they vary in size but the basic blueprint is the same.

The Humboldt Sink lies to the south of I-80, some twenty miles west of Lovelock. Here, the dwindling river evaporates into alkali flats. At this point, the pioneers faced another forty-mile dry drive across the eerie white flats, sometimes sinking to their knees in sand. The only water they found came out of the earth boiling hot; even when cooled it was too bitter to swallow. The Humboldt Sink and the nearby Carson Sink were the California Trail's graveyards. An 1850 survey found 1,000 dead mules, 5,000 dead horses, 3,750 dead cattle, and 973 graves in the forty-mile crossing. Even in the age of freeway travel, the route is deadly. This part of I-80 ranks third in the nation for fatalities; three out of four of the accidents are one-car rollovers, the drivers lulled to sleep by the landscape's monotony.

In the distance, the ghostly Stillwater Range wavers and ripples in haze. Closer, piled against the foothills, there's a preponderance of junk—junk cars, abandoned mobile homes, rusted tractors and semi-trailers, piles of tires. To keep awake, I scanned through the AM dial and came up with a community station, a woman reading the local "bulletin board." The ads touted cowboy-cut jeans, feed products, mineral blocks, and fertilizer. During the "Trading Post Program," people called in with items for sale: swamp coolers, horse trailers, parakeets. I struggled to keep from nodding off.

The monotony was finally broken by the Truckee River, a picturesque stream that tumbles down from Lake Tahoe. The Donner Party was succored by its cool mountain water, but the canyon through which the river runs provided them with still more misery—a wretched stretch that required frequent fording of a river chock-full of boulders.

Truckee Canyon was hard on the Donner Party. For four long days in October of 1846, they negotiated the canyon's twenty-five miles. Temperatures dropped below freezing at night. Crossing and re-crossing the boulder-strewn Truckee River, the oxen developed cuts and sores on their hooves. The strong headwinds were brutal. It was slow, slow going, and midway through the canyon they got their first look at the Sierra Nevada, towering dead ahead and glistening with snow.

Nowadays, the canyon is home to a power plant, a dam, a diatomaceous-earth processing plant, a trailer park, an auto-wrecking yard, and the Mustang Ranch—the largest brothel in the United States. West of the canyon lie the outskirts of Reno. The "biggest little city in the world" and its cluster of casino-hotels are built on the meadows where the Donner Party rested before attempting the ascent of the Sierra Nevada—the last and biggest obstacle before they could reach the Sacramento Valley.

They began that ascent at the end of October, with snow flurries in the air. By the time they neared the first summit it was too late. Snow fell furiously and forced the pioneers to retreat to a small lake a few miles from the summit, a lake that today bears the Donner name. Here, the Donner Party hunkered down to wait out the winter. For months on end, the snow mounted and food supplies vanished. Eventually, fifteen people would try to escape on homemade snowshoes. It took this group, known as the "Forlorn Hope," thirty days to trek the eighty miles from the lake to Sacramento. Of those fifteen, only seven survived, and for them survival necessitated cannibalizing those who died en route. Back at the lake, worsening circumstances over the long winter months forced a few other members of the party to break the same taboo. George and Tamsen Donner were among the forty who died in the mountains. Their orphaned children were taken out in March by James Reed's rescue party.

Once in California, the freeway and the trail begin to climb in earnest. The road crosses and re-crosses the Truckee. Sheer cliffs rise up, and even in the middle of a sunny day, there's a dark and gloomy air to the climb. These were the lands of the Washoe Indians, who astonished the white pioneers because they wore almost no clothing and did not seem to feel the bone-chilling cold of the Sierra.

The climb into the Sierra is steady, sinuous, and steep. At freeway speed, the curves come quickly and continuously. The road requires a more concerted effort from the driver than the vast desert expanses left behind in Nevada. No possibility of letting the attention wander. Every hundred yards or so you confront the prospect of slamming into the canyon wall or careening over the embankment into the Truckee. You grip the wheel, lean into curves, skirt past the huge, crawling tractor-trailers.

The freeway emerges from the canyon at the town of Truckee. An exit leads to Donner Lake, end of the road for me and the Donner Party. Twelve hundred miles from Fort Bridger have brought us to this deep, crystalline lake two and a half miles long, a half-mile wide, 5,924 feet above sea level. The lake is surely one of America's beauty spots, the sparkling water reflecting Donner Peak and Mount Judah, stands of lodgepole pine rimming the shoreline.

A small museum inside the park displays pioneer objects, including Tamsen Donner's kitchen utensils and a gun used by one of the party to kill a bear. Outside the museum, an impressive monument indicates the depth of the twenty-two foot snowpack that piled up during the winter of 1846, when a succession of fierce blizzards kept the Donners snowbound and starving. Plaques mark the site of their cabins and lean-tos. From the shore of the lake, you can look up at stark and beautiful Donner Pass, the final hurdle that half the party never got over.

"The cannibalism, no question," Ranger A. J. Batie says when asked why two hundred thousand people a year visit the museum. "That's what they've heard about, that's the first thing they ask about." But at the state park, Batie and the other rangers try to redirect visitors' morbid curiosity. "We try to get them to realize the difficult decisions these people faced," she says. "They made bad decisions, but traveling the trail was not easy." Meanwhile, researchers continue to ponder the more enticing and enduring mysteries about the Donner Party. How extensive was the cannibalism? Did the press of the day sensationalize the story? Were any members of the party murdered for their flesh? "We're still searching for answers," says historian Frankye Craig.

Visitors to the museum may be curious about cannibalism and fascinated with the party's multiple disasters, but these days most people come to Donner Lake for recreation—boating and fishing in the summer, snowmobiling and skiing in the winter. The lake is ringed with chalets and vacation bungalows. Cross-country ski trails lead up to the pass and several good downhill resorts are located on the surrounding mountains. What was once the site of great suffering has become, over the years, a place to go for fun.

But for all the diversions, the knowledge of what happened on the shores of the lake in 1846 forces visitors into contemplation. The serenity and beauty of the place have something to do with it. How could such suffering occur in such an idyllic spot, one wonders. The Donner tragedy haunts the pine forests around the lake, and a sense of gloom pervades the surroundings even on bright sunny days.

That, anyway, was my mood as I hiked the pioneer trail up to Donner Pass, the same three-mile climb that proved impossible on a snowy October night more than a century and a half ago. I visited in midsummer, but the air was still chilly, a harsh wind badgering the lodgepole pines, clouds racing into the gap between Mount Donner and Mount Judah. Far below me, Donner Lake receded into the mists. As I climbed, a cold rain began to fall, and the damp chill that passed into my bones encouraged empathy for the ill-fated Donner Party as they confronted their doom in the frozen heights of the Sierra Nevada. Over the years, they have been criticized as foolhardy and incompetent. They have been derided as bumbling greenhorns who had no business being on the trail. They have been accused of crimes, damned as sinners, and rebuked for violating a primary taboo. The very name *Donner* can cause a shudder. But after following their trail, I'm inclined to withhold judgment. Ill-fated they may have been, but they met that fate with perseverance, forbearance, and fortitude that I for one could never have mustered.

Forever West

A sign greets me at the border: *Welcome to Wyoming Forever West.*

The words frame the state's familiar emblem, a silhouetted rider on a bucking horse. It's a nice-sounding phrase, to be sure. Catchy. Good ring to it. Inspirational in a way, especially to one who has spent many months and several thousands of miles on the road, trending west, taking the roundabout route. It feeds my hopes for a new start out west—that persistent American urge articulated in so many phrases: *California or bust; go west, young man; across the Great Divide; there's gold in them there hills.*

And now this phrase riffing on the familiar theme: *Forever West.*

But what exactly does it mean?

The gist seems to be that Wyoming is the real deal, the true West. It's a proclamation of sorts: *Be it known that Wyoming will always stay true to its western roots.* And maybe it is a promise as well to arriving travelers: *Here you will find the West you've dreamed about, the West of your imagination.*

A mile or two into Wyoming, I spot a coyote trotting along with that habitual hangdog look so common to the species, his path constrained by the barbed-wire fence that forever parallels the road.

* * *

Forever West. When you stop to think about it, it's an odd phrase. Is it even grammatical? "Forever," normally an adverb, seems to be modifying a noun, "West"—something not permitted by the usual rules of English grammar. And yet this ungrammatical phrase seems to convey some sort of message. How is that?

It doesn't make sense, yet it does.

The more you think about it, the slipperier the phrase seems. Gives you something to ponder as you cross mile after mile of sagebrush plains.

My first stop is the town of Torrington, situated at the intersection of two highways, Route 85 and Route 26.

Large cattle-bearing tractor-trailers roll through town, gears grinding, cows groaning with each lurch. The odor of manure and diesel hangs in Torrington's air, along with choking dust that swirls in the beams of headlamps.

South of the main intersection, the town's Pioneer Park allows free camping, first come, first serve. The campground looks across the North Platte River at a huge, glowing sugar factory. Other than a teenaged couple making out under one of the picnic shelters, no one else is in the park this evening. The teenagers vanish while I set up the tent. It appears that I'll be the lone camper tonight in Torrington.

Water is heating on the propane stove when a car pulls into the parking lot nearest the campground. I see the telltale reflective lettering on the doors: a police cruiser outfitted with a searchlight on the driver's side. The beam appears.

It prowls across the park, along the riverbank, over the vegetation; it comes sniffing up to my tent, the picnic table, me, then over to the vacant campsites, then back to me.

Abruptly, the light vanishes. The car door opens; the officer steps out, adjusting his black cap so that it is low on his brow. He saunters across the park toward me. On the stove, the tea water comes to a boil and splashes over the sides of the pot, hissing when it hits the propane flame. I kill the flame and wait.

"Evening," the officer says. Touches his cap. Looks over the campsite. "Spending the night?"

"Long as it's okay."

He nods, feigning nonchalance. "Where you headed?" he wants to know. Ponders the answer, then asks, "Where're you coming from?" He's making an effort to sound casual, conversational, even polite; but it's an interrogation all the same. Suspicion of the stranger. In my younger days, annoyed by unwarranted questions, I might have answered him with some truculence. *I'm not doing anything wrong, man. It's a free country, leave me be.* Now, older and jaded, inured to these inquiries, I answer the questions straight—careful to be laconic but not curt. A harmless rambler, the cop eventually decides. He takes his leave, touching his hat again, wishing me a good night and a pleasant stay in Torrington.

Back at his patrol car he sits for a few minutes, dome light on, writing something, calling on the radio. His search beam is aimed right at the license plate of my van. Computers across the country process the information he has gathered and entered; after a few minutes, the data check out. For now, I am officially innocuous. The cop leaves me to my cup of tea and the voracious mosquitoes of the North Platte.

It's a good campground for solitude but not for sleep. All night, the sugar factory emits a glow and a steady hum. Trains skirl through town. In the early hours, truck traffic picks up, jake brakes braying in the darkness. Lying awake in the tent, I mull over that phrase, *Forever West*. Taken by itself, without the context of the state name and the welcome sign on the highway, it is ambiguous at best. How exactly does the brain decode a message like this? As near as I can tell, the phrase probably means that Wyoming is synonymous with the West, that Wyoming embodies the West. To paraphrase: "Wyoming is the place where the West—the true West—endures and will do so forever." But how exactly does one get this message from just the two words? It's an enigma of sorts.

A sign on the outskirts of Douglas, Wyoming informs new arrivals that Douglas is "Home of the Jackalope." It's no exaggeration: in Douglas, jackalopes appear everywhere. Jackalopes on banners, jackalopes on postcards, jackalopes in children's drawings taped to drugstore windows. In the town's central park, where other municipalities might place a statue of a soldier or trailblazer or statesman, Douglas has erected a fiberglass jackalope on a plinth.

As the story goes, the creature first appeared in Douglas in the 1930s when a twelve-year-old boy saw a jackrabbit carcass lying next to some antelope antlers. Practiced at taxidermy, the kid got the whimsical idea of dressing a rabbit with antlers. People liked it, and soon he started selling his humorous creations to stores and bars as décor. Eventually, the jackalope caught on with tourists to the point that Douglas now bases its identity on this chimera. Decals, postcards, posters, T-shirts, mugs, shot glasses—in Douglas, you can buy just about anything with the image of a jackalope on it.

At the LaBonte Inn, I ask the waitress what there is to see in Douglas besides jackalopes.

"Besides jackalopes?" she says with a frown. "I don't know. There's the state fair in August. Oh, and there's a museum over on the fairgrounds."

She means the Pioneer Museum, where glass cases display all the accouterments of pioneer life: saddles, boots, axes, saws, and guns—lots of guns. The docent on duty comes around to point out a few of his favorites. He is especially fond of some guns purportedly used at the Battle of the Little Bighorn. "Real beauties," he calls them.

The docent alerts me to another attraction in Douglas. During the Second World War, the town was the site of an internment camp for German and Italian prisoners. Some of the prisoners painted scenes of the Old West on the walls of the Officers' Club. The murals were preserved after the war when the Officers' Club became the meeting hall of the Odd Fellows local. "Still there to this day," the docent tells me.

He gives me directions to the Odd Fellows hall, but when I get there the place is locked tight. A historical marker out front summarizes the history of Camp Douglas. The prisoners were made to work on local farms and—the sign suggests—were happy to do so, even becoming friendly with the locals. For its part, "the Army was meticulous" in following the Geneva Accords for the humane treatment of prisoners. The sign also notes "some of the prisoners contributed artwork that still remains." But, alas, I won't get to see the art for myself.

Later, searching the Internet, I locate some photographs of the sixteen murals. They depict familiar western scenes: geysers at Yellowstone, a wagon train passing Independence Rock, a roundup in a corral, the branding of wild horses, a shootout in a saloon, and American Indians passing a peace pipe. There are plenty of horses and six-shooters in the paintings. A big sky dominates many of the scenes. They are all done in the same somewhat romanticized style, derived from Frederic Remington, that seems inevitable in Western art: rugged, mythic, impossibly idealized even as it strives for realism. Where did the Italian POWs learn this style? No one knows. Perhaps someone instructed them. Perhaps they saw examples somewhere. Or maybe they just "picked up the vibe." In any case, the murals are evidence of the powerful allure of western motifs—the very motifs that seem to be suggested by the phrase "Forever West."

Oregon Trail pioneers used to camp along Deer Creek, near present-day Glenrock, Wyoming. By this point in their long journey, the trail travelers had become sick—often literally—of the North Platte's brackish water. Deer Creek was the best source of "sweet water" that they had found in weeks of hard travel. There's a municipal park on the site now, featuring a modern campground imposed on the old pioneer camp. The facility also includes softball fields, a rodeo arena, and—something I've never encountered before in a public park—an operating oil jack.

Alone in the campground, mid-afternoon, I set up the tent, a quick task. Then I sit on the picnic table, reading Thoreau and slapping mosquitoes while the creek babbles and the oil jack churns away. Having lost my way on the career track, I am now more or less following the Oregon Trail, camping out of my van, reading the American Transcendentalists and the journals of Lewis and Clark as I go. I've told friends I'm doing research, but this journey has become more like a haphazard attempt to reclaim the westering spirit supposedly latent in all Americans—"the prevailing tendency of my countrymen," Thoreau called it. He himself wanted to walk all the way to Oregon. "Westward I go free," he said. "That way the nation is moving." And so for nine weeks now, I have been drifting westward, more or less, putting Thoreau's notion to the test. The endeavor has brought me here, to Glenrock.

Late in the afternoon, some other folks arrive, disrupting the solitude I've enjoyed for a couple of hours. First comes a groundskeeper in a county pickup truck. He unloads equipment and sets to work chalking the softball field. Looks like league action tonight. Then a truck camper that has seen better days tours the campground, driving the entire circle before selecting a site adjacent to mine, as though trying to annoy me on purpose. I can't understand why, in an otherwise empty campground, anyone would choose a site next to the only other camper in the place. But there's nothing I can do about it. It is, as Americans are wont to say, a free country. My new neighbors, an older couple, haul out their gear and set up camp. Folding lawn chairs. Strings of colored lanterns. An artificial carpet. A shelter that surrounds the picnic table—plastic top to fend off the rain, mesh walls and a zippered door to provide bug protection. Meticulously, they conduct their camp chores. Pumping water, lighting a charcoal fire, arranging kitchen utensils on the picnic table in preparation of the evening meal. They've got propane lanterns, a gas stove, a radio; in short order, their campsite is up and running, a glowing, humming borough of two. While the woman works the cooking equipment (already the smell of grilling meat fills the air), the man studies the contents of his large tackle box. He glances up to see me observing him and waves. "Hey neighbor, how's the fishing?"

"Sorry, not much of a fisherman."

A bewildered look crosses his face, a look that says something like, "What the hell? A red-blooded American male, doesn't like fishing? Well, it takes all types." Out loud he says simply, "That so?" and I feel like I've let him down. "Well, come on over and have a beer."

"I was just about to go for a walk," I say, a small lie to avoid an unwanted conversation. "Maybe later."

"All righty, then, me and Betty will keep a cold one for you."

Now committed to my little lie, I set off down the loop road to visit the park's attractions, starting with a close-up view of the oil jack. Its sucking-insect motion mesmerizes for a while, then I head over to the ball field, where warm-up is underway. I take a seat in the bleachers. The brilliant fire of sunset flares then fades. The game begins in a pool of electric light, eighteen grown men at play amid the cheering, groaning, and laughing of their families in the stands. When one older player takes his turn at bat, a tiny voice yells out, "Come on, Grandpa!" His teammates take up the chant, laughingly imploring "Gramps" to come through with a hit.

All over America at this moment, games are in progress, amateur to professional, little children trying to act like grown-up players, elderly folks trying to be kids again. Boys, girls, men, women everywhere engaged in acting out the particular choreography of baseball, a precise choreography that nonetheless allows for the idiosyncratic interpretations of both the virtuoso and the rank amateur. Here in Glenrock, it's a rather clumsy interpretation of the dance; but such is the beauty of the game, such is its inherent grace even when performed by the graceless, that I am compelled to watch to the conclusion, just to see how this one insignificant performance of the national pastime will turn out.

Even when the game is over, I tarry to watch, a sideline observer, as the teammates shake hands, slap backs, laugh together. The lights fade on the field. It's time to go, but they linger in the parking lot by their pickups, chatting, making the most of the moment. In a few hours they'll be back at the plant for another day of work. The kids clamber into the truck beds and are given the honor of holding dad's glove and bat. By the light of headlamps, the trucks crawl out of the parking lot back to the highway, and soon the park is dark and still. Cricket noise and the clank of the oil jack fill the void. I walk back to the campground, cutting across the powdery dirt of the rodeo ring. It's late, and with any luck the neighboring campers will have retired. I realize now that I've delayed my return to the tent in part to avoid the fisherman and Betty, to shirk "the cold one" he's keeping for me and whatever strained conversation would have to go with it. As I approach the campsite I feel a sense of dismay when I see the propane lanterns lit up and the colored glow of the strung-up globes decorating the neighboring site. It appears they've been waiting for me.

"Here he is, Betty," the old man says. "Hey, neighbor, ready for that beer?"

Suppressing the urge to beg off, I take the cold can and drop into the proffered folding lawn chair. Betty is working knitting needles. The old man—"George Henderson, and this here's my wife Betty"—sets aside a fly he's been fooling with, and together we form a triad on a patch of artificial grass. We've come to the moment that I seem to fear (though I'm not sure why), the moment of small talk, the tedium of chitchat.

And sure enough, George starts right in with the usual questions: Where am I coming from? Where am I headed next? What am I up to? Since the only honest answer is I don't know, I don't have the slightest idea, whatever I say comes out evasive and inarticulate: *Oh, well, just following the breeze, no particular plan, going where the road takes me.* These are euphemisms, upstanding citizens like George and Betty must surely know, meant to gloss over my lack of any vocation other than drifter, wanderer, vagabond. All of which is to say, No, I don't have a job. No, I don't have a purpose in life. Yes, I am aimless and shiftless, the poor wayfaring stranger. I am, I am.

But to my surprise, George gets a kick out of my answers. He likes the phrase and repeats it: "Just following the breeze, huh?" He comes back to it even after the conversation has moved on to the price of gasoline, good fishing spots, the weather.

"Just following the breeze," he says again. "Sound like anyone you know, Betty?"

"Yes, dear." Betty smiles wryly and continues to knit a small sweater. For a grandchild, I'm guessing. She works the needles quickly, efficiently. Everything about her is neat and organized—her ironed dress, her sprayed-and-set hair, the carefully arranged utensils on the table. Even her wrinkles seem to follow a precise pattern. No question she is a meticulous personality. She doesn't strike me as someone who would care to associate with anyone "just following the breeze."

"She means me," George says. "I was once like you."

"He still is, believe me," Betty says to George's delighted guffaws.

He's taken two more beers from the cooler. I have to admit the cold beer tastes really good sitting in a campground on a warm evening somewhere in the vast American interior.

"Oh, yes, a lot like you."

The red and green glow from the colored globes above us—the string runs from the side of the camper to a tree—warms his face and makes him look younger. He's a small, thin man with a boyish face despite the wrinkles. He gives off a sense of energy, somehow, even though his movements are slow and deliberate. I can imagine he was once called a "feisty fellow."

George goes on to tell me his story. He quit high school at fifteen and ran away from home. "Couldn't stand the old man, the way he would beat on me." George soon fell in with the hobo set and rode the rails all around the West. During his vagabond years, he got beat up and arrested more times than he can remember. He drank and did drugs. He fell out of a train car in a small Oregon town and ended up in a hospital where he met Betty, a nurse. For some reason she took a liking to him, or at least felt pity for him ("That's more like it," Betty says) and took to preaching to the lost soul and caring for him. By the time he recovered, he had fallen for the pretty nurse, but he knew he had no hope of winning her unless he proved worthy. He went to night school and got his diploma. Then the war came and Betty joined with the Red Cross and was sent to Hawaii. George enlisted, but was shipped to Europe. He wrote often to her, but nothing arrived in return. When the war was over, he went back to Oregon hoping to find her. She was there, all but engaged to a childhood friend, but inexplicably she still was drawn to the former bum. He went to college on the GI Bill and graduated with a teaching degree. For thirty years thereafter he taught high school and always kept an eye out for the wayward boys, the potential drifters like he had been. When retirement came, he got back on the road, "traveling respectable" this time and "just following the breeze" as had been his inclination all along. Now, though, he had Betty along to keep him in line and camp in order.

It's well after midnight when the story finishes and we put out the lanterns. George and Betty retire to the camper. I'm left alone, lying awake in the tent, listening to Deer Creek's splashing and gurgling backed by the continuous clanking of the oil jack. In spite of myself, and in spite of my innate reticence, I keep meeting people who seem to have something to share with me, clues possibly to what comes next. And so tomorrow I'm bound for the next stop, somewhere farther down the American road.

Casper touts itself as "an oil boomtown with a cowboy culture." With a population of maybe 50,000, Casper is the biggest city I've seen since leaving Kansas City over a month ago. I've been camping along the way, eating mostly out of cans and pouches. Casper offers the chance to spend the night in a bed and have a regular meal.

Perhaps Casper is known for its cowboy culture, but the gateway scenery on the main drag suggests that a motor-vehicle culture predominates. Seemingly every business has something to do with vehicles. Auto parts. Body shop. Brake service. Tire store. Auto repair. Auto upholstery. Battery and electric. Truck outfitter. Several large lots are dedicated to the sale of vehicles, especially large gleaming pickup trucks and RVs. Interspersed along the way are machine shops and sheet metal supply outlets. Apparently, these cowboys love their machines.

Keeping within my modest budget, I take a room at the Sage & Sand Motel, a classic roadside flophouse built from planks painted a sickly yellow. Lattice panels have been nailed over the windows for no apparent reason. The room smells of a combination of disagreeable odors—mold, cigarette smoke, hospital disinfectant. It does not seem any better than the tent, but for the price I guess I shouldn't expect much.

Driving around town in search of a local steakhouse, I find nothing but franchises—Outback Steakhouse, Olive Garden, Famous Dave's Barbecue, Buffalo Wild Wings, Red Lobster. I could be anywhere in the United States. Finally, across the street from yet another car dealership, I spot a pink and blue sign with the words "Restaurant" and "Western Grill" lit up in pink neon. A cartoonish cow's head decorates the sign, and there's a big American flag in the window. Inside: lots of signage supporting the second amendment. Toy train tracks run along the walls up near the ceiling, the track supported by trestles suspended from wires. A model train whirs around the track while I eat my strip steak and potatoes. The place is packed, offering an opportunity to eavesdrop on conversations seemingly ripped from the kind of radio talk shows I've listened to for the last several weeks. The goddamned environmentalists. The goddamned economy. The goddamned president. The goddamned Broncos.

Forever West. I've been wondering where the phrase comes from. It's not the Wyoming state motto, which is "Equal Rights." It's not the state nickname, which is "The Cowboy State." What is it then? Turns out it's a slogan, a marketing message. Or, to be more contemporary about it, a "branding tagline." This I learn during a stop at a tourist information center in Casper. The phrase appears repeatedly on marketing materials produced by the state's tourism office. It's actually trademarked: a subscript "TM" sign follows each iteration of the tagline. This interests me in part because the career I ditched back east involved writing advertising copy. I know a little bit about taglines.

What I know is that a good branding tagline is connotative, calling forth a set of imagery, hinting at multiple possibilities. The main message should be clear, and yet just ambiguous enough to inspire some thought. A good branding tagline should be both inspirational and aspirational. And on some level the message has to be manipulative. After all, it's marketing—an attempt to coerce you into believing what the marketing specialists want you to believe. Wyoming's tagline seems to do the trick. I'm impressed. But there's still the question of how it manages to suggest so much with just two words.

Back at the motel, I stare through the latticework covering the window. The neighboring businesses include an auto repair shop, Tire Rama, Wyoming Automotive, and Wyoming Alignment Supply. The motel's sign, ill lit by a streetlamp, spells out the name in red lettering. Contemplating the name, I realize that "sand and sage" is an apt description of the campsites I've been occupying for the last few weeks. In Casper, I've traded the real thing for a shabby motel with an evocative name. Well, I wanted a real bed for the night, and here I am. The bed itself—I shouldn't be surprised to discover—is a wreck, and I end up bringing in the sleeping bag and bunking on the floor.

Now and then throughout the night, the sound of freight trains from the nearby switching yard jolts me from sleep, and I find myself wishing I were out in the real sage and sand.

Today's trivia question: Where does the name "Wyoming" come from? Answer: the state is named for a valley in Pennsylvania. In 1865, an Ohio congressman suggested the name "Wyoming" for the new territory out west. In doing so, he sought to honor his home state of Pennsylvania and the lush Wyoming Valley he remembered from his youth. The congressman had never been out west, but somehow his proposal went through. So while the state's tagline declares that "Wyoming" is synonymous with the West, the name itself in fact recalls an eastern landscape. Wyoming might be "Forever West," but its name is not.

Independence Rock, the iconic Oregon Trail landmark, is now managed as a State of Wyoming historical site and rest area: toilets, vending machines, a small interpretive display, a picnic area, and a trail leading out to the distinctive granite dome. I meet the caretaker of the facility, Mr. Long, inside the men's room, where he is stocking the soap and paper supplies.

Hundreds of people stop each day, Mr. Long says. From his point of view, they are plain messy. They drop trash, spill water, and foul the restrooms. Some people are "downright thickheaded, got shit for brains." It never ceases to amaze him.

"There are folks don't even see the rock til you point it out to them. They think it's one of them boulders out front by the picnic tables. They want to know where the names are."

Mr. Long lives in the trailer behind the rest area. He's been retired for years, but "couldn't sit still no longer." So he contracted with the state to service the rest area. He mows the lawns, cleans the buildings, picks up the trash people throw into the sagebrush. Even with the mess and all, he loves it out here on the high plains. "You got your open spaces, your clean air, your fishing in the reservoir. Way I see it, it's a little bit of heaven for me." It doesn't bother him in the least to be far from the amenities of the city: Casper's a mess, ugly and congested. And he won't even think about going down to Denver. "I'm done with city life. Done for good."

After talking to Mr. Long, I walk out to the 130-foot-high domed rock to read some of the names carved there: *W. H. Collins 1862, R. McOord 1850, B. Garret 1853, P. Hollister, A. Power, J. L. Holland* and on and on—hundreds of names. Landmarks and historical sites dot the old pioneer trails. At each site there are chiseled and scratched names, footprints, ghost voices whispering their desire to move on, move on. The golden dream of the West. Somewhere up ahead at trail's end, we all want to believe, there's a promised land, the "Great West," as Thoreau called it, "enveloped in mystery and poetry."

I was hoping to climb to the top, as so many pioneers did, for an overview of the Sweetwater River and the windswept plains of central Wyoming, but these days Independence

Rock is fenced off. A sign warns that climbing the rock is strictly prohibited.

There's a ghost town on the lovely, lonely route from Independence Rock to Lander. Jeffrey City sprang up as a town for uranium workers during a mining boom in the 1950s, the population growing to over four thousand. But by the 1980s the uranium market had crashed. The mines shut down, and the workers moved away. Many of the buildings left town, too, hauled off on trucks in search of the next boomtown. Not much remains other than the town's street grid.

If you're not in a hurry, you might as well walk around the empty streets of Jeffrey City. A few street signs still stand, indicating names like Jackalope and Coyote, Rattlesnake and Uranium. But there are no houses on these streets. Only a few scattered structures remain: some erstwhile apartment complexes with boarded windows; a couple of abandoned filling stations; an outsized school. There are derelict playgrounds and tennis courts, a dismantled phone booth, and several defunct satellite dishes. Weeds have taken over pretty much everything—building foundations, playgrounds, parking lots. On the back streets, pronghorns graze on grass growing in the cracked asphalt.

Apparently, the "Forever West" ideal did not pan out in Jeffrey City, where "forever" turned out to be a delusion. Still, Jeffrey City does fairly represent Wyoming, given the prevalence of the boom-bust cycles in the state and throughout the American West. In this sense, Jeffrey City does play a part in the "Forever West" collage—just not the part the tourist commission favors in their full-page ads and brochures.

Out on the highway, there's a weathered sign that reads *Motel Yes No*. The image of a top hat rests on the sign over the "e" and the "l," but the "Top Hat Motel"—if that was its name— seems to have gone out of business long ago. The nearby Split Rock Café is supposedly still operating, but a *closed* sign hangs on the door, and the place is shut tight, the windows dark. I stand a minute in the parking lot, sand kicking up and swirling around. Across the highway, a few dust devils rise out of the sage plains. A tumbleweed rolls by. My prospects in Jeffrey City seem pretty much exhausted; nothing to do but what everyone else has already done: skip town.

During my stint in advertising, I learned about the effectiveness of "floating signifiers." The term comes from semiotics, first used by Claude Lévi-Strauss to indicate words and signs "void of meaning and thus apt to receive any meaning." Such signifiers are deliberately vague, requiring the target audience to determine meaning for themselves. In advertising slogans, the classic floating signifier is "it." *Just do it*. Do what? Depends. The meaning, open-ended and flexible, ultimately must be audience determined. In contrast, Roland Barthes talked about signifiers that are *overly* replete with multiple and contradictory meanings. In this case, too, meaning depends on audience and context. Even if meaning is fixed for one audience, the signifier still trawls around what Barthes called a "floating chain of signifieds"—all those other possible meanings bobbing along in the wake.

Maybe something like this is going on with the "Forever West" message: the precise significance awaits determination. It is suspended, floating, like a distant mirage on a desert highway. You stare and stare at the shimmer, trying to bring it into focus, thinking, what is it? Is it real, a trick of the senses, just my imagination? What?

Which brings to mind something Wallace Stegner said: "What lures many people to the West always has been, and still is, mirage."

In Lander, Wyoming, the Popo Agie Rendezvous is in full swing. Staged in the city park, the rendezvous attempts to recreate the mountain man lifestyle in the middle of a modern tourist town. Buffalo burgers are on offer, along with pizza sold from a carnival food trailer covered with weathered boards to look "old timey." The name "Dominos" has been scratched into the wood. The salesgirls are outfitted in homespun calico dresses.

Latter-day mountain men have set up tents, canvas lean-tos, even teepees. Dressed in buckskin, they sit on logs and engage in "authentic activities," such as whittling, sharpening blades, tanning hides, smoking corncob pipes, and cooking on the campfire. Children play "kick stick" and "nose ball." Babies are strapped onto cradleboards. In front of a teepee, a Pocahontas-attired woman explains to a crowd that it took her four hundred hours of scraping elk hide to make the teepee. Some of the mountain men walk around saying things like, "How's life in the big city, chief?" Mercantile tents display mountain man paraphernalia for sale: buckskin clothing, knives, hatchets, muzzle-loading rifles, leather pouches, wineskins. In one tent, A. J. White, a retired school principal and rendezvous veteran, has set up shop. His wife is a retired math teacher. For twenty years now, they've been traveling the rendezvous circuit—similar events take place throughout the Mountain West—selling antique rifles and supplies for black-powder muzzleloaders. He wears buckskin pants and a leather hat. He has a tremendous bushy beard. He "follows the shoots" around the West, a series of competitions for black-powder riflemen that culminates in a championship in Montana.

"Some rendezvous are pretty strict," Mr. White says. "They won't allow anything modern, not even shoelaces or zippers. Here in Lander, it's not so strict. You see people with wristwatches on. They might be trying to start a fire by rubbing sticks, but they still got their watches. See that group over there eating pizza? You'd never see that at the stricter rendezvous. The other participants would force them to leave. And look at those port-a-potties over there. Some rendezvous allow only wooden shacks with latrine pits. You get a few thousand people on a hot summer day and the smell will do away with any romantic notions you've got about pre-modern life."

"All in all, it's a good life," he says of their summers on the road.

Better than teaching school?

"Now and then you miss it. But we get a lot of kids coming into the tent, looking at everything. They want to know how it works, how it was made. Gives us the chance to explain, show them how folks used to live, how they made things for themselves. You see that look of wonder on the kids' faces—that's what made teaching enjoyable. But the schools nowadays are crazy, going in the wrong direction. At the rendezvous we can still teach the kids the way it ought to be."

After crossing half the state, I think I have a better read on Wyoming's branding message. It all has to do with what "West" signifies to the target audience. According to the literary critic Robert Scholes, "the human condition is a condition of textuality" in that "the conditions of our being come to us already scripted, textualized." Much of what we consider reality is actually a *textual reality* that defines and prescribes our experience by means of predetermined language and discourse conventions. "Forever West" alludes to one such textual reality. The tagline calls to mind a set of images derived from familiar texts that define the West. In American culture these texts include dime westerns, Remington-styled artwork, Hollywood films, television shows, and many other sources of popular imagery, such as Marlboro ads and souvenir postcards. As a catchphrase, "Forever West" condenses all these texts and encapsulates them. To understand the tagline, you need to access the textual reality. The marketers are counting on you to do so.

Atlantic City, Wyoming. Not quite a ghost town, but nearly so. Originally a gold rush camp founded in 1867, it is now an outpost accessible only by gravel road. In the Sagebrush

Saloon, there are more trophy heads on the walls this evening than customers. Prominent among the trophies, of course, is a jackalope head—the antlered rabbit, the ubiquitous joke that never seems to wear thin out west. The bartender talks to two men perched on stools; all three are leaning forward on the scarred wood bar like they're going over plans to hold up the mail train. Looks like they've been there for some time, well on their way to getting soused.

"Gordy, you hear what Todd here is saying? This boy wants me to buy one of them Lexus SUVs for the ranch."

"They're cool," Todd says. "Ain't they cool, Gordy?"

"Damn straight," Gordy says.

"Cool, my ass," the old man says. "Don't need no fancy leather seats when you got crap to haul. That thing's a pansy truck if I ever seen one. I spend 60,000 bucks, I want me a good piece of equipment, not no pansy ride. Lexus, shit. That thing's for ranch houses in California, not ranches in Wyoming."

Todd laughs. "That's Pop for you—he thinks an old beat-up Mack truck is the best machine going. Can you believe that, Gordy?"

"Damn straight."

The bartender, Gordy, looks the part. Typical bartender in a typical western bar: long hair, leather hat and vest, studded belt with a big silver cow-head buckle. Pure western. But at some point in the conversation, he reveals that he's from New Jersey and relates how he came west on a motorcycle after a divorce. In search of himself. Wound up in Wyoming. Dead-ended here in this near ghost town, population thirty-seven. Been here almost three years. It's a common motif running through western tales—the West as searching ground, the place of vision quests for the disaffected. The lone horseman or motorcyclist crossing the desert, the B-movie cliché reenacted in good faith by countless wandering Americans, myself included. They don the attire of freedom—leather jackets, faded jeans, turquoise and silver jewelry, maybe a bandana—and ride off into the sunset. The West is crowded with empty people seeking fulfillment in open space. Tucson, Flagstaff, Durango, Reno, Ely—you hear the same story. Different town, different era, different dude, maybe, but down through the years, all across the West, Gordy's story has been told over and over.

"You see those guys come in here?" Gordy says. "Wearing suits. Just looked around and left. Must have gone over to the Merc."

"Developers," the old man mutters. He drinks off half a beer straightaway then bangs the bottle down on the bar. "Californians. More goddamn Californians come to californicate the place."

Two of the seminal texts about Wyoming—central to the creation of a textual reality of the American West—are Francis Parkman's *The Oregon Trail* (1847) and Owen Wister's *The Virginian* (1902). Over the decades, many readers have formulated their ideas about the West from these texts. They are primary sources for popular western imagery. Yet in his preface to the third edition of *The Oregon Trail*, published six years after the first edition, Parkman seemed to think that the "Wild West" had all but disappeared. He wrote of "changes almost incredible," noting that the massive herds of buffalo had vanished. For the preface to the fourth edition (1872), Parkman remarked on "forms and conditions of life which have ceased, in great measure, to exist." The lament continued twenty years later, in yet another preface: "The Wild West is tamed, and its savage charms have withered." Similarly, in a preface to The Virginian, Owen Wister contended that the Wyoming depicted in his novel no longer existed: "It is a vanished world. No journeys, save those which memory can take, will bring you to it now. The mountains are there, far and shining, and the sunlight, and the infinite earth, and the air that seems forever the true fountain of youth, but where is the buffalo, and the wild antelope, and where the horseman with his pasturing thousands?"

Neither Parkman nor Wister seemed to believe in a Wyoming that was "forever west." Both thought that the quintessential western way of life had vanished. Nevertheless, the Wyoming Office of Tourism insists that the West endures, that it is still out there waiting for tourists who long to rediscover it.

Farther down the road, Highway 28 brings me to Route 191, which brings me eventually back to Interstate 80. After many miles on empty two-lane roads, entering the (relatively) busy flow of the freeway is like leaving solitude for a noisy party. And easily the loudest voice at the party belongs to "Little America," a way station thirty miles ahead that insistently calls attention to itself in billboards along the freeway. Leaving Green River, you see the signs appearing at regular intervals, reiterating the message—"Little America. Your Home on the Range."

Observing the time-honored ploy of roadside advertising—repetition ad nauseam—Little America has planted a billboard seemingly every half-mile or so. As you get closer to the Little America exit, these billboards appear with greater and greater frequency. The place is hyped so insistently that you really can't pass it by without stopping to find out what it's all about. By the time it appears on the horizon atop the next rise in the sagebrush plains, you have no choice but to acquiesce to your curiosity.

Coming up the ramp into the Little America parking lot, you find yourself in an artificial oasis. A forest of birch and pine trees shades picnic grounds and a swimming pool. These pines might well be the only trees within a hundred square miles. A series of buildings in faux colonial style fronts the parking lot: a hotel, a restaurant, a post office, a convenience store, a souvenir shop. At one end of the complex, a fueling station, with a good fifty pumps or so, does a brisk business.

Road weary, you might as well stretch your legs a bit and stroll around the "Frontier America Shop," a store with every kind of western kitsch you could imagine. There are bison statuettes in a variety of sizes, for example, and American Indian coffee cups, including a souvenir series featuring portraits of the Great Chiefs. A sign suggests that you "collect the whole set, 12 in all." There's also a Vanishing Wildlife series, with images of wolves and bears and bison stamped on eight-ounce mugs. And there's a whole row of cowboy-boot novelties like cowboy-boot dinner bells and boot-shaped candles. There are boot incense burners and an entire boot tea service in silver. Here, too, are the usual fake Native tchotchkes: moccasin candles, bead purses, Indian princess statuettes, pots made into lamps, sand paintings turned into clocks. There's one whole row of items with fossil motifs, and another row with items made from petrified wood. And in every aisle there's a cowgirl in costume waiting to assist customers in their quest for curios.

Any curio you can think of, folks, they've got it in the Frontier America Shop. Wind chimes, clocks, key chains, magnets, shot glasses, wolves and eagles made out of petrified wood, mini bison heads and antlers and coonskins and beaver skins. Jackalopes. Of course there are jackalopes. Geodes, trays of gemstones, aspen leaf-shaped jewelry. All kinds of hats and Wyoming-themed T-shirts. And penguins, hundreds of them, tiny and huge. Why penguins? Turns out a penguin is Little America's mascot—apparently because there's a Little America in Antarctica.

A fill-up, a couple of souvenirs, an ice cream cone, and you can say you've had the complete Little America experience (unless of course you want to spend the night in the Little America Hotel). Back out in the midday glare of the sage plains, riding off into vast nothingness, you have to wonder, as Little America quickly fades and vanishes in the rear-view mirror, was it all just a mirage?

Forever West. The slogan prompts us to accept a textual reality in place of the reality we encounter. We are supposed to attune ourselves to a mediated version of the West rather than the place we actually see. We are directed to tourist sites set up to enact the textual reality, sites that replicate the familiar tropes and motifs.

According to Jean Baudrillard, the *hyperreal* is a further level of textual reality wherein "everything is so textualized that there is no space left for the real." Instead, "we encounter simulations and simulacra at every turn." When these simulations and simulacra pile up, replacing reality, we find ourselves immersed in a hyperreality.

Moreover, Baudrillard suggests, we often prefer hyperreality to reality. The state's marketing campaign seems to encourage this preference. The marketing materials repeatedly refer to "your Forever West experience" and "your Forever West adventure." And what, according to the brochures, will you find on your Forever West adventure? Simulacra. A recreated West. Costumed characters in staged gunfights on the streets of Cody. Cowboy music revues. Reenactments of mountain man rendezvous. You can go on a covered wagon cookout or a "wagon train adventure" featuring a stop at a depopulated "Indian village." You can take the family for a root beer in a movie-set saloon. You can camp in a teepee or spend the night in a "fully restored frontier hotel." You can enjoy a "carefree stay" at a dude ranch, which promises to be "a transformative experience that you'll never forget." In promoting these "western-themed attractions," the Wyoming Office of Tourism apparently wants you to seek out a hyperreal Wyoming and mistake it for reality, a sort of "Forever West World."

As part of the Forever West campaign, the tourism office has produced a television commercial. In it, a twenty-first-century boy and his mother are traveling around the state in a car. As they travel, the boy sees familiar images of the Old West: a pioneer boy (his doppelganger?), a stagecoach, wild horses. But these images are not real. They are merely reflections—on glass, on the shiny side of an Airstream trailer, on river water. The words "Forever West" appear at the end of the commercial. Yet all the images that the boy sees (save a herd of fenced-in bison) are illusions, figments of the imagination derived from the standard texts.

Does the West endure in Wyoming? Or is the state merely a stage for the enduring illusions of the West we want to believe in? Ultimately, the marketing campaign requires a kind of wishful thinking. It is sadly nostalgic, wistful in its attempts to create presence from absence, to restore to existence what no longer exists and may never have existed. But the campaign's wistful, wishful thinking depends upon a delusion: "When the real is no longer what it used to be," Baudrillard has said, "nostalgia assumes its full meaning."

In southwestern Wyoming, the "Bridger Valley Historic Byway" takes me through a couple of small towns on the way to Fort Bridger Historic Site. According to the guidebook, there's a campground at the site, and that's where I intend to pass the night. It's a beautiful place—meadows watered by a creek, mountains for a backdrop—where Jim Bridger once operated a trading post. Bridger was a legendary figure, the paragon of a mountain man, one of those characters—like

Daniel Boone, Kit Carson, and Davy Crockett—lauded in our schoolbooks once upon a time. They were an American archetype: the independent, free-spirited, wide-roaming dudes of the frontier and wilderness. When I was younger, Bridger was well represented not just in our textbooks but in the wider culture as well. He was on television (*Wagon Train*) and in the movies (*Tomahawk, The Gun That Won the West, Jeremiah Johnson*). He even showed up in a pop song by Johnny Horton. Who didn't want to be Jim Bridger, western wanderer, trailblazer, bear fighter?

The historical site that memorializes Bridger includes a handful of restored buildings, most of them from the military era that followed Bridger's tenure. A recently built cabin replicates the trading post that Bridger operated. There is also a museum and a gift shop. The big event at Fort Bridger is a rendezvous reenactment that features (judging from the film in the museum) hundreds of people dressed in mountain man costumes.

The guidebook confidently promised a campground at Fort Bridger, but the ranger in the visitors' center informs me that in fact there is no camping on site. This is a problem. It's late in the day and there's no campground anywhere nearby, nothing but an RV site, and I'm not about to set up my tent among those noisy behemoths.

Seems I have no choice but to retrace my steps and head back into the little town of Lyman. I drive slowly, taking a look at what the place has to offer. Main Street is nice and wide, tree-lined, lovely in the evening light. There's a fast food place—Taco Time—with a message board that reads,

"2 x 1 Crispy Burritos July 4 Celebrate Freedom." There's city hall, closed for the day. And there's Ted's Bar, open for business, its poker-themed windows shaped like clubs and diamonds. And there's the Mormon Church, certainly one of the bigger buildings in town. Down the road a bit, I come upon a motel, but I don't want to waste any more money on dingy motels.

A few kids ride bicycles on the sidewalk. Two older boys zoom by on all-terrain vehicles. People are out walking dogs. In the evening light, everything looks picturesque, idyllic. At a bend in the main drag, I pass a cop car and give a little wave to the deputy. I've got the window down, and I'm breathing in the evening air, tapping the van roof with my fingers as country music plays on the radio. Celebrate freedom, the sign said, and who could disagree? Freedom, after all, is a key theme in the West's textual reality.

In fact, the Wyoming Office of Tourism, playing on this theme, uses a secondary tagline, a corollary to "Forever West" in its marketing campaign: "Roam Free." One of their television commercials features gorgeous shots of Wyoming landscapes as a voiceover tells us, "Not everything is meant to be tamed. Part of you wants to roam free. Wyoming is a place that encourages it, a place Forever West." It's a compelling message, no question. Hard not to buy into it.

Another mile or so down the road, I come upon the local high school. Big parking lot, a lush football field lined with bleachers. Looks like a fine spot for eating a couple of sandwiches, drinking a beer, enjoying the sunset. A year ago, I could not have imagined this: sitting here on the bleachers of the high school football field in Lyman, Wyoming. The moment gives me pause: What am I doing here? How did I get here?

I have come west for the same reason that has compelled so many Americans over the years: I lost my way. The career track led to a dead-end job, and I had to escape. I was suddenly filled with the westering spirit that has long animated Americans. Thoreau said, "Westward I go free," and under his spell westward I went. Stacked on the back seat, I carry with me copies of Thoreau and Parkman, Wister, Steinbeck, Kerouac—the textual reality to which I, too, have uncritically subscribed. An observation from Robert Scholes floats to mind: "We may wish to wander freely through our world, and may even believe that we are doing so, but we always—and sooner rather than later—find the warp and woof of the cultural text guiding our steps."

I don't know where to go from here, but for the moment it doesn't matter. Just now, the Lyman football field is a good enough place to be. Nice grass, quiet place, good as any campground. Thinking I might as well spend the night here, I get out my sleeping bag and tarp.

An hour later, I'm thinking what a perfect moment this is—bedding down for the night under the stars, a place with soft grass, the sound of crickets, and almost no light pollution, just the sparkling stars, the extraordinary presence of the Milky Way seemingly just beyond my reach.

Why are such pleasant moments so fleeting? Just when you reach a calm, meditative state, the inevitable disturbance comes along. In this case, it's one of the good citizens of

Lyman, out walking the dog. I hear her voice above the crickets: "Oh, no, no you don't, Ranger. Get over here and do your business on the grass." I follow the flashlight beam as it tracks along the far edge of the parking lot and then into the end zone. I can hear the dog's collar and tags jangling. I figure if I lie low the disturbance will pass. But no. The dog is aware that something is different. It growls at the darkness then barks sharply. "What is it, boy? You smell a raccoon?" The flashlight beam plays across the field until it stumbles over the lump in the grass that is me. The light pauses and hovers. The dog barks and growls and pulls at the leash. I can imagine the thought process of Ranger's owner as she wonders what the heck is that out there. The beam moves around a bit more and picks up on the fact that there's a van near the bleachers. It's coming clear to her now. "Come on, Ranger," she says. Ranger keeps growling and yelping as they walk on, pausing at the van to check—out-of-state plates, sure enough—and quickly now they're heading back to the main road.

I can guess what will happen next. Just a matter of how long. The answer: about ten minutes. Ten minutes, and here comes the deputy, his patrol car turning into the parking lot, heading straight for my van, the mounted searchlight focused on the license plate. Already, no doubt, the computer check is underway.

No point in waiting it out. I emerge from the darkness and into the headlight beam, giving a friendly little wave to the person behind the glare, the person I cannot see. The subsequent interview is pleasant enough. The young, chubby-faced deputy hears out my story, nodding knowingly as I talk, the police radio crackling from inside the patrol car. His tone is polite, even apologetic and deferential. He's very sorry but he can't let me stay here, law's the law. There have been some break-ins of late, people are nervous about it, it's a friendly town on the whole, but you understand how it is. He suggests I try the rest area out by the interstate, where I can sleep in the van, he says, if I can't afford the motel. Apparently, he has sized me up as the down-and-out sort, short on funds, a drifter.

Nice enough fellow, but no use appealing to his good nature. We know who holds the authority—and the handcuffs—in this encounter. Without argument, I pack up my stuff and reload the van while the deputy watches. Once he has the results from the computer check of my license and registration, he sends me on my way.

"Have a nice evening, sir," he says. "Take care."

I'm free to go. Free to roam free.

To get to the deputy-recommended rest area, I have to drive back into Lyman—slinking through town under cover of darkness, playing the role of outcast, looking for the road that will take me back out to the freeway. After a right turn at the Gateway Inn—the motel I can't afford—and then a couple miles of dark road, I come upon the tiny rest area. It sits just off the freeway where the tractor-trailers are churning past, one every couple of minutes, sometimes a pack of three or four together, cabs outlined in yellow lights. A circular drive, a couple of picnic tables under shelters, insects flitting in the glow. A hard wind blows over and through it all. It has the look of a rest area that Edward Hopper might paint.

And here I am, sitting on top of one of the concrete picnic tables to assess the situation, playing the part of the solitary Hopperesque figure, the sad sack beat down by circumstances, devoid of purpose, a lost soul stuck in the moment staring off into nothingness. I've spent the night in rest areas before and could do so now. But sometimes it's simpler to forgo sleep and just keep driving. Which is it going to be tonight?

While I'm pondering my options, a coyote appears, emerging from the shadows, skirting the edges of the rest area about thirty yards off. Something—the alien scent, the slightest movement—alerts him to my presence and he stops to stare at me. For a long, long moment we watch each other. Coyote—the iconic western figure. Legendary trickster, messenger, vagabond, rogue. Reviled wherever he goes, shot at, chased off. His telltale trait: slinking around, checking out the territory, forever wandering from place to place, celebrating freedom.

This coyote maintains a steady gaze until he has learned what he needs to learn about me. Then he trots off, disappearing into the night.

When he's gone, I take the cue: it's time for me to move on, too. So long Lyman, so long Jim Bridger, so long coyote. *Roam free*, as they say in these parts. And now I'm picking up speed on the interstate, fifty, sixty down the onramp, until once again I'm on the open road, cruising along at seventy miles per hour, plunging ahead into darkness, heading west, forever west.

Unapproachable Evanston

Evanston, Wyoming: yet another place that calls to mind Emerson's somewhat ambiguous line about an "unapproachable America." Back in Nebraska, I had learned about a bed and breakfast hotel in Evanston, a "real nice place," I was told, with nice folks running it. A bed and breakfast was not the kind of lodging I usually favored. Far from it. I was drifting across the country, camping in a tent, seeking out budget campgrounds, usually remote BLM sites with limited facilities and no more than a nominal fee. I was "roughing it" on purpose—*for* a purpose, or so I wanted to believe. At any rate, I had no intention of staying in some posh bed and breakfast. No way.

Yet here I was, tooling the streets of Evanston in search of the "Bear River Country Inn."

A talkative stranger had informed me about the place. This was at a truck stop diner outside Grand Island. By chance, we were seated side by side at the counter, sipping coffee, waiting on our food. The stranger tried chatting up the waitress as she busied herself at her station. Failing in getting much out of her, he turned to me. Wanted to know, was I a truck driver? Traveling salesman? Where was I going and why? Over the miles and after many such encounters,

I had learned to keep my answers simple and—unlike my roundabout route—straightforward. Keep it minimal, that was my guideline. Reveal as little as possible.

Heading west, I said. Just heading west.

He nodded knowingly. In America, "just heading west" says plenty—much more than the surface meaning of those three words. There's a subtext, a deeper meaning that Americans implicitly understand. It's all about a common rootlessness: dissatisfaction with the here and now, a need to move on, change the scene, find yourself. Call it an Emersonian quest. *Ghostlike we glide.*

The stranger mulled my words and nodded again. "I got you," he said.

He wondered if by chance I'd be passing through Evanston, Wyoming. I couldn't say for sure. Well, if I went through Evanston, he said, I should stop for the night at this place he knew, what they call a "B & B." His cousin was the owner and operator. Nice folks, her and her husband. Good Christian people. They'd take care of me. The stranger produced a business card. "Here, take this," he said, signing the back of it. Just tell them Cousin Dwight recommended me to the place and if they had a room available that night they'd let me stay there free of charge.

I wasn't all that interested, but I took the card anyway. Sometimes it's easier just to go along, take what's offered. Being agreeable usually brings the conversation more quickly to a close. I stuck the card in the book I had been reading, Kerouac's *Desolation Angels*—one of my guidebooks, along with Emerson and Thoreau, for my meander across the continent.

He cocked his head to see the title and his brow furrowed slightly. "Tell you what," he said, "I got something else for you." From the chest pocket of his jeans jacket he produced a palm-sized New Testament, green-covered, a gift of the Gideon Society.

This, too, I accepted without protest.

"Atta boy," he said and slapped me on the shoulder as he slid off the stool. "Well, pardner, be seeing you somewhere down the road."

He ambled off to pay his check, chatting for a while with the clerk as the transaction took place. With all the din and clatter in the coffee shop I couldn't make out the conversation, but I could guess its drift. He took a toothpick from the dispenser and left the diner. Through the window, I watched him climb into a huge, gleaming pickup truck. I waited until he drove off and was out of sight before asking the waitress for my check.

"Your friend already paid it," she told me.

Weeks after the encounter with Cousin Dwight, I approached Evanston, Wyoming—touted as a "Preserve America Community," a "Wyoming Main Street Community," and "Tree City USA," on the welcome sign at city limits. A subsequent sign issued a warning or possibly a threat: "Keep our place clean . . . you know what we mean."

Earlier in the day, I had remembered Dwight and the business card stuck in *Desolation Angels*. The thought of staying in a B & B—even for free or whatever deep discount Cousin Dwight's signature entitled me to—still seemed wrong, a violation of the spirit of my journey. Kerouac surely would have balked. But the last week or so had been a slog: thunderstorms, chilly nights, soggy mornings. Wouldn't be such a bad thing, I thought, to indulge a bit, enjoy some soft comfort for a night.

But once in Evanston I had trouble with the address. It didn't seem to exist. At a convenience store, I bought a town map and sat in the car searching the street index to no avail. I went back into the store and asked the clerk. He knew of no such street. I showed him the business card with the name of the bed and breakfast.

He shook his head. Nope. Didn't ring a bell. He'd lived in Evanston his whole life—which by my guess would have been about eighteen years—and he'd never heard of no such place.

A cop wandered in and we consulted him. He frowned at the card. Didn't look right to him. He was pretty sure there was no establishment by that particular name and he was darn sure there was no Sheridan Street, neither in Evanston proper nor the surrounding environs. Down at the Chamber of Commerce they could tell me about any bed and breakfasts in town, he said as he filled an enormous plastic cup with cola at the soda machine. But he didn't think there were any, none that he knew of. Evanston was not really a bed and breakfast sort of town.

It was now late in the day, too late to reach the nearest BLM or National Forest campground. On the outskirts of town I had noticed a trailer and RV park with a small area set aside for tents. I drove back to check it out. Not ideal by any means—too expensive and too congested for tent camping—but it would have to do. Sure enough, all the other campers that evening had arrived in RVs or trucks pulling travel trailers, and they were making full use of the electrical hookups; the campground hummed with machinery. I set up my small tent in the allotted sandbox.

The place wasn't much. It was bordered by repair shops, tire stores, and a large truck stop whose lights promised to glow all night. Tractor-trailers groaned and revved and screeched. But at least there were a few scattered trees, and somewhere just beyond the campground's perimeter fencing flowed the Bear River, said to be a lovely stream—at least in the stretches beyond Evanston's boundaries.

With the sun setting, I sat at a picnic table eating a peanut butter sandwich and wondering what that bed and breakfast business was all about. Miscommunication? A strange prank? Who knew. Surely there was nothing sinister to it, but I felt vaguely uneasy about the episode nonetheless.

From a rack in the campground office, I had picked up some brochures about the area. I thumbed through them and learned that Evanston, like many Wyoming settlements, was once a boomtown. Its great claim to fame: once upon a time, long ago, it had more neon lights per capita than any place in the world. But out west booms are short-lived; busts are the rule, and all too soon Evanston's neon had flickered out.

Evanston began as a railroad town on the Union Pacific's transcontinental line. The railroad brought development (or exploitation, depending on your point of view). Logging in the nearby mountains provided railroad ties. Trains crossing the vast empty stretches of high desert needed coal along the way, and southwestern Wyoming held rich deposits. Mines were opened and hundreds of miners came to work.

The railroad gave Evanston its origin, but the mines gave the town its character: rough, dangerous, prone to violence. Year in, year out, methane gas explosions killed scores of miners. When mine workers went on strike for better pay and safer work conditions, the coal company turned to goon squads and scabs. Many of the strikebreakers were Chinese, and for decades Evanston became the scene of periodic race riots until the Chinese were driven out of town.

Vestiges of this past are evident here and there. The old Union Pacific depot still stands, and some 1940s-era train cars are on display. Evanston boasts the only roundhouse left on the Union Pacific line. Meanwhile, at the abandoned coal mines, smoke leaches from the earth, the byproduct of fires still burning one hundred years after the methane gas explosions that started them.

Along with perpetually smoking coal mines, southwestern Wyoming is home to one of the world's biggest strip mines, a huge open pit operated by Chevron. World-class extraction is something of a local theme. World's biggest coke production plant. World's biggest trona mine. World's biggest helium plant. It's all thanks to the Overthrust Belt, an uplift formed by two colliding land masses. Eons ago, the western mass folded over the eastern mass and trapped oil, natural gas, and sulfur within. And it all lay dormant until twentieth-century man came along to drill and dig for it. Around Evanston, "Energy Project" is the watchword.

Darkness fell. Feeling restless, I took a walk into town to see what was happening in Evanston on a Saturday night. A mile or so along a wide highway—Bear River Road—brought me to an underpass that cut beneath the railroad tracks. On the other side was downtown Evanston, which was all but shut down for the night. Bank, courthouse, post office, church, hardware store: all closed and dark. Only one place out on the edge of downtown showed signs of life—The Painted Lady Saloon, a handful of Harley-Davidsons parked in the poorly lit lot. I thought about going in for a beer but opted instead for a walk around the side streets.

I headed back to Center Street and kept turning corners, following a zigzag path through Evanston's residential sector. Strolling the streets of an unfamiliar town at night, you can't help but feel ostracized. In town after town across the country, few people seem to go outside after dark, these days, except perhaps to walk the dog. Come nightfall, everyone is locked up in their homes, consumed with their private lives. When I was young, people spent more time outdoors. Kids used to play catch or tag or kick the can until well after sundown. Adults sat on porches chatting. At least that's the way I remember it, but maybe the fog of nostalgia has obscured my memory.

Many of Evanston's houses had nice porches. Did they ever get used? Did those nice-looking swings ever creak with the weight of people? House after house, nothing but the bluish light of televisions emanating from within, like flashes of heat lightning. Now and again, my passage tripped a motion sensor and a porch light clicked on. The presence of a stranger seemed to prompt suspicion: Who goes there and why? the awoken porch light asked. A front door cracked open and a woman emerged to set down a dish for a cat with a quivering tail. Hearing my footsteps, the woman glanced up then ducked back inside. I heard a bolt slide shut.

At most of the houses, the curtains were drawn. But in some windows I could see the ubiquitous televisions—huge screens flashing a dazzle of images, brilliant and rippling in the window panes. A dewy can of beer. A bikini-clad woman running in slow motion down a beach. Teenagers dancing around and singing while eating potato chips.

I thought again of that phrase from Emerson's essay "Experience": *unapproachable America*. In his writing, Emerson seemed to think of "America" in two different ways. One America was a Dreamland, a mythic place, the "heaven without rent or seam" that did not and could not exist anywhere but in the imagination as an unapproachable Ideal. The other America was the actual place where he lived, a place that often disappointed and perplexed him. "Alas for America," Emerson fretted in his journal. "It all runs to miscellany. The air is loaded with poppy, with imbecility, with dispersion & sloth." This America was dense and sordid with "inharmonious and trivial particulars," an America strung out on narcotics (or "poppy"—opium—in Emerson's terms) and deluded by chimeras.

Two Americas. Both unapproachable.

A distant train whistle sounded in the quiet night. For some reason, I imagined myself wandering through one of those little towns that surround model railroad displays—a toy town of miniaturized depots, crossing gates, drugstores, churches, banks. Everything tidy. Everything perfect.

Across the street, on another big screen glowing in an otherwise darkened room, a murder was in progress.

During my walk, I had heard distant thunder. Now the persistent grumbling grew louder, drawing ever closer. A storm seemed imminent. The warm breeze turned to a cool wind, and a gust knocked over an empty garbage can, the can rocking back and forth in the street. Lightning lit up the neural pathways of black clouds. I hurried back to the campground, dirt and sand skittering down the highway and whipping up into my face. Somewhere in the darkness, riled by the wind, a pack of dogs howled. I reached my tent as the first splattering drops hit.

All night long squalls pushed through Evanston. I fell asleep to the rain's soft rhythm and passed several comfortable hours. But sometime in the night a stronger storm cell brought intermittent bouts of downpour, the pitter-patter giving way to a rapid drumming. A puddle developed underneath a leaky seam. Reports of thunder followed close upon flashes of lightning, which for a searing moment turned the tent walls fire red.

With the drop in pressure, I could feel the usual aura coming on, a headache likely. I popped some ibuprofen and lay awake wondering where this journey was taking me—hundreds of miles, town after town, one Evanston after another. I kept going farther down the road only to be stuck on the outskirts of some unapproachable place.

* * *

Come morning, the storm had passed and I headed back downtown for breakfast at Mother Mae's Kitchen, located right on Main Street beneath a hand-painted sign. Over coffee and pancakes, I leafed through the *Uinta County Herald* to find out what was happening these days in Evanston.

The chatty waitress was all too happy to tell me what was happening. There's the county fair at the end of July, she said, and after that the Roundhouse Festival when people set up their model trains and the like. There's the Bear River Rendezvous, lots of mountain man types in town for that. And then Cowboy Days when folks come from all over for the rodeo. They say it's the biggest little rodeo in the world, right here in Evanston.

She didn't mention Evanston's main curiosity, a joss house that replicates the Taoist temple originally built in the nineteenth century as a place of worship for the town's Chinese population. A historical marker explains that the joss house, one of three in the United States at the time, "attracted thousands of Chinese for Chinese New Year's Day ceremonies" until "the joss house burned on January 26, 1922." What the sign does not say is that the fire was no accident: the white citizenry deliberately torched the temple during the razing of Evanston's Chinese sector. After the purge, only two Chinese people remained in the town: "Mormon Charlie" and "China Mary." Nowadays, looking for anything that might appeal to tourists, Evanston plays up its Chinese heritage with a Chinese New Year Parade. Artifacts rescued from the debris of Chinatown's destruction are on display in a small museum. A street is named after China Mary.

I walked over to the joss house hoping to tour the museum only to find that it was closed on Sundays. But there was a nice little garden with a pagoda and a koi pond where I sat for a while to read the rest of the local newspaper. Police reports. Obituaries. Local sports. Eleven people had been arrested in Evanston during the previous week—ten for intoxication, one for burglary. A veteran of the Second World War had died after a long bout with dementia. Expectations were high for the upcoming high school football season.

Apart from energy, Evanston's economy depends on its proximity to Utah, a state where everything categorically venial seems to be restricted or forbidden. Utahans come for betting at the Wyoming Downs racetrack. They come for cheap liquor and legal fireworks, sold together at stands and shacks along the freeway exit ramps. Early in the morning the firecracker tents are crowded with shoppers looking to load up on petards for the summer holidays. Heading west toward the state line, you can see the big signs in bright colors shouting *Liquor—Bargain Prices! Roman Candles! Factory Outlet! Direct! Cheapest Beer in Town! More Bang for Your Buck!*

I had come to Evanston looking for something. I hadn't found it, but there were other discoveries in store. There always are. Patterns emerging from the "inharmonious and trivial particulars." Images appearing in shape-shifting storm clouds. Forms taking definition in the pale glow of automated porch lights. "All is riddle, and the key to a riddle is another riddle," Emerson said. And because of that,

Kerouac seemingly answered, "We lean forward to the next crazy venture beneath the skies."

Following the code, reading the signs, I too leaned forward, exiting Evanston, heading for the next riddle.

West of the fireworks stands and liquor stores, Evanston peters out and Wyoming comes to an end. Up ahead, Utah beckons: gold-plated temples, a white-out desert, a dead sea. A place for prophets and saints and desert mystics. A place for bombing ranges, proving grounds, wildlife preserves, mirages. Another stop on the seeker's itinerary, another starred attraction in the road atlas of unapproachable America.

Liminal Wendover

West of the Great Salt Lake, the highway crosses the Great Salt Lake Desert. Salt, salt, salt: everywhere the blindingly white expanse of the salt flats. You've got about fifty miles or so to cover, a long stretch of bleak terrain, seemingly the dead center of wastelands real and metaphoric. The glare is fierce. You might feel a bit lightheaded as you peer into the distance trying to make sense of this eerie, moonlike land, the now-dry bed of a lake that fifteen thousand years ago was as large as—and much deeper than—Lake Michigan. It's intense, but it's not a hard drive, not on the interstate freeway. In under an hour, you've crossed it east to west.

Nothing at all compared to what the early pioneers endured when they tried to negotiate this desert. There was the Donner Party in 1846, for example. In Wyoming, they left the main trail to follow an untested cutoff across Utah, hoping to reduce the long journey to California by a few hundred miles. But the shorter route in distance proved the longer route in time. The unexpected desert crossing was a nightmare—hot days, cold nights, no water. Animals died, wagons broke down, and the pioneers suffered hallucinations as they trudged across the salt flats. This ordeal was not even the worst of it: the labored passage in Utah cost the Donners precious time and further delayed their eventual attempt to cross the Sierra Nevada. By then it was too late: heavy snows caught and trapped them in the mountains, and the story of their ill-fated trek became infamous.

But today you face no such difficulties. Less than an hour and the salt flats are behind you. You can linger a while if you want—stop to visit the Bonneville Speedway out there on the desert's flattest, smoothest part (so flat you'll see the curvature of the earth). Or you can drive a couple of miles off the freeway on a gravel road, then hike up to Danger Cave, an archaeological site where ten thousand-year-old artifacts have been found, including knives, scrapers, baskets, moccasins, projectile points, and a host of other objects that demonstrate how the Early Peoples were able to exist within this harsh environment. It's hot and bright out there, and the dry sodium air burns your throat and nostrils; but you've got polarized glasses, a hat, sunscreen, plenty of water. There's an ice chest in your trunk. You can explore a bit, if you like, keeping the car in sight, crunching salt balls as you walk and leaving your footprints in the mineral crust. Then it's back to the car, a cold drink, and you're on your way. In no time at all, you've made the crossing.

And what's on the other side of the salt flats? Your map says there's a town—the town of Wendover, straddling the Utah–Nevada border. And Nevada means—as the many billboards suddenly cropping up have made amply clear—casinos, casinos, casinos. They're up ahead, looking like beached cruise ships in the desert. And here's the Wendover exit, the business loop that will take you straight to them. You're tired of driving for the day and in no particular hurry. Might as well spend the night here, see what the town is all about.

In the beginning, circa 1900, Wendover was a watering stop for the Western Pacific Railroad, a tank town wedged between the outcroppings of the Leppy Hills and the glaring, blinding salt flats. Railroad workers called it "the town on the edge of hell."

In the decades that followed, Wendover became a military town. Its sublime isolation made it an ideal locale for the military's secret activities. During the Second World War, the air force built a base to train pilots in the techniques of heavy bombardment. The air force also built a dummy town out on the flats to make target practice more realistic—a tacit acknowledgment that civilian populations had become routine targets. Ordnance teams were sent to Wendover to assemble and test special inert bombs, known in military lingo as "shapes." In 1944, Colonel Paul Tibbets brought his select bomber crew to Wendover and made practice runs in a brand new B-29 with a bay modified to accommodate an unusual shape that they called "the pumpkin." A year later, both bomber and pumpkin had new names—Enola Gay and Little Boy—and the Tibbets crew put their Wendover training into practice over Hiroshima.

During the Cold War, bombing and gunnery practice continued out on the salt flats. The air force added missiles to the mix: the Minuteman and the Cruise were both tested at "the Oasis"—the air force's night-clubbish name for the proving grounds near Wendover. You can find remnants of Wendover's military heyday if you're willing to wander out into the desert: south of town, at the site of the old airfield, the barracks still stand. Out there, too, you can find what's left of Enola Gay's hangar, a deteriorating rusted hulk that looks eerily similar to a Hiroshima ruin.

To commemorate its role in the "first atomic bombardment," the town has erected a pillar, to which a high-relief model of a B-29 bomber (aka the Boeing Superfortress) has been affixed. At the base of the pillar, a plaque memorializes President Truman's words about the atomic bomb: "We pray that (God) may guide us to use it in His ways and for His purposes." The legend demands a double take, a second reading, a shake of the head at this strange attempt to ascribe a providential teleology to the bomb's existence. It's dismaying to know that a president ever uttered these words, and more dismaying still to discover that decades later a town would see fit to preserve them.

But these remnants and memorials are all that remain of the town's erstwhile militarization. The air force has long since abandoned Wendover, and casinos have taken over. In fact, a casino stands directly across the street from the monument to atomic bombardment.

Entering town from the Utah side, you tool past gas stations and convenience stores, budget motels and anachronistic motor courts, a wide-hipped Mormon church (pretty much the biggest structure this side of the line) and trailer parks, their dirt pales chockablock with junk cars, cast-off furniture, construction materials, toys, and satellite dishes.

Looming up ahead is Wendover Will, the "world's largest mechanical cowboy," according to the *Guinness Book of Records*. Will is constantly gesticulating: one arm waves a greeting while the other arm moves up and down, pointing out the entrance to the Stateline Casino. A loose cigarette frenetically wags in his mouth, which is frozen in a somewhat stupid grin. Will looks maybe a little pie-eyed as he beckons one and all to come on over to the Nevada side of town. That's where the casinos are: the Stateline, the Peppermill, the Red Garter, the Silver Smith. Giant Will, the cartoon cowboy outlined in neon, presides over it all, waving, puffing, pointing. And at night he becomes much more than a droll gimmick; according to the postcards for sale around town, the lit-up Will takes on a symbolic glow: "The neon brilliance of this cowboy signals the beginning of an evening of excitement."

Excitement indeed. But where to spend the night? You've got your choice of glitzy casino hotels on the Nevada side or dowdy chain motels on the Utah side. And if you want to pitch your tent, there's only one option: the KOA. The initials stand for "Kampgrounds of America," a commercial chain of ersatz campgrounds strung out along the interstates and main highways of America, primarily sited near tourist attractions. KOAs emphasize comfort and convenience, providing "kampers" with electricity, showers, swimming pools, playgrounds, and asphalt. According to KOA literature, the idea is to "take the rough out of roughing it." The company believes that you want a "hassle-free outdoor experience" with "on-site recreation and entertainment venues."

Of course, no self-respecting tent camper would willingly resort to a KOA. The electrical hookups bring in the RV crowd, and a tent camper can feel nothing but disdain for those behemoths and their enormous consumption of energy. The pious tent camper considers RVs the antithesis of the true camping experience and will therefore deign to pitch his tent in a KOA only with the greatest reluctance. But in Wendover, there's no other choice.

In the office of the Wendover KOA, Dolly, the manager, is in a harried state, what with all the evening arrivals trying to check in at once. On top of that, there are the questions and complaints from already registered "kampers." Dolly thinks she's getting one hell of a headache. No, she can't do anything about the Mexicans crossing the kampground— they're just the casino workers going to their jobs, honey, they don't hassle nobody. All right, just a minute, she'll find someone to lead you to the site, just hang on till Alberto gets back.

The RV sites are all taken (quite a crowd in Wendover tonight), but getting a tent site is no problem. All of Row J, a handful of sandboxes along the back fence, is reserved for tents, and so far Row J is entirely empty. No tent campers as of yet. Take your pick, Dolly says.

The sandboxes abut the KOA's boundary fence. On the other side of the fence, there's a residential sector consisting of mobile and manufactured homes. The smell of beans and tortillas and the sound of Spanish radio in the air indicate that it's a Mexican barrio, home to the casino workers. On the KOA side of the fence, opposite these shabby little houses, the kampers' gargantuan vehicles loom, many of them "luxuriously appointed," to use the marketing phrase, with furnishings and household conveniences. The tableau neatly replicates the socio-economic divide of the US–Mexico border: wealth on one side, poverty on the other. Indeed, as on the border, every few minutes someone from the barrio slips through a gap in the fence and crosses the campground, headed for work at the casinos. The trespassing Mexicans clearly worry the RV folks. They watch suspiciously from the lawn chairs they've set up on patches of artificial grass. When they're fed up with this alien intrusion, they stomp off to the KOA office to complain.

With camp chores done, there's time to sit on the picnic table and marvel at the onset of evening, the desert sublime: shifting beams of light, metallic glints, a spectrum of hues in the vast western sky, a luminous sheen on the salt flats. The foothills and outcroppings turn a rich, intense gold, and then as the sun nears the horizon the rocks shimmer and glow. The glow eventually gives way to gloaming, and then the RV generators rumble on and light up the place with serious wattage—enough to power their televisions, stereos, and spotlights.

The diligence of the RV people in recreating the comforts of home is impressive. Outside their well-equipped rigs, they've set up neat little patios: lawn chairs, squares of green carpet or artificial grass mats, canopies, strings of lanterns and glowing colored globes. But for all these comforts—

and for all the wealth needed to enjoy leisure travel—no one seems terribly happy tonight in the KOA. Discontented voices rise above the generator noise:

"But I wanna go swimming *now.*"

"No, I told you not for half an hour."

"Hey, watch what you're doing. You're messing everything up, your feet are filthy!"

"That don't give you no reason to whine. Quit your complaining right this minute."

The families on the Mexican side of the fence—with their mariachi radios and smoking barbecues and merry children—sound much happier than those parked in the KOA for the night.

But happiness is beside the point just now; there's gambling to be done. The neon lights of the casinos beckon. Closest to the KOA is the Red Garter, over on Wendover Boulevard. Perched atop the Red Garter's neon sign, a leg-wagging wench winks a come-hither to passers-by. Down the road a bit, the Rainbow's neon sign renders a pulsating polychromatic arc. The Peppermill's signage contributes a spinning star to the razzle-dazzle, while two searchlight beams continuously separate and crisscross in the desert sky. And then there's Will, the spindly cowboy winking, puffing on his cigarette, and pointing to the Stateline door.

Inside the casinos, it's like Mardi Gras on the catatonic ward: a party atmosphere without the human revelry. There's a curious combination of joyless monotony and sensory frenzy. In the midst of spinning lights and colored neon tubing and the onslaught of sound, hundreds of unsmiling people are engaged in one repetitive act or another: slipping tokens into slots, smoking cigarettes, staring at cards as they are turned over. Weirdly, the people look lifeless, while the machines are hyperactive.

And there are rows and rows of these brightly lit machines, all bonging and whirring and blinking. They all have different names, and their façades feature different cartoon imagery, but this surface variety belies the functional similarity of the slot machines. *Quartermania, Slam Dunk, Haywire, IRS Special*— the pictures and names promise different games, but they all play the same way. Put in the token, pull the lever or push a button, watch the spinning icons. Repeat. In fact, they are not games at all, just machines with one mode of operation, one thing to do, no thinking or skill involved. The façade of a machine called *Naughty Nickels* depicts a girl, apparently nude (her midsection is discreetly covered by a coin), leaning back, kicking her bare legs up in the air. *Naughty Nickels* is being played by an elderly lady, the most prominent demographic at the Stateline tonight.

A shuttle bus circuits the several casinos, making it easy to tour and view their peculiar interior décors. In the Silver Smith, a balcony overlooks the game room, allowing for a panorama of the casino floor. Below, a faux fountain splashes strings of light. A coin made from neon tubes spins around. Purple and orange neon tubing snakes along the walls. In the Peppermill, it's all mirrors and neon: a mirrored ceiling, mirrored pillars, mirror balls. Crazy swirls of neon tubing adorn the walls. One oft-repeated motif made from this tubing is hard to figure out. Is it a ball of neon yarn? A cluster of multicolored worms? Spaghetti gone bad? Who knows.

In the Rainbow, the décor of the buffet restaurant plays with rainforest themes. There's a lot of plastic tropical vegetation—an odd touch given the vast desert that surrounds the casino. Plastic palms embower the booths, their fronds populated with fiberglass parrots sporting neon-bright plumage. Ceiling mirrors reflect splashes of blue, lavender, atomic orange, and lime green. A jungle fountain and a row of plastic trees separate the restaurant from the casino, but the game room noise filters through and competes with the canned music issuing from speakers implanted in the plastic tree trunks. The Rainbow's décor aggressively plays up these rainforest motifs without foregoing the neon decoration that is de rigueur in Nevada's casinos. It's a wacky combination, all this neon tropical imagery—flitting neon butterflies, neon parrots, clusters of neon vines, neon palm trees, and some unidentifiable neon fruit (mangos?). On the wall, words appear in neon script: *Rainforest Poker! Win!* The motley décor is mind-boggling. Here the carpet has a tropical flower design, and over here it has an incongruous outer space design; here, plastic trees are growing right up through the round tables; over there crystal spheres are flashing colored light; and over there neon bars and stripes flicker off and on, off and on. The words *Nickels* and *Win* pulsate repeatedly from random placements on walls and pillars. Plastic vines slither up plastic trees, which are blooming with purple-white-pink plastic flowers. Through the fake trees, a keno board flashes bright red numbers—a mystical code being studied by people on barstools. Every surface gleams like obsidian or gold, and the noise—the thrum, the hum, the drone, the ding-dong bing-bong—is incessant. This is not a place for anyone prone to headaches.

No casino has natural light of any kind. Lost in a liminal zone, patrons have no idea what time of day it is. One casino's coffee shop supplants natural light with the illusion of natural light: the round windows along the booths are pasted over with photos of pastoral scenes—meadows, cows, mountains—all backlit to give the impression of sunlight. These inert scenes don't change—there's no movement in them—thus reinforcing the impression that time is not passing.

Meanwhile, late as it is, children are bouncing around the high-volume kiddie playroom, trying their luck at junior versions of the adult games. The lobby, too, is swarming with screeching, giggling kids. Long into the night, they're running around blowing bubbles, chaperoned by a couple of casino employees.

At some point, the sensory overload becomes too much, and it's time to escape.

Well after two AM, outside the casino, the weather has turned. A fierce, stinging wind whips sand and salt and even red ants into the face of anyone out walking. The wind deposits a layer of grit on cars and piles sand up against the tires.

Then something happens. A laughing threesome emerges from a casino. Two men in cowboy hats and boots, a woman in a studded denim jacket. She's carrying a chihuahua, baby-talking to it as she stumbles along. Suddenly, the dog wriggles from her arms, drops to the sidewalk, and takes off running.

"Pumpkin!" the woman cries. "You come back here! Help!"

An oncoming pedestrian stoops to snatch the dog, but it veers away and darts into the street—just as a shuttle bus comes along. The bus skids, the dog yelps. Then comes the dull thud, and just like that, the chihuahua has gone under the tire. The woman and her companions come running up. "No, no, no, Pumpkin!" the woman cries. "Christ almighty," one man says. The driver comes around the bus looking horrified and speaking Spanish. He's followed by a handful of passengers and everyone stands over the dog. Pumpkin is clearly a goner. Blood trickles from the mouth, nerves causing him to twitch even after he has died. The woman sobs and sobs. In a matter of seconds, a little ridge of wind-blown sand has built up against the dog's body and against the onlookers' shoes. Above, giant Wendover Will grins and glows, his mechanized arm continuing through its inexorable motions, up and down, up and down, pointing out the spot.

Back at the KOA, the windstorm has played havoc with the tidy campsites. Lawn chairs have tumbled into the driveway; strings of colored globes have blown down; screen houses have collapsed. Tomorrow, the kampers will have a mess on their hands.

For the rest of the night as you try to sleep, you hear the tent fabric rippling and shuddering; you hear tumbleweeds scraping against cyclone fencing; and from far off in the desert night, you hear the ghost moan of the windstorm rattling the rusted hangar, the liminal ruin that once upon a time sheltered gravid Enola Gay—she who left these barren salt flats for a land faraway where, as legend tells, she bore and delivered a divinely ordained Little Boy.

Author's Note:

Not long after the trip and research that led to this essay, ownership of the Stateline Casino changed hands. The new operators no longer needed Wendover Will's services. After fifty years on the job, Will had become superfluous. Not wanting to lose its most prominent citizen, the town acquired the sign, refurbished it, and moved it to the far western edge of town. Wendover Will now stands in the middle of the highway, still waving, still smoking, and still pointing—though now it's unclear exactly what he's pointing at or toward.

Open House at Trinity Site

On the morning of July 16, 1945, a tremendous explosion shook the widely scattered towns of central and southern New Mexico. People in cities as far apart as Gallup and Las Cruces felt the rumbling. In Roswell, the pre-dawn sky lit up as though seared by a divine bolt. In Socorro, windows broke from the tremor. Nationally, the big news that day was the impending meeting of Churchill, Stalin, and Truman at Potsdam. But in Albuquerque, the evening *Tribune* made the explosion its lead story under the headline, "Munitions Explode at Alamo Dump." According to an army spokesman, an ammunitions magazine had exploded "in a remote area of the Alamogordo Air Base reservation."

A month later, the residents of New Mexico and the rest of the world learned the truth about the explosion. The "remote area" referred to in the article was known to the military by the secret code name of "Trinity Site." The "brilliant flash and blast" were in fact caused by the first successful test of an atomic bomb.

Today, Trinity Site remains the most remote and restricted National Historic Landmark. Accessible only by rough roads and isolated in an extreme sector of the White

Sands Missile Range, Trinity is open to the public only twice a year—the first Saturdays in April and October—when the Public Affairs Office of the White Sands Missile Range leads a convoy from Alamogordo, New Mexico out to Ground Zero. The army calls the occasion an "open house."

One Easter weekend, I drove out to Alamogordo to join the convoy. Despite vast vistas, Alamogordo feels isolated and insular, as if the edge of the earth were a few miles outside of town in any direction. Its founders envisioned an oasis to serve railway passengers, but passenger trains no longer go through town. Only three roads access the Tularosa Basin, in which Alamogordo lies between the eerie rippling gypsum dunes of White Sands to the west and the stark Sacramento Mountains to the east. Windswept, dusty, and sun-broiled, Alamogordo epitomizes the sleepy Southwestern town that progress has passed by. Even so, the town considers progress, especially technological progress, central to its identity. Alamogordo is home to the International Space Hall of Fame, a five-story golden glass building at the foot of the Sacramentos that glows in the afternoon sun like something fallen from orbit. Rockets stand erect in the town's parks and street medians. Model missiles crop up here and there. Aerospace-themed images adorn signs and façades.

The source of Alamogordo's space-age self-image is the nearby White Sands Missile Range—"birthplace of America's missile and space activity"—where promising military "products," to use the terminology of the Range's information brochure, undergo testing. Cruise missiles,

Patriot missiles, smart bombs, stealth aircraft: they were all put through the paces here. Of course, the army decided to locate a missile range in this region precisely because of its supreme isolation, an isolation that would mitigate the consequences of any haywire experiments. The Alamogordo Chamber of Commerce, however, chooses to overlook this unflattering fact. To the Chamber, Alamogordo is "Spaceport, USA."

Visitors to Trinity Site gather at the Otero County fairgrounds for the eighty-five-mile drive across the missile range. When I got there, military policemen were busy organizing several hundred vehicles into a convoy. "Remain in line," an MP said, leaning into my window to hand me a Rule Sheet. "No passing, no turning off the road, less you all wanna become part of target practice." Drivers were required to turn on their headlamps and follow a slow-moving military police vehicle; it looked a little like a funeral procession.

Shortly after leaving Alamogordo, our caravan turned off the highway and passed through a gate onto the fenced-in missile range. A sign warned that this was a "Missile Impact Area." Another suggested that equipment operating on the missile grounds might affect cardiac pacemakers. Here and there across the desert floor stood huge white billboards with black numbers on them—codes to pilots practicing their bombing skills in the scrubland.

I was at the back of the procession. Up ahead, like a desert sidewinder, the line of vehicles wriggled along the bumpy road into the continuous shimmer of a heat mirage.

Pickups, truck campers, and recreational vehicles made up a good portion of the caravan. Many of the vehicles were decorated with bumper stickers: *Thank God You Can Still Pray in the USA*, *I'm the NRA and I Vote*, *Warning: Vehicle Insured by Smith and Wesson*, *Don't Mess with Texas*, *Support Our Troops—Operation Desert Storm*. Several vehicles flew miniature American flags from side-view mirrors. Given my compatriots' apparent predilections, there seemed little chance of a violation of Regulation #2 on the Rule Sheet that the MP had handed me: "Demonstrations, picketing, sit-ins, protest marches, political speeches and similar activities are prohibited."

Regulation #1 seemed equally unnecessary: "No photography is allowed on the missile range." During the seventy miles I drove on what the army calls Range Road 7, I saw nothing to photograph that would compromise America's security—unless the particular arrangement of the desert's spiny yucca plants, gnarled mesquite shrubs, and tough creosote bushes could be construed as Top Secret information.

It was hard to imagine a more forbidding landscape. This part of the huge Chihuahua Desert evokes a strong sense of otherworldly alienation. Long, scarred escarpments and ridges thrust up from the desert floor to form the Oscura (or "Dark") Mountains. The sierra looms as a formidable barrier. Sand dunes spill onto scrubland. The approach to Trinity Site is guarded east and west by two massive basalt lava beds, one a petrified lava river forty-four miles long and six miles wide. The Spanish called these beds the *malpaís*, the badlands. The old trail connecting Mexico City and Santa Fe passed through here, forced by cliffs and marshes to swing away from the life-preserving waters of the Rio Grande. The passage was so desolate and dry that Spanish travelers gave it the ominous name of *Jornada del Muerto*—the journey of death.

Despite the austere beauty of the land and a backdrop of snow-capped mountains, my drive into Trinity was tedious. The rough road required drivers to pay close attention to upcoming bumps and ruts. Dust kicked up by the cars ahead made it difficult to take in the scenery. I read and re-read the decals on the camper truck in front of me. By my count, the camper's owners had been to forty-six states. Somehow, in all their far-ranging travels, they had managed to miss Ohio, or perhaps they had not bothered to pick up the requisite decal for such an ordinary state. The range road cut through a military-altered landscape; there were scores of bunkers, platforms made from steel girders, concrete shelters. And there were numerous signs: *High Explosive Test Area, Danger Unexploded Munitions, NATO Missile System Left, Hardhat Area*. The danger signs had been thoughtfully translated into Spanish, presumably for any "illegal aliens" who might wander up from the Mexican border, ninety miles to the south.

Finally, after two hours, the convoy passed an old instrumentation bunker built in 1945 to record data for the atomic test, and shortly thereafter we found ourselves pulling into a makeshift parking lot where MPs emphatically whistled us into smart rows on the hardpan desert floor.

If the historical associations of the place seemed ominous and apocalyptic, the notion was apparently lost on or insignificant to my fellow visitors. There was, in fact, a festive air to the occasion. Even as I rattled into the lot with the sidewinder's tail, various groups were busy setting up tables and chairs, opening bags of snacks, and preparing for an All-American tailgate party. It was clearly not a moment for solemnity, never mind the anxious and watchful eyes of a dozen MPs. Two boys tossed a Frisbee. Somebody's car stereo blasted a Garth Brooks tune.

Forgoing the impromptu party, I walked two hundred yards north to a fenced enclosure that demarcated Ground Zero. Purple and yellow signs depicting the universal radioactivity symbol were posted on the eight-foot fence. A boyish MP handed out flyers informing visitors that "a one-hour visit to the inner fenced area will result in a whole body exposure of one-half to one milliroentgen," an amount supposedly less than a third of the exposure that one would receive flying cross country on a jet airliner. "Although radiation levels are low," the flyer noted, "some feel any extra exposure should be avoided. The decision is yours." Despite these assurances, the army felt compelled to put up another sign warning visitors not to eat, drink, or (of all things) apply make-up within the fenced enclosure. Dutifully, no one opened a cosmetic case.

At the entrance to Ground Zero, the rusty remains of a 214-ton bomb hulk named "Jumbo" sat on display. Built to encase the original atom bomb, Jumbo was never used as a container (instead it was left near Ground Zero during the explosion and survived with minimal damage). To get Jumbo to Trinity Site in 1945, scientists needed a custom designed sixty-four-wheel trailer. The total cost of building and transporting the unused artifact ran into the millions of dollars. In fact, the development of this surrounding wasteland into a sophisticated testing ground required numerous expensive and Herculean tasks of this sort. Harvard physicist Kenneth Bainbridge selected Trinity in 1944 over seven other possible sites in California, Colorado, Texas, and New Mexico. During the course of a year, Bainbridge oversaw the construction of laboratories, instrumentation bunkers, a detonation tower, and a base camp. From hundreds of miles away, over rough ranch roads, army trucks brought in the necessary materials: prefabricated steel struts for building a one hundred-foot tower, concrete slabs and oak beams for bunkers, heavy-duty electrical winches, hundreds of six-foot wooden T-poles, five hundred miles of electrical wiring, searchlights, banks of high speed cameras, seismographs, geophones, ionization chambers, spectographs, and eventually, on the eve of the grand opening, the star of the show, the plutonium core—which arrived like a true dignitary in the back seat of an army sedan.

But of all this effort, there was little left for us to see at Ground Zero. All of the materials brought in were either vaporized in the test or dismantled shortly thereafter. The main attraction now is a ten-foot lava rock obelisk marking the spot where Bainbridge's tower stood. In 1945, the bomb was hoisted to the top of the tower, one hundred feet above ground, and detonated on July 16 at 05:29:45 Mountain War Time—a nineteen-kiloton explosion—some six kt greater than the Hiroshima explosion twenty-one days later. But compared to the unimaginable destruction inflicted on the Japanese city, the New Mexico desert suffered little obvious damage. The tower was vaporized except for one of the concrete pilings (still visible to the northwest of the obelisk, a small mound from which steel rods protrude like hairs on a mole). A search of the area after the blast turned up blown-over cacti and the carcasses of flash-burned jackrabbits.

The most obvious result of the blast was a shallow crater, wherein the desert floor melted into a green glassy substance subsequently named "Trinitite." This five hundred-yard-wide, quarter-inch thick plate of radioactive green crystal was bulldozed into an underground concrete bunker. Later, the army graded over the crater and backfilled it with sand. Later still, the Nuclear Energy Commission removed the Trinitite from the bunker, loaded it into steel drums, and hauled it off. Today, some scattered shards of Trinitite still sparkle in the soil. Otherwise, little impression of the blast is left upon the land. To the west of the obelisk, a low shelter protects a portion of the original crater. Windows in the shelter reveal the fused glassy crust scientists found at Ground Zero after the blast.

As if to make up for the lack of visual effects, the army has set up a couple of other displays inside the fence. A replica of Fat Man, the Nagasaki bomb, rests on a flatbed trailer, fronted by a sign explaining when and where the bomb was dropped and counterintuitively informing visitors that the atomic bomb "represents mankind's greatest hope for lasting peace."

The second display—a series of lacquered photos affixed to Ground Zero's fence—shows a second-by-second sequence of the Trinity explosion—the now familiar fireball expanding, then collapsing on itself, before expanding again in a huge mushroom cloud.

I was reading the sign in front of Fat Man, when a young man in a cowboy hat strolled over, arm around his gal.

"See here," he said. "This is the one they dropped on China."

"The sign says Japan," the woman said.

"Whatever," the cowboy said.

At the photo display, a father called over his young son. "Look at this, Jason, see how it looks like a mushroom. That's why they call it a mushroom cloud."

A few photos down the fence, a mother held up her four-year-old to a picture of the explosion.

"Ka-boom!" the boy shouted, raising his arms.

The merriment in the parking lot had carried over into the blast site. People photographed each other smiling and waving in front of Fat Man, grinning at Grandma from Ground Zero. Kids ran around laughing, playing games of tag. A small group of Japanese exchange students huddled over a book and gestured at the surrounding landscape. I found it odd that Trinity Site might be included in a Japanese guidebook, but by then the whole day was taking on bizarre, incongruous overtones.

I don't know why, but I had expected more solemnity at Trinity Site, maybe because it was Easter weekend and the juxtaposition of the bomb with the Resurrection seemed like an unmistakable irony, an irony that our procession-like pilgrimage into Trinity had only enhanced. One person who might have appreciated that irony was Robert Oppenheimer, the overseer of the Manhattan Project and the man who nursed the bomb into maturity. It was Oppenheimer, after all, who code-named the site "Trinity," giving peculiarly religious overtones to the name of the bomb site. Years later, he couldn't remember exactly what had prompted him to choose the name, though he suggested a connection to a devotional sonnet by the metaphysical poet John Donne, a sonnet that paradoxically associates the Christian doctrine of the Trinity with awesome violence:

Batter my heart, three-person'd God; for you
As yet but knock, breathe, shine, and seek to mend;
That I may rise and stand, overthrow me, and bend
Your force to break, blow, burn and make me new.

A man given as much to mysticism as physics, Oppenheimer embodied the odd connection of religion and the bomb. Watching the Trinity explosion, Oppenheimer recalled some verses from the Hindu scripture, the Bhagavad Gita: "Now I am become Death, the destroyer of worlds." Oppenheimer's pensiveness was perhaps more what I had in mind in visiting Trinity, but the crowd would have none of it. A roving band of MPs presided over the fun, watching to make sure no one pocketed Trinitite or egregiously violated any of the other regulations. Despite Regulation #7—"You may not pick up or take Trinitite from Ground Zero"—visitors hunted for shards of Trinitite to take as souvenirs. The fact that the stuff was radioactive enough to fog photographic film did not seem to bother anyone.

The army carefully prescribed every activity at Trinity Site, yet it also wanted to appear accommodating. This was, after all, an open house, and a happy crowd was an untroubled and unreflective crowd. Instructed to be friendly and helpful, the MPs hoisted kids up to see Fat Man, answered questions with a smart "Yes, sir" and "No, ma'am," and talked weaponry with the many gun enthusiasts. One soldier sat at a card table with a neat little science display for the kids—a Geiger counter and Trinitite chunks. The kids were invited to pass the Geiger's copper rod over the chunks. The sudden hyperactive clicking elicited squeals and giggles.

It all seemed so innocuous. A little too innocuous. I walked around the circle several times thinking there had to be something amiss. After all, this was the point of origin for the nightmares that had haunted us for half a century. For those of us who had gone through "duck-and-cover" drills in school and had grown up fearing the holocaust that might descend from the skies at any moment, Trinity Site was the place where the fundamental conditions of human existence were forever changed. And yet, visiting the place, one found that there was nothing particularly horrible about it. Not even an awe-inspiring crater. "All life on Earth has been touched by the event which took place here," read the plaque on the obelisk. But all evidence of the "event" had been effaced or removed, leaving behind nothing that could be considered disturbing. Instead, Ground Zero had been transformed into the scene of an impromptu tailgate party, the partygoers enjoying snack foods, photo opportunities, and Frisbee games. I was sorely tempted to break Regulation #2 and hold some sort of demonstration. I considered the tried-and-true standby of chaining myself to a fence, but I didn't have a chain and I knew such a melodramatic gesture wouldn't accomplish anything anyway. Instead, I left Ground Zero for the parking lot and stopped at the army's information tent.

I asked if there had ever been protests or sit-ins. Presumably there had been, if the army felt the need to expressly forbid them.

"I can't say, sir," the shaved-head MP said.

I admired the ambiguity. Did he mean that he did not know, or that he was not allowed to say? When I asked for clarification, his delivery remained prompt and deadpan: "I can't say, sir."

I stood apart from the crowd, mulling the words that had been inscribed on the obelisk. *All life on Earth has been touched by the event that took place here.* To me, the words seemed inadequate, a grotesque understatement, a glib attempt to gloss over the magnitude of the event. It was Epcot-style prose: superficial, reductive, bland. This "event," as the obelisk called it, had delineated and inscribed the lives of everyone, everywhere. Throughout my lifetime, this manifest ability to destroy ourselves had been the most fearsome thing of all, hard to grasp and yet all too tangible.

Even those of us who had experienced relatively tranquil childhoods knew the fear, the anxiety that the Bomb—upper case now in the imagination—instilled and has continued to instill. Death could come spiraling from the clear blue sky at any moment. A peaceful morning—whether in Hiroshima or Hartford—could instantly transform into a hell of blinding light. The knowledge that it could happen at any moment—well, it did much more than *touch* you. It left an indelible mark, a palpable fear that one fine day you, too, might be obliterated.

Apart from Ground Zero, visitors are allowed to tour the nearby McDonald Ranch, which in 1945 was transformed into a makeshift laboratory. A school bus takes people the three miles to the ranch house, a one-story adobe building surrounded by a low stone wall. Inside the house, the Trinity team assembled the various parts of the bomb in the days before the test. In the dusty, wind-whipped desert, the house had to be constantly vacuumed and the windows sealed with plastic and tape to create the sterile environment necessary for the assembly of an atomic bomb.

Today, the dust has returned with a vengeance, and the house smells old and abandoned, like a crypt. A few displays and posted signs help visitors interpret what life was like at Trinity for the scientists and soldiers stationed there. Scorpions, fire ants, centipedes, rattlesnakes, and tarantulas were constant nuisances. For entertainment, the soldiers on guard duty shot antelope with machine guns. Gypsum sullied the well water and stiffened the hair of those who drank it. For relief from the one hundred-degree heat, the crew swam in a huge water tank near the barn. The water tank is still there. A nearby barn remains partially collapsed from the impact of the atomic blast.

During our tour, someone spied a rattlesnake curled in the shade of the stone wall, and it quickly became the main tourist attraction. Everyone maneuvered to get a picture, and a MP came out to keep people back. "You gotta be careful," he said. "Them suckers move pretty fast when they want to."

When it was time to go, the bullhorn called us back to the parking lot. An MP closed and locked the gate to Ground Zero. We were given questionnaires about the "experience" of visiting Trinity Site. Then the lead jeep started off and the MPs whistled and waved us back into the caravan. After the eighty-mile drive back to Alamogordo, we were granted our freedom.

Alongside the highway in Alamogordo, several vendors sat outside vans, rear doors propped open to display "Authentic Trinitite Artwork"—necklaces, earrings, and—oddly, it seemed to me—imitation arrowheads. One by one the tourists pulled over to check out the souvenirs. I asked one vendor about the arrowheads. Wasn't it kind of ironic to fashion a primitive weapon from the by-product of an ultramodern one?

"Never thought of it that way," he said. "They're just easy to make. But now that you mention it, that's a good point. Ironic, like you say. Kind of cool." I could see his mind at work: maybe this was a talking point he could use to close sales.

On the way back to Albuquerque, I stopped at a diner in Socorro, New Mexico, seventy-five miles from Trinity Site. Over coffee, I read a brochure describing the town's attractions, one of which was a piece of debris from Ground Zero, now prominently displayed in a city park. I walked up the street to check it out. Above town, the setting sun struck the San Mateo Mountains with its fireball. In the park, the pitted black chunk—a fragment from Jumbo—lay on an altar-like plinth, an inscrutable relic absorbing the sun's last light. A little water—apparently snowmelt from last week's storm—had pooled in a depression, turning the chunk into a font, the water darkly reflecting the sky. A nearby historical marker said that the steel fragment was "a souvenir of the worlds [sic] first nuclear explosion," the municipal version, apparently, of the Trinitite souvenirs that visitors to Ground Zero pocketed.

Back at Trinity, I had refrained from submitting my questionnaire. Two of its questions had me stymied:

Why did you come today?
What did you expect to see?

I hardly knew what to say. I guess I had imagined something more reminiscent of the Vietnam Veterans Memorial in Washington: reflective, somber, sobering. I hadn't expected gaiety. I was puzzled by the unquestioned and nonchalant celebration of the Atomic Age. I was puzzled by souvenir snapshots of Fat Man. I was puzzled by Trinitite art. I was puzzled by reverent displays of bomb debris in city parks.

Staring at the blackened fragment, Socorro's pride, I recalled Oppenheimer's Hindu chant: *I am become Death, destroyer of worlds*. I wondered why, after nearly half a century, the scientist's apprehension had changed into the blithe apathy of those touring Trinity. Had we become so inured to its imagery that we could exhibit fragments of its wreckage in our parks as a tourist attraction? Did the Bomb now invoke civic pride?

Perhaps the atomic bomb's strange but persistent connection to religion offers an explanation by analogy. What is a *holy day* for the original believers becomes in subsequent generations a *holiday*, emptied of the significance it once held for the first faithful. Solemnity in observance yields to frivolity and revelry. An occasion for prayer becomes an occasion for partying. The Holy Mass mutates into a secular Easter egg hunt. Decades later, awe and fear of the Bomb had dissipated. Its effect on the people visiting Trinity was like its impact on the desert itself. Minimal. Less and less apparent with time. The army had succeeded in packaging the event as something innocuous, an "open house." How nice. How inviting. In the late 1940s, the army removed all evidence of the blast from Trinity; and now it had successfully cleansed the site of any overtly ominous associations.

The army wanted to know why I had gone to Trinity. At first I thought it was mere curiosity. Now I understood that I had gone out of a sense of obligation, an obligation to see for myself, to experience this place where we as a people became death, the destroyer of worlds. And with that recognition, the blackened and pitted fragment before me seemed hideous. I hurried away from the park, pursued by church bells calling the flock to Easter vespers. But few parishioners were in evidence, only a trio of elderly, shawl-wrapped women who huddled on the steps before the shuttered doors of the sanctuary.

II

Ground Truthing

I learn by going where I have to go.

—Theodore Roethke, "The Waking"

Land of the Lost

When the train lifted from the tracks I woke up, thinking I was back in the USSR. It was not yet dawn, and through the soiled curtain I could see a snow-blown train yard. Weak light from a watchtower gave vague shape to a row of old boxcars imprinted with faded Cyrillic letters. The carriage I rode in hovered in the air. From below came hard metallic blows and emphatic Russian imprecations.

It was a bogie change, a border procedure necessary because back in the nineteenth century Imperial Russia had built tracks of a broader gauge than those used elsewhere in Europe. A crane lifted each train carriage a couple meters off the tracks while rail workers changed the bogies by hand. Judging from the proletarian curses coming from below, the procedure wasn't going so well this winter's night.

An hour earlier, at the Romanian border post, two guards had passed down the aisle, giving a cursory glance at passports and taking the yellowed strips of paper (hand cut with uneven edges) that served as official Romanian visas. The elder guard, a grim-faced Ceausescu-era leftover, took far more interest in the pretty female trainee following him than he did in who or what was leaving Romania. But he paused over my passport and murmured a joke about me that caused the woman to glance away and stifle a giggle. The older guard stamped my passport, snapped it shut, and handed it back. *Drum bun*, he said, his sarcasm needing no translation. *Da, drum bun*, the woman repeated. Good road. Bon voyage. Happy trails.

They snickered on to the next berth, leaving me to wonder at the joke. I checked my pocket dictionary for an unfamiliar word and then my slow Romanian caught up with what the guard had said: "This American must think he's on the train to Vienna." Therein lay the joke: no tourist in his right mind these days would travel west to east—the direction I was headed—not in this part of the world. The general rule was the farther east you went, the worse things got. In terms of direction, west was best.

With the border formalities concluded, the train had then crossed the River Prut, long the boundary between Romania and the Soviet Union and now Romania's boundary with the newly independent country of Moldova. Shortly after crossing over, the train stalled and a cold wind rocked the dead coaches. In the long moments between lurches, I drifted asleep until the moment the carriage levitated and the banging began and the curses rang out from below.

I awoke confused. Everything was eerily familiar: the musty smell of the ticking draped on the berth, the stronger smell of tar-spiked cigarettes, the dim low-watt bulbs now humming alight as Soviet-trained guards came aboard for inspection. They passed from compartment to compartment, sliding aside the panel doors of fake wood grain that led to the aisle outside the four-person compartments. Vodka-laced voices up and down the aisle managed to express with the same tone and the same words both impatient discontent and weary resignation.

It was all so familiar that in my groggy confusion I thought it really was the Soviet Union, that I was back on the Trans-Siberian, just as I had been twenty years before when, during a long, bitter, late-winter night, a Russian traveler and I passed a bottle of vodka back and forth, back and forth, and I tried to focus enough to understand what he was telling me. His constant, furtive refrain had been clear enough. "Carter, *da*. Brezhnev, *nyet*. America, good—Soviet Union, no good."

Now twenty years later, Brezhnev was long gone. The Soviet Union was no more. It was 1999. On one level, everything had changed. On another, nothing had changed.

The Moldovan passport official appeared in the compartment doorway. Like the Romanian guards, he found my documents something of a novelty. "You are American?" he said dubiously, in English. He turned the pages slowly, studying the visa and entry stamps. Behind him in the aisle, soldiers in search of contraband were tapping panels and groping into presumed crawl spaces. The official sat down on the berth opposite me and patted my passport in his palm, as though contemplating judgment. But instead of the ingrained Soviet scowl, his face broke into a broad grin. "American," he repeated. "I once wanted very much to go to America. But now of course it is not possible." He was a heavy-set man in a bulky military coat, but he sat lightly on the edge of the berth, leaning forward into me. He reminded me of Rod Steiger in *Doctor Zhivago*. On the official's military-issue fur hat, you could see a discolored outline where the red star had once been. He sighed. "Before," he said, using a pregnant word I was to hear often in the weeks to come as my interlocutors spoke of Moldova's transition to the new world order, "before, I could travel many places for no money at all. Moscow. St. Petersburg. Kiev. Tashkent. All over Soviet Union. And now, nowhere. I am prisoner on this border. Yes, freedom I have to go to Paris, America. But I have no money, my friend, not even to go to Bucharest."

He closed his eyes and shrugged in the slow-rocking Russian way—total resignation to a hard life. "What is to be done?" he said at last.

The official placed my passport on the little table between berths. Then he stood and bowed slightly. "Please enjoy your visit to my country," he said. "Welcome to Moldova."

Moldova. Formerly a Soviet republic. Before that, a province of Romania. Once upon a time an outpost of the Ottoman Empire. A wedge of steppe land no bigger than Belgium, traded back and forth in the various treaties that have temporarily resolved disputes and wars among the regional powers. Truly a pawn in the chess match, or maybe not even a pawn—just a square on the board waiting to be occupied. Finally, after the breakup of the Soviet Union, Moldova found itself an independent country struggling for survival and identity.

I was traveling from Bucharest to Moldova's capital, Kishinev, on the overnight "Rapid"—a three hundred-mile journey that required a good fourteen hours, the train's designation notwithstanding. A good chunk of that time involved waiting out the bogie change and the passport formalities at the border posts. But even at top speed the train merely crawled along as though reluctant to make the journey, as though it too dreaded passage to the east.

Once the train left the border, I saw by the gray light of dawn the rolling, snow-covered undulations of the steppes. Much of the land was under cultivation with fruit trees and vineyards, the barren branches now covered with frost. Occasionally, the train passed through a muddy village of tin-roofed houses. In the middle of frozen lakes, men sat on boxes, ice-fishing. Horse-drawn carts waited out the slow passage of the train, the burly peasant drivers swigging from wine flasks. It was as though in crossing the border I had gone back a century or more. Even backward Romania now looked modern in comparison. At the end of the twentieth century, Moldova remained an underdeveloped, primarily agrarian outpost.

Even when we reached the outskirts of Kishinev, the landscape was only reluctantly urban. Orchards and vineyards bordered city streets. Grapevines climbed house walls. Apartment buildings and warehouses, too, were draped in vines. Kishinev was a city of 700,000, but it seemed more like an extended village. It certainly did not look like a national capital, and yet it was, thanks to the events that led to the breakup of the Soviet Union in 1991.

In the years following independence, attempts to dismantle the Soviet system had been chaotic and inconsistent. Yes, democratic elections had occurred in Moldova. Yes, the invisible hand of capitalism had tinkered, or rather fumbled, with the economy. But by the late 1990s, the anticipated economic, political, and cultural transformations were still incomplete. Important structural reforms had not yet taken place, and the International Monetary Fund and the World Bank were pressuring the Moldovan government for more drastic changes. The economy and the government were still largely in the hands of Soviet-era apparatchiks who had simply adopted new titles in the transition. Many were now linked to the emerging Russian Mafia.

Meanwhile, from the moment of independence, a group of hardliners who preferred the Soviet system had holed up in a sliver of territory known as Transnistria along Moldova's border with Ukraine. These hardliners refused to accept Kishinev's authority, and they were willing to fight for their autonomy. In fact, for a period of time in the early 1990s, war had broken out. Seven years later, the uneasy standoff still required international monitoring and had proven to be a further drag on Moldova's modernization.

As the first decade of independence drew to an end, income distribution in Moldova was widening considerably, with a very few getting rich—primarily through corrupt capitalist ventures—while the vast majority grew poorer and poorer. In some cases, desperately poor: according to reports, large numbers of Moldovan women were being enticed to work as prostitutes in Western Europe, where many of them had disappeared into the netherworld of sex slavery. There were rumors that traffickers in human organs were buying Moldovan kidneys to sell on the black market. Before my year in the country was over, Moldova would officially become the poorest of the former Soviet republics and the poorest country in Europe, dropping below even woebegone Albania. This was the gist of the situation in Moldova when I arrived.

I had come to Moldova for several reasons. My primary purpose was to lecture at the national university. While doing so, I wanted to see what was happening in one of the small, newly independent countries that had emerged after the Soviet breakup. Moldova, it seemed to me, was a microcosm of the other troubled areas in the former Soviet Union, where separatist struggles over territorial control were leading to the rapid disintegration of coherent political units. Finally, I wanted to see if the vaunted triumph of capitalism and democracy was genuine. Francis Fukuyama, a former US State Department policy planner, had written a much-bruited book called *The End of History*. In it, Fukuyama claimed that the epic contest of political systems had been fought and won by "our side," the West. "What we are witnessing is not just the end of the Cold War," Fukuyama wrote, "or a passing of a particular period of postwar history, but the end of history as such: that is, the end point of mankind's ideological evolution and the universalization of Western liberal democracy as the final form of human government." The worldwide ideological struggle, Fukuyama maintained, was now replaced by "the satisfaction of sophisticated consumer demands." In short, the underlying world order—what George H. W. Bush had called the New World Order—was now "an unabashed victory of economic and political liberalism." That sounded just fine from the tranquil vantage point of middle America. But what was happening out on the frontlines, I wondered. If Francis Fukuyama was right in declaring a capitalist paradise as the end of history, then places like Moldova should be progressing toward prosperity and engaging in the pursuit of happiness. Such, however, did not appear to be the case.

On the morning of my arrival in Kishinev (Romanian speakers call the city "Chişinau"), I came out of the depot into a fog-bound, bone-cold town. A raw wind blew but did not seem to stir the fog. On the small square fronting the train station, a row of battered buses awaited passengers for Istanbul. This morning there were none. Nor were there customers at the sidewalk kiosks selling Polish cola, Russian newspapers, and American cigarettes. Several old women wrapped in heavy coats and scarves—their doughy, wrinkled faces fixed in dour, stoic expressions—stood over sacks of black sunflower seeds, Moldova's ubiquitous snack food.

Leaving the square, I turned onto Kishinev's main boulevard and walked toward the city center. After a few blocks, I passed a small outdoor market in a muddy lot. Farmers from the outlying villages proffered jugs of milk and plastic bottles of blood-red wine and cakes of crumbling cheese. Passers-by, trampling in mud, took samples, but few deigned to buy. Light, crystallized flurries drifted down through the fog.

The market abutted an intersection, a traffic circle where several pothole-ridden boulevards came together. Across from the circle stood the towering concrete block of the Hotel Cosmos, Stalinesque and uninviting, a high-rise mausoleum that had had few guests in its previous incarnation as an Intourist hotel, and perhaps even fewer now that Moldova had slipped into the "newly independent" vortex. To the right, just off the plaza, was another huge concrete tower, or rather a mere shell of a tower, apparently still under construction, though no one was working and the project appeared defunct. Looking up the street between the two towers, I saw a desolation row of vacant lots and disintegrating buildings lining a wide boulevard with little traffic. What traffic there was came together at the roundabout in a cacophony of horns, backfire, unmuffled growls, squealing brakes, and electric spark-showers from overhead trolley lines.

In stark contrast to the bleak scene, a sleek, colorful billboard dominated the center of the traffic circle. It had once displayed propaganda posters. Now, like everything else in Moldova from members of parliament to flower stalls, the hoarding had converted to capitalism. It touted a computer concern.

Following the lead of Kishinev's citizens, I spent a good amount of time loitering in parks and walking around town more or less aimlessly. Summer or winter, warm or cold, people bided time in city parks, some reading the week-old newspapers tacked on display boards, most sitting on benches doing crossword puzzles or just watching the flow. The elderly gathered in groups to smoke and argue. The young paired off for kissing and groping. Freelance photographers stood around, ready to memorialize special occasions with a Polaroid. Some photographers brought along props to enhance the photos. Animals were a popular motif: stuffed deer, jaguars, rabbits. I arrived in Kishinev just after the New Year, the week of Orthodox Christmas, and for the occasion freelance photographers had set up backdrops—fanciful scenes of winter wonderlands with Happy New Year messages painted across them. There were live models, too: a hoary Father Christmas in a blue velvet suit and a buxom snow queen to complement the usual stuffed animals. But by far the most popular model this year was a black Santa, an African who had come to study in Kishinev during Soviet days. After the break-up, he was stranded. His Soviet scholarship was cut off, and his homeland had no funds for his return. Now he lived hand-to-mouth. By a stroke of fortune, he had discovered that Moldovans regarded a black Santa a novelty worthy of their spare change.

Kishinev reveled in its parks, and the parks were without question the city's best feature. There was the Park of the Cathedral with its flower stalls and diminutive copy of the Arc de Triomphe (not big enough for a street, it straddled a sidewalk). Across the city's main boulevard was the park dedicated to Stefan the Great, Moldova's greatest hero. A huge statue of the Turk-fighter—sword in one hand, cross in the other—guarded the entrance. The park's central fountain, a replica of the Roman coliseum, spewed water in warm weather and sported a layer of ice in winter. Nearby stood a column dedicated to Pushkin. It was to Kishinev in 1820 that the poet was banished for his liberal proclivities. Young and unknown, Pushkin spent three long years in the Bessarabian town. At that time, Kishinev was little more than a village of peasants in the far southwestern corner of Russia, a place of few amenities and unsophisticated culture. Pushkin wrote poetry while in Kishinev, but he wrote little if anything about his place of exile. A few songs about gypsy girls—not among his best work—may or may not reflect Bessarabian themes, one can't be certain. Fittingly, Kishinev's most celebrated resident lived there involuntarily and spent his three unproductive years in the town longing to leave. He referred to the place as "accursed Kishinev."

Beyond Pushkin's column, the walkway led past the busts of Romanian luminaries, all unknown outside the Romanian-speaking world (with the possible exception of Mircea Eliade). With time, I became familiar with the faces, if not the achievements, of Mikhail Kogalniceanu and Nicolae Iorga and a host of others. They scrutinized my daily passage with the same paradoxical expression—xenophobic curiosity—that outsiders so frequently encounter in Eastern Europe.

I soon settled into a routine. My daily walks took me down the main boulevard, through Stefan the Great's Park, past the president's house, and then past the US Embassy. Down the street from the embassy, I came to a small park where every day, in every kind of weather, a group of hardy pensioners played long games of chess, two playing while twenty watched intently. Wearing shabby sport coats decorated with faded ribbons and medals won in the Soviet Union's wars, they spent hours lingering over the boards, nodding or frowning at the contestants' moves.

From the chess players' park, my boots crunching the icy walkways, I descended a long flight of snow-encrusted steps to another park, this one featuring an artificial lake dug in Stalin's time by Komonsol, the Communist Youth Organization. During my first three months in Moldova, the lake was frozen over and scores of fishermen sat on crates hunched over holes hacked in the ice. At one end of the lake was an antiquated fun fair—a collection of erratic amusement rides—that operated on weekends even in the dead of winter. There, I would pause to watch bundled children riding a decrepit train, their breath frosting in the air.

Adjacent to the fun fair, the path led to a large expo grounds and a number of stores—formerly exposition halls for showcasing Soviet economic prowess—where import items were on display. Stereos, televisions, computers, bicycles, washing machines, cosmetics, and coffee makers were found here, the wonders of the Western world, perused but rarely purchased. In fact, on my visits to the place (grandly titled "MoldExpo"), very few perusers were in evidence. After eight years of independence and the free-falling economy of capitalism, Moldovans were no longer much interested in gazing at goods they had no hope of buying. Just recently, an Ace Hardware franchise had opened up in MoldExpo, an "American-style" store according to a sign out front, and it was brimming with gadgets and devices for equipping and decorating a proper modern home—latex paint, insulation, brass doorknobs, smoke detectors, home invasion alarms, stereo speakers for the garden, even kits for testing swimming pool water. A whole row was devoted to home lighting products, but the Ace Hardware store itself was unlit; there were so few customers management had elected to reduce operating costs by keeping the lights and heat turned off. Bundled in huge coats, the employees sat on stools and stared straight ahead, immobile even when the occasional customer happened in. They knew the likely drill: customers browsed the aisles, fingered products out of curiosity, and moved on.

At the bottom end of the expo grounds stood three statues—Marx, Engels, and Lenin, the great trinity of a lost world. Elsewhere in Eastern Europe similar statues had been destroyed. But the Moldovans had not been so drastic in their treatment of fallen heroes. Removed from their positions of prominence near the Congress building and exiled to this remote spot, the three titans of communism gazed at the well-stocked but depopulated expo halls of capitalism from afar. The busts of Marx and Engels brooded ineffectually, while Lenin stood full of ferocious energy, one leg forward, as though he were ready to mount a charge against the forces that had banished him.

The fallen heroes chafed in their exile, ignored for the most part—but not entirely. Visiting them on midwinter days, I sometimes found a handful of frostbitten flowers had been laid on the pedestals. A fresh dusting of frost made their heads hoary, and windblown snow whited out Marx's deep sockets, blinding him, turning him into the Tiresias of Kishinev.

* * *

The people of Kishinev shopped not in MoldExpo but in the bazaars scattered around town. I loved roaming through the jam-packed rows of the main bazaar on Saturdays, when everyone in the country seemed to cram into one place. From the villages came peasants with their bags of black potatoes, turnips, onions, beets, and carrots. The city folk came to shop and bargain. There were chickens and pigs and lambs ready for slaughter. There were live fish in murky tanks and dead fish splayed on tables. There were scores of sausages dangling from wire and stacks of cheese packets oozing curds. There were baskets of breads and rolls and pastries. At the tables and established stalls, licensed vendors displayed packaged goods, mostly imported. But many of the hawkers were peripatetic freelancers. With no fixed base and no license, they roamed the bazaar proffering two or three odd items they had managed to procure somewhere, somehow—plastic clothespins, rat poison, shoelaces, batteries, Spice Girls stickers, cheese graters. And plastic bags: everyone in Kishinev carried a plastic bag at all times. The bags often bore a bogus design suggestive of some Western corporation; and like anything else in the capitalist world, those with the classier logos cost more—even though the bags were themselves identical and the logos were merely fanciful copies.

Elsewhere in the bazaar, ancient shawl-wrapped women held out bundles of slender brown candles or jars of red powder used in religious ceremonies. Some of the items for sale suggested wild hopes and desperation. A small girl sold pussy willows. An old man offered peacock feathers. A wizened proletarian stood his ground in midst of the flowing, pushing throng, gripping something to his chest with two trembling hands: a tattered Lenin cap. I thought he was a beggar until the third time the current of the crowd forced me past him, when I realized he was trying to sell the cap.

In certain places, pockets of freelance vendors had established themselves more or less permanently. One of these places I came to think of as the Gauntlet. Along a sidewalk leading into the bazaar, freelancers formed two rows between which pedestrians passed. In the crooks of their arms the vendors—mostly stout women—cradled their inventory: stockings, socks, girdles, and a selection of startlingly voluminous bras. Vendors with an especially nice item to sell—a child's party dress for example—displayed the items on hangers dangling from the buttonholes of their coats. The vendors' own bodies served, in effect, as display cases. For hours on end they stood in the cold, merchandise-laden arms outstretched—a position that looked like either torture or rehearsal for capitalist martyrdom—patiently awaiting some passer-by to stop and haggle. They were paragons of obdurate patience and Sisyphean stoicism. After putting in hours to make one sale, they were just as likely to lose the sale at the last second to another vendor in the gauntlet, the competition was so intense, supply way outstripping demand.

Vendors took their places in the gauntlet out of necessity, not choice. Most were the unemployed relatives of factory workers who had been paid in the product that their place of employment produced. The bras, for example, came from a small local manufacturer that, lacking the capital to pay its employees, paid them in kind. To convert the bras into money, someone from the worker's family had to go out and sell them or barter them for another product. This practice had become the norm in Moldova, and in the bazaar or on the streets you came upon any number of products—from electric heaters to sparkling wine to glass jars—that were the in-kind wages of the workers who had made them. Even the government often paid the employees of the state in goods rather than currency. Schoolteachers were paid in sugar, the government having accepted beet sugar as a tax payment from farmers. The teachers would try to sell the sugar or trade it for something—perhaps a bra from the gauntlet. In this way, Moldova was moving closer and closer to a barter economy.

I did not go to the bazaar solely for the fun of immersing myself in the crowd; like everyone else I went in search of daily necessities. Most of the time these necessities were available in quantity if not quality. Yet at any given time, something or other was in short supply. One week it was milk, another week eggs, then butter. Later, bread was suddenly scarce. No one I knew had an explanation for these shortages. Shopkeepers and bazaar vendors shook their heads and shrugged—an ambivalent gesture common in the country, at once a confession of ignorance and a denial of responsibility. No, nothing is available today. Who knows when there will be more?

On the other hand, some unexpected items were always readily available in the bazaars and street markets. A stunning variety of flowers, for example, could always be found, no matter the weather. A strip of flower stalls stayed open twenty-four hours, the flowers carefully arranged and displayed inside heated tents. Even when the temperature dropped below zero, the sturdy vendors stayed on, ready to supply Moldovans' inordinate need for flowers. Tulips, crocuses, hyacinths, and daffodils were arranged in bouquets according to local custom: an odd number of blooms for happy events, an even number for funerals and other sorrowful occasions. Moldovans, I was told, might spend ten to twenty percent of their income on flowers, and it was absolutely essential to bring along a bouquet whenever you visited someone's home. People could go without milk, butter, eggs, even bread—but not flowers.

Elsewhere in the various bazaars around town, you could count on a steady supply of pirated products, mostly Western knock-offs made in places like Uzbekistan beyond the pale of trademark laws. Jeans, perfumes, watches, and especially compact discs were sold from rickety tables and homemade display cases for double-take prices. CDs, for example, were going for two and three dollars, with a selection that would impress even the most acquisitive of Western shoppers—the latest in rock, pop, rhythm and blues, and rap available in copies so faithfully reproduced that even the *Parental Advisory: Explicit Lyrics* warning label was included, though no one, least of all the counterfeiters, understood or cared about the warning's intent. In Moldova, the words were as meaningless and irrelevant as the phrase "intellectual property rights."

The popularity of pirated music I could understand. But who in this impoverished country, I wondered, was buying copies of computer games and programs? Yet there they were, rows and rows of jewel cases with the latest software direct from outlaw factories out on the Eurasian steppes. Unctuous and eager salesmen sidled up when I stopped to browse. What are you looking for, they said in English, shuffling CDs for my perusal. Jazz? Blues? Country? War games? Shania Twain? Death Star? Will Smith? Thirty *lei*. Fifty for two.

What about viruses, I asked, fingering a three-dollar copy of a one hundred-dollar program upgrade. The vendor shrugged and pulled a pirated anti-virus program from his stack. No problem, my friend.

Besides picking up bargain-priced software, the few Westerners who found themselves in Moldova liked to hunt the bazaars for war medals and other Soviet memorabilia—hammer-and-sickle belt buckles, for example, or Red Army holsters—items that had been sold by people desperate for cash. War medals, along with antique icons, were prize souvenirs to take out of Moldova, and while it was technically illegal to do so, nothing in Moldova was impossible for the person with money. There might be hassles passing through customs on the way out of the country, but a small bribe would likely clear up any difficulties.

Walking around Kishinev, I felt increasingly dismayed at evidence of the country's stagnation. The imagery of despair in Moldova had its own bleakness that worked and worked on you until you too felt beat and hopeless—even if you had what everyone else wanted and couldn't get: a ticket out. Emblematic of the stagnation and despair were the scores of elderly beggars stationed at store entrances and church portals. When the Soviet Union collapsed, these pensioners had lost everything. Savings accounts became worthless with the disintegration of the Soviet ruble. Pension funds vanished. Jobs no longer existed. Because Moldova had once been regarded as a good place for Soviet citizens to retire, it now had a large number of pensioners and no money for their support. Like schoolteachers, pensioners might be paid in commodities such as sugar—when they were paid at all—and many were forced to beg on the streets. Bundled in tattered coats, they waited patiently outside stores and prayed for God's reward on those who gave them some spare change; and in Moldova there was precious little change to spare. They might wait all day for a handful of nearly worthless coins.

And there were other beggars, too. Gypsy children. Baby-bearing girls from the villages. Disabled veterans of the Red Army's war in Afghanistan. Street musicians in gimmicky attire, such as an accordionist who wore an elephant mask while he played. Competing with the beggars, dogs roamed Kishinev's streets, hundreds of strays scrounging garbage and snarling for scraps. Sometimes Kishinev seemed like a vast dog kennel on the loose.

The city's infrastructure provided further evidence of the hardships of collapse and transition. Wherever you walked, you saw the decaying apartment blocks of the Soviet era, some buildings eroding before your eyes as the wind wore away mortar and sent pellets of concrete eddying down to the sidewalks. One abandoned shopping center had a post-apocalyptic look to it—disintegrated stairways, collapsed storefronts, exposed rebar, corroded girders. Was it an earthquake ruin, I wondered, or a casualty of the 1992 conflict with breakaway Transnistria? No, people told me, just another shoddy Soviet project falling apart of its own accord. The shopping center was especially noteworthy because it dated to the late-Brezhnev era, that period in time when, to Western eyes, the Soviet Union appeared monolithic, fearsome, even evil. But from the inside, from places like Kishinev, the imminent collapse that was to seem so shocking to the West had already become apparent by 1982. As this and many other ruins in Kishinev attested, the USSR was a superpower that couldn't build a halfway decent shopping center. It had been driven by a bureaucratic system designed to meet production quotas not standards of quality; projects like the shopping center began falling apart the moment the ribbon-cutting ceremony lauding socialist achievement had concluded.

To me, this particular shopping center was elevated to something of a symbol when I saw it featured on a postcard. A Moldovan acquaintance gave me a packet of Soviet-era postcards of Kishinev—tourist souvenirs, I guess, though very few tourists had ever visited the city. The grainy photos depicted government buildings, museums, socialist monuments, and churches (the latter used in Soviet times as union halls and art galleries). Several of the postcards celebrated examples of Soviet achievement, such as tenement complexes, factories, and this same shopping center, newly completed in the photo. The postcard suggested that (along with a truly peculiar notion of tourist aesthetics) the Soviet Union took official pride in these "glorious achievements of the socialist worker," achievements that were laughably bad to the point of obvious irony. In this one shopping center, then, you had a perfect symbol for the end of the Soviet empire.

So it was wherever you looked: decaying buildings, choppy roads, crumbling sidewalks. And unfinished buildings, too: scores of tottering shells, construction projects abandoned in 1991 when Moscow's largesse dissipated along with the quotas and five-year plans that had put the projects into motion. But the plans and projects were all obviated now; the money had vanished. The remnant skeletons remained, inconclusive and untouched for ten years.

The appearance of abandonment was enhanced in the evening when daylight faded and the streets went dark. Functioning street lamps were few and far between, and a walk in the city after nightfall became an eerie and dangerous exercise. Huge crows circled and cawed in the gloaming. Pedestrians suddenly emerged from shadows, disrupting your pace and peace of mind. Dogs snarled in alleyways. The darkened shells of abandoned buildings loomed. Unseen depressions and potholes riddled the walkways. Lampposts existed, but most of the lamps had no bulbs—and even with bulbs would not have functioned, as there wasn't enough electricity to power them. Moldova relied on power plants located on the eastern banks of the Dniester, under control of the separatists who had no interest in cutting deals. Otherwise, Moldova had to buy its power from Russia, and the government simply didn't have enough credit to meet the country's electrical needs.

My walks also took me past a place that I mistook at first for a nature preserve. From the street, all I could see was a tangle of growth—an unkempt forest—behind a high wall. Eventually, I learned that this was the old Jewish cemetery, long abandoned now that there were almost no Jews left in Moldova.

Other than being the locale of Pushkin's exile, Kishinev had secured its small place in history as the scene of horrific pogroms. At the beginning of the twentieth century, nearly half of the city's population was Jewish. Kishinev was under Russian jurisdiction at the time, and Russia in 1900 was a virulently anti-Semitic state. Jews were loathed and feared. The czar's authorities considered them revolutionaries. The Russian peasants envied Jewish successes in business. Folk stories of ritual murders—Jews killing Christians for their blood—circulated and the authorities did little to squelch them. Profit-driven newspaper publishers worked rumors into fully realized reports of atrocities. The typical report told of Russian boys and girls falling into the clutches of butcher Jews collecting Christian blood for Passover feasts. Such a story surfaced in Kishinev just before Easter, 1903. Over the Easter weekend, the city's good Christians ran riot, exacting their revenge by burning and looting Kishinev's ghetto. Hundreds of Jews were pulled from their homes, clubbed, and mauled. A few were pulled to pieces. Some forty-three Jews died. The twentieth century had just begun, and remote Kishinev was foreshadowing its major motifs. Indeed, the 1903 pogrom was only a prelude for what was to come in Kishinev. When Romania aligned itself with Nazi Germany, 400,000 Bessarabian Jews (and 40,000 Gypsies) were sent to concentration camps in Transnistria. Many were eventually deported to Auschwitz.

By the end of the century, very few Jews lived in Kishinev; they accounted for about one percent of the population. My Moldovan acquaintances knew very little about the city's Jewish history. A small, unassuming stone slab in a park on the edge of the city was dedicated to the victims of the 1903 pogrom, but the history museum ignored the matter altogether. Most people I spoke to were puzzled by mention of the pogrom. Such a thing had never happened in Kishinev, they were sure. Nor did they believe that the city had once been nearly half Jewish. During their lifetime, the city's Jewish background had been all but obliterated. For example, the official city map did not indicate the location of the old Jewish cemetery. To passers-by, it was just a large, abandoned tract of land hidden behind deteriorated walls. When I finally learned what was behind the walls, I made several visits and found thousands of uprooted and overturned gravestones entangled in a dense thicket of vines and briars. But according to the maps, the cemetery did not officially exist. Nor was the location of Moldova's World War II concentration camps marked or memorialized in any way. My Moldovan acquaintances expressed their surprise—and their doubt—that such places had ever existed in the country, and they questioned the validity of my information.

Despite the dangers of night walking in Kishinev, I was often out after dark, usually to attend some social event. My status as a Fulbright scholar and my consequent connection to the American embassy put me in close contact with the expatriate community in Moldova. This community included personnel at the Western embassies and aid workers representing various NGOs. Some of the expatriates had formed a "diners' club," which met once a month at local restaurants, where we were often the only patrons except for perhaps a handful of government officials and Russian Mafia functionaries huddled in a corner. Many Moldovans I knew had not been to a restaurant in years; none had been to the fancier establishments (probably Mafia-owned) that the diners' club favored.

On a typical outing, twenty-five or thirty of us were seated at a long table. Musicians played loud gypsy-style versions of movie and show standards—the themes from *Dr. Zhivago*, *Titanic*, and *James Bond* were in heavy rotation—meant to entertain us during the long, inexplicable waits between courses. When a break in the music permitted conversation, the expats returned to their favorite themes: the rapid disintegration of the country and their intense desire to get out. Many expressed anxiety about being trapped in Moldova. True, some claimed that "Moldova could get in your blood" and professed to truly love the place, its people, its culture. These were the foreigners who had married Moldovans or who had some ongoing research project, something that tied them to the place. But for most of the foreign community, Moldova was a temporary post in a disagreeable backwater. They spoke longingly of previous assignments or speculated and dreamed about where they would go next, once they had "put in time" in Moldova.

The anxiety that these expats felt led them to carp about the country and its citizens. A long list of complaints was drawn up and reiterated at each gathering. Almost anything could be the subject of complaint—the mud, the cold, the bread, the milk, the hard water, the baffling pattern of one-way streets, the Moldovan custom of hanging rugs on walls. The emblem for their irritation was the typical Moldovan lift, whether in a tenement, a government building, or a store. The grumbling, lurching elevators inspired fear and loathing in expats. "I just won't do it," someone would grouse. "I won't take one of those things. I'd rather walk up ten flights, thank you." Who got stuck in a lift, when, where, and for how long was one of the favorite news items amongst the foreign community.

And then there were some in Moldova's foreign community who thought that the Kishinev group had it relatively easy. These were the international aid workers with assignments in the outlying villages where conditions were even more rustic. To these people, Kishinev was the big city, a place of wonders and comforts that one could only dream about back in the villages.

One day, I met one of these hinterland expats, a pomologist from Washington State who was in Moldova to help with the development of commercial horticulture. He and his family lived in Edinets, a village in the northern part of the country. There they endured bleak conditions at best: sporadic electricity, unreliable food supplies, no running water. Because they lived in an apartment building (for even in the rural areas the Soviet government had housed people in Stalinesque blocks), they had to haul water from a well to the building and then up several flights of stairs. The two children could not go to school because the teachers, unpaid for months, no longer showed up for classes. The family had adjusted admirably to these conditions and carried on as best they could, committed to doing their part to help those less fortunate. Deprived of every amenity, they savored their forays into Kishinev and found it a marvel to stroll the streets of the big city.

The pomologist told me a story that seemed something of an apposite parable for life in Moldova. The little village of Edinets had received a gift bear from Russia. Why Edinets merited this favor was not exactly clear; the Russians had made similar gestures elsewhere in the "Newly Independent States," bestowing some token gift on a town or village apparently to remind the people of their historical ties to Russia. Not everyone in these villages, however, saw those historical ties in a favorable light. For many, "historical ties" meant imperial domination, and in such a context, Russia's gifts could easily be perceived as a subtle threat of the potential reassertion of its former hegemony. To the citizens of Edinets, the gift bear served as a rather credible symbol of such a threat, and as a consequence they came to loathe the otherwise innocent creature. They kept it caged in the center of town, ignored, unloved, and all but starved. Nobody could afford to feed the bear anyway, and because it was Russian, nobody in the staunchly Romanian village particularly wanted to.

That was only the beginning of the symbolic ironies. The emaciated bear eventually found a savior of sorts in an American Peace Corps volunteer assigned to Edinets who brought scraps of fish to the caged wretch. But it wasn't enough. One night, a drunken woman stumbling home got the capricious idea of talking to the bear or petting it. She ended up staggering against the cage and passing out, whereupon the starving bear gnawed off her arm. According to the apple farmer, the villagers now wanted to put the bear to death but had not yet decided how to do so.

Despite its incessant disgruntlement, the expat community proved to be a valuable source of information. It was during expat meet-ups that I heard confirmation of the many rumors now circulating about the dark side of Moldova's economic decline. Peace Corps officials, USAID personnel, and staff at some NGOs—people with inside information—confirmed that what we had heard was true: Moldova had become one of the principal countries of origin for the trafficking of women. Criminal gangs had lured or kidnapped thousands of young women and sent them into sex slavery abroad. An official of the Organization for Security and Co-operation in Europe called Moldova the "largest supplier state" of sex slaves in Europe.

Members of medical missions told us that the black market organ stories were true as well. Moldovans were being taken by bus across the Turkish border—sometimes with false promises of a job—where they were pressured into selling a kidney for a few thousand dollars. But what could be done? Most Moldovans earned well under a thousand dollars a year. When someone showed up offering "jobs" paying two thousand dollars, of course desperation would lead people to take a chance. And once they found themselves across the border in a hospital room with all their documents taken from them, they probably felt that they had little choice but to go through with it.

That was Moldova at the end of a sad century: a land of poverty, a land of frustration, a land of cynicism, a land of despair. And yet, there was always wine, the one product for which Moldova had won some renown, and as long as there was wine, the Moldovans themselves weren't going to go down without a toast. Perhaps because there was so little to celebrate, Moldovans celebrated anything and everything with enthusiasm and aggression. Weddings and religious feasts could last not just for hours but from one day to the next. A *sashlik*, or picnic barbecue in the woods, could turn into a bacchanalian marathon. Invitations were easy to come by, as foreigners were prized and honored guests. I received several invites from people I met at the state university. The presence of a foreign guest intensified the affair manifold, the toasts coming furiously often, the food foisted to the point of nausea. Expats in Moldova referred to it as "terrorist hospitality." Once a celebration began, even a simple dinner party, you had no hope of escape. You were held hostage, plied with food and drink, forced into toast after toast, no objection or excuse tolerated. The point was, seemingly, to make you crapulous for days thereafter.

In my several experiences, terrorist hospitality began at ten in the morning with a quick shot of Moldovan cognac. It was obligatory to drain the glass at once. From cognac you progressed to various homemade wines poured from plastic bottles. Plates of food were brought forth—herring, sausages, cheeses, radishes, pickles, cucumbers, tomatoes. Bottles were lined up on the table: brandy, wine, vodka, whiskey. You raised glasses for the first toasts, microcosmic in theme: to your health, to your mother, to the success of all your endeavors. Then came *mamaliga*—a cornmeal mush— and then came noodles, then a beet and walnut salad, then spaghetti. At last the main dish appeared, a steaming lamb joint slathered in gravy. But first another round of toasts, now advancing to more macrocosmic themes: to America, to Moldova, to world peace, to space exploration.

At this point, you might try a few ploys to stem your intake. You could explain that you needed to curtail your drinking because of some ongoing stomach complaint. Or that you were taking medicine that forbade interaction with alcohol. Or that your religion imposed moderation if not teetotalism (a word even the best English speakers amongst Moldovans could not understand). But there was simply no begging off allowed. Every possible excuse was parried, and a new bottle produced to meet the objection. Stomach complaints? Try this special cognac, known to settle stomachs and cure digestive ills. And try this white wine, too, known to enhance the properties of any prescription drug. As for religion, what could be more spiritual than wine? One by one, the bottles appeared and continued to appear. This one for arthritis. This one for asthma. This one for fever or flu or headache. At several households, the hosts told me with great solemnity that the kind of wine now being poured could prevent and cure radiation sickness.

You had no choice but to acquiesce. All right, you would say, but this is the last round.

"Or next to last," your host would respond as he drained the glass in a gulp and urged you to do the same.

Then it was time for dessert: cheese blintzes, fruit blintzes, cakes and cookies—a sugar-shock inducing spread of confections washed down with champagne and syrupy wine. As the evening wore on, the pressure to consume more kept intensifying. Oh, but you must try this. And this. And some of these, too, the host insisted. Eat up, drink up, for life is surely short and the wolf is at the door. Toasts now ventured into the realm of the inane. To road repair. To Monica and Hilary. Success to the McDonald's corporation's new restaurant in Moldova. Escape was impossible. Afternoon became evening, evening became night, and you could scarcely get permission to leave your chair. Any attempt to excuse yourself was preempted when someone in the host family brought out something for show-and-tell: photos of a trip to Bulgaria, a CD collection of American pop (sure to include artists you'd never heard of), old internal passports and other mementos of the Soviet era.

And in truth it was this sharing that made the visits worthwhile. It took an enormous effort to focus away the haze and the spinning in your head, to shut out the din of music and joke-telling and political argument that turned the room into a whirling Chagall canvas. Some of the stories were incredibly moving; every family seemed to have a Zhivago-esque epic somewhere in its recent history. Stalin was a constant presence on these occasions, a ghost haunting the fêtes of a people still not free of his legacy. Hushed voices told a tortured history, sometimes barely audible as though afraid the ghost still listened. Everyone in Moldova had at least one relative sent to Siberia after the war. Most of the exiled had never returned, and their ghosts, too, lingered in the room alongside that of their persecutor, as samples of their handicrafts or their writings or their photos were brought to you for examination.

A university professor told me about finding a pair of wooden boots in the family attic when she was a child. When she asked about them, her mother told her to forget she had ever seen them, to say nothing about them to anyone. The boots were never seen again. Only years later, after the fall of communism, did she learn the truth about those boots: after the war, her father and uncle had been sent to a labor camp in Siberia. Eventually they escaped and managed to walk back to Moldova, three thousand harrowing miles, wearing the wooden boots. Her uncle died of tuberculosis shortly after returning home; her father never told the children the story, fearing that knowledge of it would put them in danger.

The table talk always included as well reminiscences of the early days of independence, a brief, hopeful interlude in long lives of hardship. Moldovans wistfully recalled the energy and excitement that accompanied the events from 1989 to 1992, as Moldovan nationalism asserted itself, and then suddenly the Soviet Union fell apart, leaving Moldova independent and on its own. A carnival atmosphere had presided in those days—rallies, parades, citywide parties late into the night. Everyone was eager to experience this newfound freedom, to know democracy, to taste capitalism.

And it turned out that freedom did have a particular taste to it: the taste of bananas. Several Moldovans told me that in Soviet times bananas were unknown, seen perhaps in pictures but never in real life. Bananas were in effect a forbidden fruit, even if no policy specifically prohibited them. They were simply unattainable. Then came independence, and suddenly bananas from Iran appeared, expensive but not prohibitively so. People were so curious they stood in long lines to buy bananas from street vendors. Bananas became part of everyone's conversation: Have you tried one? What did you think? They discussed the flavor of bananas like they discussed wines—describing the taste sensations, the sweetness, the texture. The fruit came to symbolize freedom, and Moldovans thronged to consume it.

Then the ruble collapsed, and political tensions led to skirmishes and the standoff with the rebels in Transnistria. Everyone's money turned worthless almost overnight. Five thousand rubles, enough to buy a car one month, couldn't buy groceries the next. The banana queues dwindled. Few people could afford to indulge. They had to be content with seeing the bananas displayed on sidewalk tables, but buying them? Tasting them? No. Impossible. As one of my Moldovan hosts put it, "What was once unavailable is now merely impossible to attain." For Moldovans, the unattainable banana had transformed from a symbol of freedom to a symbol of discontent and frustration.

During the long days and nights I was subjected to Moldovan hospitality, I heard that frustration voiced by nearly everyone, young and old alike. For the young in particular hope was wanting. They had now lived half their lives or more in an independent Moldova. They had only indistinct memories of the communist years, and no real memories of terror and oppression. They remembered Young Pioneer camps, the long marches in the woods singing hymns to Lenin and silly ceremonies honoring heroic production on state farms. They were glad to be shut of that boring nonsense, but they felt vulnerable and uncertain in the new Moldova, and they all wanted to leave their homeland as soon as possible. Their future was constricted, they said, with no careers to go into, no opportunities available to them. They badly wanted out, but the possibilities were few. Hoping to win a scholarship to study abroad, they diligently practiced English, French, and German. But even in their studies, they were frustrated, for the Moldovan educational system reflected many of the problems in society at large. It was an antiquated system that still followed Soviet procedures in everything from administration to pedagogy. The only textbooks available were out-of-date leftovers from the Soviet Union. Rote memorization was the principal means of instruction. Upon enrollment, students were assigned to a group with fourteen other students. They remained part of that group throughout their years of study, and they were never allowed to choose their own classes or schedule. They and their group went where they were told and studied what was chosen for them. Worse, it was a corrupt system, with bribery the norm. Gaining entrance into the university would likely involve greasing the palms of administrators. Teachers often expected payment before permitting a student to sit for an exam.

The students I spoke with were clearly disgusted with the status quo, but they were resigned to it and saw little hope for reform. This despair led them to dream of leaving Moldova. And if they had the good fortune to win a scholarship abroad, they had no intention of ever returning to help in the building of a new Moldova. What for? What "new Moldova?" They were certain that the metastasizing ills were too virulent. Moldova was a terminal country on life support. They were smart, eager, capable students, full of promise. And yet they viewed the future with despair. They were young, but already they believed that their lives were doomed to be wasted. Their eyes pleaded with me: *Do something.*

Yet there was no heat to their pleas. They did not believe that I could help them. They knew I would not stay long in Moldova. Like shades in the Inferno, they stared as I passed through, hopelessly hoping that someone might rescue them but resigned to their fate.

* * *

Winter gave way to spring. The cherry trees blossomed and the grapevines budded. The lakes around Kishinev thawed and the muddy margins came alive with croaking frogs. Warm winds blew across the frozen steppes, and finally I had the chance to visit a strange and isolated region of Moldova called Transnistria, a trouble spot with a complicated and conflicted history.

In the early days of independence, many Romanian-speaking Moldovans favored some sort of reunification with Romania. But there were insurmountable obstacles to these hopes. For one thing, Romania was still reeling from Ceausescu's downfall and enduring the violent aftermath of its own transformation from communism to democracy. Even more problematic, however, was the large Russian population that had been settled in Moldova under Soviet policies. They were nationalists, too, and wanted Moldova's historic ties to Russia maintained. They could not accept reunification with Romania (a country that had always had an uneasy relationship with Slavic countries), nor did they much like the adoption of Romanian as the official language of Moldova. Their discontent scuttled any hope of reunification and soon soured the initial euphoria of Moldova's newfound independence.

Some of the Russian population, in fact, yearned for a return to the communist era. The hardliners gravitated to the Transnistria region, a narrow strip of territory barely ten miles wide between the Dniester River's east bank and the border with Ukraine. Transnistria had never been part of Romania or Bessarabia, and its population remained resolutely pro-Russian and pro-communist.

Armed with weapons left behind by the Soviet Army, the hardliners in Transnistria dug in and declared themselves autonomous. They set up a government, raised an army, issued a currency, and doggedly attempted to resurrect the managed economy of the Soviet heyday. This self-styled "Dniester Moldova Republic" saw itself as distinct in its traditions, its history, and its ideology, and it was willing to fight for its right to territorial autonomy and self-rule. Russia openly supported the DMR's cause and provided tangible military and economic support. In fact, Russia's Fourteenth Army remained stationed in Transnistria even after Moldova's independence.

A territorial battle was inevitable. In 1992, disagreement over the status of Transnistria led to an armed conflict between the Moldovan government and the separatists. The brief civil war involved hundreds of casualties. On both sides, violations of international humanitarian law were commonplace. The military engagement ended after a few intense months, but the ensuing stalemate continued to plague Moldova. Most important, the problems that led to the conflict remained and showed no signs of abating. Some of the problems resulted from the instability of an inchoate civil society trying to emerge from an authoritarian form of government and a centralized economy. The deeper problems involved the overwhelming need of people in the region to correct what they considered historical wrongs, especially the injustice of changes in territorial control. So strong was this need, it had to be satisfied no matter what the human cost.

Because of travel restrictions, I had no expectations of visiting the Transnistria. Then I met Nigel, the Tin Man. I happened to sit next to him at one of the Diners' Club soirees. During the inevitable hour-long wait for the entrée, we fell into conversation.

The Tin Man was one of those Englishmen who seem willing to live in any execrable part of the planet just so long as it's not England. He had come to Moldova from Nigeria as an employee of Crown Cork & Seal, a tin can manufacturer that specialized in cornering the can market in backs-of-beyond the world over. Now Crown Cork & Seal was endeavoring to capture the potentially vast Newly Independent States market, and to do so it had negotiated a joint-venture deal with the de facto government of Transnistria, the first and only deal between the breakaway government and a Western corporation. To get the factory up and functioning, Crown Cork & Seal brought Nigel from Nigeria. His vast experience in the Third World made him the ideal person to handle Transnistria's special conditions.

Operating under the name Carnaud Metalbox, Crown Cork & Seal was the only Western concern attempting to run a factory in Transnistria. Indeed, Carnaud Metalbox was just about the only functioning factory in the entire semi-autonomous breakaway region. According to Nigel, several of the biggest factories he had ever seen lined the left bank of the Dniester, idle every one of them. "Amazing, simply amazing they are," he said. "The floor space, the assembly lines, the equipment. These are factories on a scale you'd never see in the West."

During Soviet times, Moscow had chosen to build most of the factories for the southwest region of the USSR in and around the city of Tiraspol, now the capital of Transnistria. By contrast, the Moldova side of the Dniester River was left essentially agricultural. As a consequence, what industrialization, or potential for industrialization, that Moldova had was situated within the jurisdiction of Transnistria. But the de facto government of the DMR had yet to figure out how to actualize the industrial potential, and so the factories sat idle, obsolescing with the passage of the years. The joint venture with Carnaud Metalbox was an experiment to determine whether Western corporations and Transnistria's hardline believers in a state-managed economy could work together in a mutually profitable partnership. Nigel was charged with bringing this partnership to fruition and refurbishing a factory that hadn't operated for nearly a decade.

While we talked, Nigel and I went through a bottle of wine and then started on another. A peas-and-mayonnaise salad appeared, then bread but no butter (not even the fanciest restaurant in Moldova put out butter). The entrée seemed stuck in limbo. Seated not ten feet from us, the house band enthusiastically raced through yet another loud version of "Somewhere, My Love."

Learning of my frustrations at not getting a chance to visit Transnistria, Nigel offered to take me along to the factory for a day. He could facilitate my crossing of the security zone and provide me with a driver in Tiraspol who could watch over me and handle any difficulties that might arise. By the time the entrée finally appeared, we had settled on the details.

On the appointed morning, I met up with Nigel outside the Hotel Codru, and we set out for Tiraspol, a fifty-mile drive from Kishinev. Sergei, Nigel's Moldovan factotum, took the wheel. Nigel and Sergei made the round trip every day, Nigel finding it preferable to live in depressed Kishinev rather than ultra-depressed Tiraspol. It was a difficult commute, especially with all the checkpoints in the security zone; but living in Tiraspol would be too much of a hardship even for this hardened veteran of deplorable living conditions, and so each day he put his life in Sergei's hands for the hair-raising ride to Tiraspol.

With us in the car were two English assembly line workers from the Cork Crown & Seal plant in Great Britain. Teams of experts from Crown plants had been parachuting in for brief stints when Nigel needed them. These two were part of the latest team. They had come to Moldova to lend their expertise to the start up operation. For the past two weeks, they had been repairing equipment that had fallen into desuetude and training Transnistrians to operate and maintain the equipment properly.

As soon as we reached the outskirts, the two specialists nervously lit cigarettes in preparation for the ride on the "highway of fear," as they had christened it: fifty miles of a breakneck slalom around potholes, car parts, animals, and horse drawn carts. The constant weaving effectively nullified the niceties of lane laws, forcing vehicles from one side of the road to the other. We passed on-coming traffic first to the left of us then to the right then left again. A head-on collision seemed imminent. The car filled with cigarette smoke. Sergei fooled with the radio knob and looked bored with it all.

The trail of potholes led to a thicket of checkpoints that began outside Bendery, a town on the Moldovan side of the Dniester facing Tiraspol. The principal fighting of the 1992 battles between Moldovan police and the rogue Transnistrian forces took place in and around Bendery and Tiraspol.

In simplistic terms, the armed conflict in 1992 concerned the territorial and political status of Transnistria. Many factors contributed to the escalation of the conflict. Certainly antipathy among ethnic groups was a big factor, an antipathy exacerbated by the passage of language laws in Moldova that promoted Romanian over Russian. These laws encouraged Moldova's Russian population, especially those living in Transnistria, to believe that they would suffer discrimination in the newly independent Moldova. Hardliners in Transnistria immediately started a separatist movement in response to the laws.

In late 1991, just months after Moldova declared independence, paramilitary detachments of the DMR clashed with Moldovan police over control of government buildings in Transnistria. A state of emergency was declared throughout Moldova. By the middle of 1992 these clashes had escalated into a sustained military conflict centered in the Tiraspol-Bendery area, where the fighting reached its chaotic climax in battles for control of the bridge over the Dniester connecting the two cities. For several months, Moldova was the scene of politically motivated killings. Civilians and civilian structures were frequent targets. Land mines were laid. Reports of pillage, attacks on medical staff, and mistreatment in detention were common. At its height, the violence was indiscriminate, with renegade forces engaging in killing and looting sprees. The civil war ultimately resulted in hundreds of casualties and caused material damage in the millions of dollars. Around one hundred thousand refugees were forced from the theater of conflict.

Because the DMR was better armed with rockets and missiles inherited from the Soviet Army, the Moldovan side of the Dniester sustained considerable damage from shelling. Russia was the primary supplier of both arms and moral support to the DMR. The presence of the Russian Fourteenth Army in Transnistria only exacerbated the tension. The Fourteenth Army, heir to the Soviet Army, had remained stationed on both banks of the Dniester River, even after Moldova's independence. It was a large presence—some ten thousand active servicemen, along with tens of thousands of reservists and former Soviet military personnel who had chosen to retire in the area. Even though Transnistria was more than three hundred miles from the Russian border, the Russian government felt obliged to aid the Russian minority in the region. Critics argued, however, that Russia was simply trying to maintain hegemony in certain parts of the former Soviet Empire. In addition to receiving tacit Russian aid, the DMR counted on the contribution of hundreds of mercenaries from Russia, including Cossacks in their famous uniforms of blue wool coats, knee boots, and long sabers. The DMR also paid for the release of young men in Russian jails in exchange for their services.

After several abortive cease-fires, Russia and Moldova finally agreed to an internationally enforced truce. A tripartite peacekeeping force made up of Russian, Moldovan, and Transnistrian troops was supposed to work together to maintain the peace. Seven years later, when I arrived in Transnistria, the international forces were still in place, still overseeing a fragile stalemate.

One by one we negotiated the checkpoints, concrete barricades placed mid-road with heavily armed soldiers standing by. I couldn't tell from the tattered uniforms which peacekeepers were Moldovan, which Transnistrian, and which Russian. We came to the principal checkpoint, a small metal structure. Nigel and Sergei took our passports inside. The rest of us sat in the car. Three soldiers, forearms resting on automatic weapons, stared at us. Beyond, the broad steppe undulated toward the eastern horizon. A wan spring sun struggled against scud. The black earth had been plowed, but I could see no one in the fields, no one but soldiers for miles around. And every one of them, every soldier present on the scene, seemed to be staring at us.

At last, Nigel and Sergei came out of the Control Post.

Nigel handed me my passport. "Good news," he said. "They gave you a six-hour visa. You can stay in Tiraspol until three o'clock."

We entered Bendery, the former theater of conflict. Captured and successfully defended by the forces of the DMR in 1992, Bendery was now converted into a security zone. The international peacekeeping force—predominantly Russian—was based in Bendery. Here, in what was supposed to be a demilitarized zone, militiamen were everywhere. And military hardware. And military vehicles. From what I saw, the demilitarized zone was completely militarized, with no indication of civilian activity at all.

The road took us to a heavily guarded bridge, and the bridge took us over the Dniester and into Tiraspol. Now, truly, I was back in the USSR, or rather its surviving remnant. We passed a statue of Lenin and a government building adorned with the hammer and sickle. It was like entering a time warp. Sergei drove us through the city center and out toward the industrialized outskirts, where the Carnaud Metalbox compound was located. At the entrance to the compound, a security guard lowered a chain to admit our car. Like most Soviet factory sites, the compound was huge. A driveway took us past the outbuildings that had once been the workers' social hall, the workers' dormitory, the machine shop, the warehouse, all now fallen into disrepair and abandoned.

I sat in Nigel's bare makeshift office while he went over the day's assignments with his Transnistrian assistant and the visiting English experts. The main task at the moment, Nigel later explained to me, was to refurbish some of the Soviet equipment left in the factory. They were also trying to install brand new equipment imported from the West. Obtaining this new equipment had proven to be his biggest challenge and headache so far. He could get the equipment to Tiraspol well enough. Odessa, Ukraine's port on the Black Sea, was only fifty miles away. The problems lay in getting any of it out of Transnistrian customs. For weeks on end, crates of parts had been sitting in warehouses a few scant miles from the factory—so close, yet so far away—while Nigel attempted.to negotiate for their release.

Corruption was only part of the problem. To be sure, bribes were necessary, he knew that. In these situations, there were pockets to line, that was just the way things went. Coming from a place like Nigeria, he was well used to it. Bribes amounted to little more than an import tax, and here in Transnistria he was learning the proper etiquette for bribes—that was all well and good. But the real problem he faced was a total lack of organization in the government of Transnistria, if government you could call it. They just didn't seem to have any idea how to run the show. It was doubly frustrating to him because Carnaud Metalbox was a joint venture. It had the approval of the parliament of the DMR. An important government functionary from the Politburo was on Carnaud's board. And yet no one showed the slightest interest in facilitating the processes. The delays clearly were not due to volume. Nigel had been to the customs warehouse often enough to check on his parts, and he knew that *nothing but* his parts was there. No one else was importing anything to the DMR, at least not legally.

He had come to the conclusion that the real problem was that no one in Tiraspol was sure what to do or how to do it. They knew they wanted to maintain the ideology and the policies of the Soviet Union. Fine. They knew they wanted a state-managed economy. Fine. But how to do it? In the Soviet heyday, functionaries in places like Tiraspol took their orders from Moscow, and that was that. They never had to think or make decisions. They just did what they were told to do. But now that they had to make their own decisions, no Moscow to direct them, the Soviet-trained bureaucrats were completely lost. As a consequence, Nigel was forced to wait and wait and wait on the release of his hostage parts, while valuable time was lost in Carnaud's scheme to corner the tin can market in the post-Soviet East.

As to that market, prospects were promising, Nigel said. True, the recent ruble collapse and economic woes in Russia were problematic. But look, you had three hundred million people in the former USSR. Eventually an economy had to emerge. And when it did, those three hundred million were going to need tin cans; or better, the corporations marketing to those three hundred million would need cans to package their products. Already Carnaud had contracts with Purina pet food and a few other corporations looking to get into the potential Russian market. Those corporations needed a near-to-hand source of tin cans, and by God Carnaud would be there for them, if Nigel had his way. Certainly, they were well positioned to do so; Carnaud had the largest tin can-producing facility in Eastern Europe to work with. They just needed to get the factory up and running. Then, *if* the Russian economy pulled out of its nosedive, and *if* Transnistria's government cooperated . . . the sky was the limit.

"That's a lot to ask for," I said.

Nigel nodded and fell silent for a moment, frowning at the floor as if in discussing it the project suddenly daunted him. He was a genial, easygoing, and generally upbeat sort, but he had a constantly sad, long-in-the-face look to him, the kind of countenance familiar at closing time when the taps are shut down, the football's finished, darts are done, and we're all reminded of the pains and sorrows that brought us to the pub in the first place. There in his office that morning, outlining the long process of factory restoration for a visitor, Nigel bore a sadder look than usual.

When we toured the plant, however, enthusiasm returned to his voice. It was the equipment that did it. With evident affection, Nigel pointed out the qualities of the machines he had inherited. Some were antiquated but serviceable; some were "state of the art," newly installed in the late 1980s and hardly used before the collapse. These machines in particular were marvels, the likes of which did not even exist in the West. What most amazed him was that they had been sitting idle for eight years now, abandoned and deteriorating. Still, it was gorgeous equipment, fascinating for a career tin can man like himself. Apart from restoring it to functionality, the major problem confronting Nigel's team was retooling these machines to produce cans of standard Western volumes. Soviet cans met an entirely different standard, one that didn't match Western production values. Purina couldn't accommodate cans of Soviet volume, so Carnaud had to retool and give Purina (and other potential clients from the West) what they needed.

Walking around the cavernous factory, I could see the enormity of the task. Everything needed overhauling, refurbishing, retooling. The ceiling. The floors. The wiring. The ventilation. The place was loud with projects— hammering, sawing, drilling. The British experts were training the local proletariat on the new equipment. Other workers were painting the old machines in bright colors. "Pride in the workplace, that's one of the first things we teach them," Nigel said. "They're fantastic learners and eager for the work."

Despite the progress, the new Carnaud plant was still far from ready. Nigel estimated that they were twenty-five percent along. There was some urgency to get things operational, but until the Russian economy rebounded they would have little business anyway, so for now they would concentrate their efforts and resources on devising a model facility. Nigel envisioned a plant producing hundreds of thousands of tin cans, enough to containerize the multifarious products of Russia's pending capitalist revolution. In fact, only one assembly line was actually producing. Nigel walked me over to a back corner of the plant where a handful of stout women in white smocks watched a small, primitive press stamp out tin lids, used locally to seal glass jars of homemade mayonnaise, jam, pickles, and whatnot. This was the extent of Carnaud's product line at the moment.

Talking with Nigel and touring the plant had used up nearly half my allotted visa. The plan now was for Sergei to take me around Tiraspol in the car. Not a mile from the Carnaud plant, Transnistrian security forces whistled us to the roadside for a routine inspection. Two soldiers scrutinized the car, a minute inspection of everything, the trunk, the engine, the wheel rims, the glove compartment. They felt under the seats. One soldier slid under the car for a look.

"What were they looking for?" I asked Sergei after the soldiers waved us on.

"First, guns and weapons of any kind. Second, smuggled goods. Third, anything that arouses suspicions."

In spite of the tensions associated with latent civil war, and in spite of the omnipresence of armed security forces, Tiraspol looked like a pleasant city, with parks along the riverfront and big leafy trees shading the streets. It seemed tranquil enough, too, though that impression was probably related to the air of stagnation about the place. Everyone appeared to be waiting, waiting for something unspecified that may or may not occur. Many waited in queues. There were queues outside the Transnistria Savings Bank, queues at telephone booths, queues at bus stops. Vendors manned kiosks devoid of products. In the streets, traffic was light or nonexistent. Cars sat stalled at roadside, drivers asleep or reading yellow newspapers. The only movement in the whole scene seemed to be that of the ubiquitous patrolling soldiers. Suspense and suspension dominated the mood of the place, blending together to create an aura unique to Tiraspol. I couldn't pinpoint the sensation, but "post-Soviet" seemed an apt descriptor.

Sergei took me down to the river, the Dniester. Here, at nine-tenths of its 850-mile course from the Carpathians to the Black Sea, it was a slow brown meander laden with chemicals and heavy metals carried down from Ukraine: more of Moldova's inheritance from the country's Soviet past.

We walked halfway across a footbridge and paused. Sergei pointed downriver and told me to watch carefully. Some fishermen labored in weathered boats near the bank. A couple of children launched leaves and imaginary boats. I wasn't sure what Sergei wanted me to see. Then he tapped my arm and pointed. I heard the rattle of an outboard motor. A powerboat emerged from foliage on the Transnistrian bank and churned across to the Moldovan side.

"Smugglers," Sergei said.

"What would they be smuggling?"

He rolled his shoulders. Who knew? Anyone's guess. "Maybe guns, maybe baby diapers. Maybe plutonium."

We were watching the Transnistrian economy at work. Smuggling, arms-trafficking, money laundering: these were about the only productive activities available to the citizens of the DMR.

After this scenic view of a smuggling operation, Sergei didn't know what else to show me. Tiraspol had no tourist sites. There was a museum dedicated to a local poet who had founded a school of chemistry during the Soviet heyday. There was also the preserved headquarters of an obscure local hero from the Russian Revolution. There were numerous memorials, too, to commemorate either the 1918 October Revolution or the 1992 war with Moldova. And of course, there was the obligatory statue of Lenin adorned with fresh wreaths; but Sergei didn't think any of it would hold much interest for me.

Then he thought of the bazaar. Perhaps I wanted to see the kind of goods for sale? I was all for it, and off we went in the company car, past the city hall with its hammer-and-sickle emblem, past the Lenin statue, past the Heroes' Cemetery, past a place called "Café-Bar Eden."

At the bazaar, a guard in a generic uniform waved us into the rutted car park. Even though the lot was but half full, he exercised his vague authority by whistling us into a narrow space between two decrepit Soviet Ladas. Then he had Sergei back out and realign the car to his liking. Finally, he issued a ticket stub for the dashboard.

The bazaar, spread out over a muddy lot, had the same atmosphere of suspension that permeated Tiraspol. In many respects, the Tiraspol bazaar was the saddest place I had seen in my Eastern European travels, sadder than the gypsy encampments, sadder than Bucharest's industrial wastelands, sadder than the desolate villages of Moldova. Here, vendors presided over piles of shriveled potatoes and tables laden with the meretricious trinkets of outlaw capitalism. Most of the items for sale were counterfeit contraband: shoddy jeans, bogus watches, cheap vinyl gym bags stamped with meaningless English phrases like "American Sexy Boy Chicago Bull." Products from the reject pile of Turkish and Syrian sweatshops. Nearby, an old woman wearing a headscarf hawked day-old bread. A young woman, no scarf, paused to handle a loaf, didn't like the feel, and passed on. "It was better in Stalin's day," the old woman yelled after her, apropos of nothing as far as I could tell.

"Did she say Stalin?" I asked Sergei.

He shrugged. "They worship him here."

By far the highlight of my visit to the bazaar was exchanging money. Sergei spotted a black marketeer biding his time outside the butchers' stalls. The air was thick with the scent of bloody carcasses, and a torrent of flies rushed and buzzed about us as we huddled for the transaction. The black marketeer was a young man, twenty-something with a military buzz cut, a Soviet Army jacket, and tattered jackboots. Two words had been scrawled on the jacket in splotchy black ink: "Prodigy" and "Nirvana." I held out a ten-dollar bill, and the trader nodded, flicked his cigarette, pulled a wad of brown money from his coat, and began to count. I was getting nearly five million rubles and it came to me in an assortment of baffling denominations. The DMR's money was a work in progress. Most of the bills I received were ten-ruble notes to which a stamp with four zeros had been affixed, making the bills worth 100,000 rubles. Inflation was such that the former ten-ruble notes had been recalled so that the Transnistrian government could revise their value. I also had some five-ruble notes that were actually worth 50,000, Sergei assured me, because they too had a stamp affixed to them. My fifty-ruble notes, in turn, were worth 500,000. Additional zeroes were pending.

Now that I had made my millions, I had to decide what to spend them on. Sergei suggested we blow it all, the entire five million rubles, on beer. And so I handed over the wad in exchange for two bottles of warm and excruciatingly bitter Ukrainian beer. There was just enough left over—300,000 rubles—for a ring of hard bread. Bread and beer complemented each other perfectly, the bread too hard and dry to be swallowed without the beer and the beer too vile to drink without something to absorb the aftertaste. It took me the better part of an hour—most of the drive back to Kishinev—to choke down my multimillion-ruble snack.

By mid-afternoon, my time in the time warp was just about up. We left the bazaar, drove past statuesque Lenin in his petrified pose, then crossed the Dniester again for Bendery and Moldova. Sergei pointed out Bendery's landmarks: civil war bunkers, bombed buildings, gravesites, and flaming memorials. He pointed out, too, the dry-moated fort where the Russian Army remained hunkered. And then came the security zones, the checkpoints, the patrols. I surrendered my visa, and we were back in Moldova with its wide-open fields, black earth, grapevines, fruit trees in blossom, hamlets with stores, gas stations, and brightly painted cottages adorned with filigreed tin. Moldova looked good, and I wondered why I had found it so depressing before. Then I remembered the maxim for travel in Eastern Europe: Everything looks better as you head west. Moldova wasn't so nice as Romania, to be sure, but it was a hell of a lot better off than Transnistria.

I was scheduled to leave Kishinev on an Air Moldova flight to Athens. On the way to the airport, the taxi took me along Kishinev's main boulevard and around a traffic circle near the train station, the same traffic circle I had circumambulated on first arriving in Moldova months before. Now I was experienced enough to perceive the significance of the imagery here. First, there was the towering Soviet hotel, built out of all practical scale to fulfill the self-perpetuating, self-aggrandizing plans of the bureaucratized economy. Across from it stood the sister tower, a shell abandoned nearly a decade now, left undone when Moscow's money fled Moldova. And over there was the muddy open-air market where stout villagers hawked homemade milk, butter, and wine for negligible profit—the only true free market economy Moldova could create. And in the middle of it all was the computer company billboard, a company I now knew to have ties to a Russian crime syndicate, as any profitable business in Moldova must have. The taxi sped me around the circle and down the boulevard past yet another long row of deteriorating buildings, and I said goodbye to Kishinev. A traffic-free road cut across orchards to the airport.

The airport terminal was as sad a building as you could find in a country of sad buildings. Built in 1974 on the occasion of Brezhnev's return to the city where he had begun his career, the terminal was yet another concrete block in the process of decomposing, a process it was approaching with celerity. Of course, there was no pressing need to renovate Kishinev's airport, since it received little use. According to official statistics, fewer than one thousand passengers passed through the place each day. And the number had been declining for several years running.

On the day of my passage a smallish crowd had gathered for the departure of flights to Moscow, Bucharest, and Athens. Most in the crowd had come to see off a friend or a relative in the traditional Moldovan way: by getting good and drunk before departure. It was eight in the morning and the brandy was flowing freely. The drinking gave way to cigarette smoking when we left the well-wishers behind and passed through the Customs portal. Our bags were checked for old icons and the like, items of "patrimonial value" that should not leave the country. Then it was a passport check and a long wait in a smoke-filled departure lounge. Unintelligible loudspeaker announcements were interrupted by drilling and hammering as construction workers tried to shore up the sagging terminal.

My flight was delayed, no explanation, and by the time the Moscow and Bucharest flights had departed, I was left with my traveling companions to Athens: a score of look-alike women, peroxided hair, short skirts, and fur coats evidently the travel fashion for the day.

The delay extended. Still no explanation. The women smoked and grew surly. A few of the more vocal among them took to demanding information from an Air Moldova agent. At first the agent ignored them, but the demands became more shrill and threatening. Two soldiers arrived to quell the disturbance. Undaunted, one brash woman continued to declaim vociferously (and lewdly, I took it, because all the women burst into laughter at one of her comments and continued to laugh throughout her harangue). Red-faced, the guards retreated. Well, I thought, there's one difference since Soviet times; back then, no one would have dared challenge authority so openly.

Whether by coincidence or not, another agent arrived mid-disturbance to announce boarding, and the lot of us descended a crumbling stairway to a bus that took us across the tarmac to our airplane. It was a Soviet Tupolev jet of uncertain vintage, maybe mid-1970s to judge from the gaudy colors of the interior décor.

I took my seat and looked out the porthole. There were perhaps ten airplanes lined up on the tarmac. At least five looked defunct. All these airplanes had once been part of the Soviet Union's Aeroflot fleet, the world's largest in its heyday. Whatever airplanes happened to be in Moldova on the day of Moldova's independence had become Air Moldova's inheritance by default. The breakup of the Soviet Union had also meant the breakup of Aeroflot into a dozen different national airlines—Ukrainian Air, Air Uzbekistan, Air Kazakhstan, Air Turkmenistan, Armenian Air, Air Georgia. I imagined the other fleets had as tenuous a claim to airline status as Air Moldova did (what, pray tell, could Air Tajikistan be like?) and certainly Air Moldova's claim was tenuous. There, on the tarmac, was another jet with the name MOLDOVA painted in red above the windows. But you could also see, still legible beneath the red letters, the faded blue paint of the Cyrillic letters for AEROFLOT. Perhaps at the time of the collapse no white paint was available to blot out the Aeroflot letters. Or perhaps in the rush to appropriate no one really cared to do a proper job. No matter which explanation you went with, the image captured perfectly Moldova's situation—a lack of resources, a lack of care, the old Soviet system lurking just beneath every surface.

The tarmac scene provided yet another quintessential Moldovan image. Taxiing toward the runway, the jet passed an emaciated old man in tattered clothes who went through a series of emphatic gesticulations that ended with him looking up at the cockpit and jabbing his hand toward the horizon as if to say, "You go thatta way." Again, any conceivable explanation (A drunk on the runway? A legitimate airport worker dressed in rags trying to point the pilot in the right direction?) seemed to typify Moldova at the end of the century. Ironic. Sad. Creatively bizarre.

"Now we prepare for takeoff," the stewardess said. "You will see the four emergency exits." That concluded the safety announcements. Nobody around me bothered with seat belts. The stewardess came down the aisle dispensing hard candies and asking people to extinguish cigarettes. No one obeyed. I told the stewardess that my carry-on bag did not fit on the narrow overhead shelf or beneath the seat. She advised me to put it on the open seat next to mine. Whining and groaning, the airplane set off down the runway and rattled over potholes. Once airborne, the airplane climbed vertically with the verve of a fighter jet and emitted terrible new noises seemingly indicative of torque and G-stress and other physical forces I didn't want to know about. I focused on the English instructions inscribed above the emergency door: "For escape open hatch and throw rope out."

Soon the stewardess handed out plates of cold, greasy sausages. The cigarette smoke, mingling with the cloying scent of cheap perfume, made my eyes water. I attempted an unsteady stroll down the aisle to the toilet. I was surprised again at how many young women—all with exposed cleavage and bare legs—were on the flight. There were only two other men, and they both stood in the back drinking from a duty free bottle.

"English?" one asked me when I emerged from the WC.

"American." They shook my hand and introduced themselves as Dima and Yuri.

They offered me a shot of brandy and put me through the usual inquisition interspersed with obligatory toasts. How long had I been in Moldova? What had I done there? What did I think of the country? They nodded approval at my assessment: Wonderful people, much potential, sad situation at the moment. Inexplicably, they raised their glasses, toasting that assessment, and drained the shot. We stepped aside for yet another buxom passenger on her way to the WC.

I asked Dima and Yuri why so many women were on the flight.

"They are going to Athens," Yuri said. "To work."

"Is it possible for Moldovans to work in Greece?"

"Of course. Moldovan women are prized for their beauty. Very popular with the Greek men."

Only then did it dawn on me: Young women. Revealing outfits. Going to Athens, "to work." Before I could say anything else, Dima raised the bottle reflexively. "To the beauty of Moldovan women," he said.

We were called back to our seats—a nod to safety—as we neared Athens. I stared out the window at the barren Attic peninsula, and then the outskirts of Athens came into view, and then the huge city, a dizzying array of white buildings, jammed streets, smog. We circled over the birthplace of democracy and all its attendant capitalist chaos—a completely different world from the one we on the airplane had left behind. In a recent issue, The Economist had called Moldova a "nowhereland, stuck in a wretched economic and geographical plight, a country not so much forgotten as never remembered." True, but was "nowhereland" really that bad? I looked down on cluttered, smoggy Athens and thought of backwards Kishinev with no traffic, no air pollution, no fast food, no noise, no media, no advertising: Was that so much worse than the mess of Athens? Maybe The Beatles were right: The boys back in the USSR didn't know how lucky they were.

Maybe so, but the passengers had no doubts. They clucked and chattered excitedly about money and shopping and glitter. They were Moldova's pilgrims to Democracy's Holy Land. Was it ironic that the pilgrims were prostitutes, like the priestesses who once served Athena in the emblematic temples down below us? Perhaps. But it was no time to reflect on irony: now the airplane was banking sharply out over the Saronic Gulf for the final approach to Ellinikon East. The Tupolev jet banked and banked again at almost forty-five degrees. Pressed against the window by the airplane's severe tilt, I watched the wings wobble and the gulf waters rush up, then abruptly we leveled and the tarmac appeared. At the moment of impact, the empty seat backs collapsed forward, my unsecured bag tumbled from the seat to the floor, and an empty wine bottle came careening down the aisle.

A moment later, the hatch was opened and we filed out, Dima, Yuri, and I, the prostitutes trailing behind as they gathered their faux Prada bags from the overhead bin. The stewardess saw us out the door, and I said *"Dosvedonya"* to her—my tacit goodbye to Moldova. Behind me were months of cold, bleak deprivation, economic stagnation, hours of idling on park benches, long walks to nowhere, the pointless appointments of the unemployed. Just ahead were a traffic jam, an argument over an impossibly expensive cab fare, and a noisy night among the bargain-shopping tourists in jammed Plaka. Behind me was a land lost in history; ahead was the much-ballyhooed End of History, the great triumph of neo-liberalism. Here I was, back on the threshold of the great capitalist free-for-all, the new world agora on the make. I hesitated before descending to the tarmac, but the prostitutes were pushing hard from behind and there was nowhere to go but down.

Our Mailman in Havana

On my first visit to Havana, I devoted my time to gathering information for a magazine article. I spent three days shuttling around on tour buses to the city's famous sites: Hemingway's old haunts, the centuries-old Spanish forts, the Tropicana cabaret, the hotel strip built by the mob during Havana's heyday as a sin city. But almost every moment of those days was pre-arranged, leaving me little opportunity to explore Havana on my own.

On my last evening, I was standing at the seawall along the harbor when the mailman came along and put a completely different spin on my visit to the city. He sauntered up and stood at my side, a young man wearing a New York Yankees shirt. He carried a satchel. For a moment, he stared at the sea and said nothing. But I was pretty sure a spiel was coming. In an hour's time a few dozen just like him had approached me with the same pitch: You want cigars? Girls? What you want, mister? They were called "jockeys" in Cuban Spanish, trying to ride the tourists, trying to sell something—anything—for a few dollars. Without US dollars, life in Havana was hard.

I don't want anything, I told him. I came to see Havana, that's all.

"Come on then, I will show you Havana. You can join me on my rounds."

Rounds?

He patted the satchel. "I am a mailman."

We started off down a main street, then turned onto a side street and turned again. Soon I lost all sense of direction in the narrow maze of Old Havana. As we walked, the young man kept up a steady monologue in rapid-fire Spanish. His name was Vladimir, but he wanted me to call him Eddie. English names were better than Russian, he said. Normally he didn't deliver the mail this late—evening had fallen and the unlit streets were now dark—but his bicycle had broken down and he was forced to proceed on foot.

As we entered different buildings to deliver the mail, Eddie told me something of their history. A famous archbishop's residence, a viceroy's house, the place where Cortez stayed—all dating to the sixteenth or seventeenth century, and all teetering on the verge of collapse. The United Nations had declared this part of Havana a World Heritage Site, but so far little attempt at preservation was in evidence. Only the tourist hotels were restored these days, Eddie said. Each building, no matter how glorious its past, was now a tenement where several families lived in dilapidated flats. By the light of dim bulbs I saw old but tidy furniture, faded floor tiles, peeling paint, shrines to Catholic saints and *Santería* deities. I smelled boiling rice, mildew, dust, and crumbling mortar.

It was soon clear that Eddie was showing me off. In building after building, he introduced me to the tenants.

"This is my friend," Eddie said. "An American." Everyone seemed unduly impressed. People shook my hand, offered me glasses of murky liquid, showed me pictures of cousins in Miami. Entire extended families gathered at the threshold to stare and ask questions. Often Eddie had nothing to deliver but knocked anyway. He wanted everyone to see his godsend.

In one dark passage, an impossibly old man leaned forward to hear Eddie's boast and gave me a wide-eyed perusal. Then he grabbed my arm and pulled me into his flat. I couldn't understand his cackling speech. He led me to a corner where candles burned before the blackened statue of a saint. There were folded pieces of paper and little plastic animals arranged around the base. The old man reached behind the statue and drew forth a small paper rectangle. With great pride and élan, he handed it to me. In the candlelight I saw it was a postcard, a much-handled postcard of—I squinted—Cinderella's castle in Disneyland. Mickey Mouse waved from the foreground.

The old man rummaged through a wooden cigar box until he produced a stubby pencil. His speech was animated and constant. I looked to the mailman for interpretation.

"He wants you to sign the picture," Eddie said.

The request baffled me. I couldn't think of any reason why he would want my signature on the postcard. But I couldn't very well refuse. The old man rattled off another long sentence and tapped the card to indicate where I should sign. When I had done so, he snatched the card, cackled, and returned it to the altar.

Back on the street, I said to Eddie, "That was strange."

He nodded. "Well, you wanted to see Havana," he said. "Havana is strange. Now you have seen Havana."

When we finished with the mailman's rounds, we made our way back to the tourist district and my hotel. I invited Eddie in for a drink at the hotel bar, but an armed guard was posted to keep Cubans out. So I bought two bottles of beer and we sat on the plaza outside. Scores of girls in spandex promenaded on the arms of European tourists. Someone somewhere was playing a violin. A cigar-smoking crone sat on a stool and waited to read fortunes. A bored girl dutifully occupied her assigned post at a corner pizza stand that no longer had pizza to sell. A man passed by carrying a squawking, upside-down chicken. Across the plaza, the lambent moonlight cast shadows on a former convent's façade of saints and angels.

When the mailman took his leave he hit me up for a few dollars—medicine for his baby girl, he said.

Hours later, I stood at the window of my hotel room, ten stories up, and stared down at the city. In three days I had gathered twenty pages of information for an article on what to do and where to go in Havana.

Yet all the note-taking, all the research, had barely scratched the surface.

In Search of San Juan Hill

According to the textbooks I studied in school, Teddy Roosevelt and his Rough Riders made their famous charge up San Juan Hill on July 1, 1898. The event is well known to Americans, if only in scanty detail. Most people can conjure up a fanciful image of the mounted Roosevelt, saber raised overhead, leading a thundering cavalry—bugles sounding, guidons fluttering—on a defiant charge into the desperate fire of a startled, doomed foe. A fair number of Americans can name the foe—Spain—and identify the battle as part of the Spanish-American War. Far fewer can place San Juan Hill in Cuba, near the city of Santiago. Almost no one knows that the popular image of the charge is more fiction than fact.

Growing up, I for one was more versed in the fictional version of the charge. I remember as a boy reading about Roosevelt in one of those series of books with inspirational titles like the "Library of Great Americans." Along with George Washington, Thomas Jefferson, and George Custer, Theodore Roosevelt was presented as a paragon of heroism. Tough, brash, independent, scrupulous, and courageous to the core, "TR" rallied the troops, ignored enemy fire, dashed to the frontlines, and all but single-handedly vanquished the corrupt, rapacious army of Spain in the stirring charge to the top of the hill.

I remember, too, reading a boys' novel that followed the exploits of a fictional Rough Rider, an Arizona cowboy who idolized his leader, the charismatic Teddy. Like the "Library of Great Americans," this book emphasized manly bravado, glorifying it in clipped yet bombastic prose: "Many were the heroes on the field that day. No cowards, these Rough Riders. Not one was derelict in his duty. All went forward to support their stalwart leader. Acts of heroism were so numerous that to count them was to count the number of men on the field." Not a page in these books passed without the repeated use of the words *valor*, *courage*, and *bravery*. At the time, I accepted the accuracy of these stories. Later, my high school history textbooks did nothing to alter that perception. In the few paragraphs accorded the War with Spain—the so-called "splendid little war"—Roosevelt's exploits were given prominent treatment, accompanied by a romanticized illustration of the great man leading the charge.

Over the years, I discovered that the "Library of Great Americans" and the young adult novels I had read were full of legends, half-truths, and outright bunkum. George Washington, it turned out, told plenty of lies. Thomas Jefferson, the champion of universal rights, owned slaves. Custer could be more accurately viewed as an arrogant and foolhardy swashbuckler who finished last in his West Point class and was unworthy of history's accolades. As the one hundredth anniversary of the Spanish-American War approached, I recalled the stirring accounts of Roosevelt and the Rough Riders, and I wondered if there wasn't another side to this celebrated story as well.

And indeed, when I went to the library to scratch the surface of the story, I learned that things were not as they seemed with the "splendid little war," as John Hay, then Secretary of State, called it. My old history textbooks had implied that the war had brought out the qualities—altruism, resolve, courage—that would allow America to become a world power in the coming century. And all of these qualities were supposedly embodied in the war's great hero, Teddy Roosevelt. But in fact, I found out, the war also exposed other aspects of the American character, including racism, greed, warmongering, and a penchant for meddling. And these, too, were traits that Teddy Roosevelt embodied.

The more I studied the Spanish-American War, the more intriguing I found the true story of the war and the renowned characters in its cast: Roosevelt, of course, but also Stephen Crane, Richard Harding Davis, William Randolph Hearst, John Jacob Astor, Frederic Remington, John Pershing, and Clara Barton. I was taken by the idea of visiting the sites of the war to see what remained one hundred years later. Was it even possible, I wondered, to visit San Juan Hill? What could you learn by going there? Would there be something as surprising as the slave quarters at Monticello? Would there be something as sobering as the graves at Little Big Horn? The fact that San Juan Hill was located in a forbidden country only added to the allure. With these questions in mind, I set out to find San Juan Hill and the ghosts of the Rough Riders.

* * *

Before I left the States for Cuba, there was a flurry of media stories on the centenary of the sinking of the USS Maine, the other famous event of the Spanish-American War. In Havana, I found no flurry, but I did find a memorial. Walking along the Malecón, Havana's picturesque seaside boulevard, I came upon a pair of nondescript columns at the base of which sat a bronze statue, gone green with patina, of an anguished woman holding a dead child. Above her head, a tablet read, in Spanish, "To the victims of the Maine, who were sacrificed by imperialist voraciousness." Another tablet at the woman's feet listed the names of the two hundred-plus victims of the explosion that destroyed the battleship as it rested at anchor in Havana's harbor.

That explosion, culminating several years of tension between the two countries, impelled the United States to declare war on Spain. Since 1895, the American press had been covering the efforts of Cuban insurgents to win their island's independence from Spain. In a battle to boost circulation, the New York newspapers embarked on a campaign of "yellow journalism," each trying to outdo the others in feeding the public sensationalistic stories. Led primarily by William Randolph Hearst's *Journal* and Joseph Pulitzer's *World*, the newspapers ran report after lurid report of Spanish atrocities. The press corps discovered a news bonanza in stories detailing Spanish mistreatment of American citizens and women. One of the most famous stories (false it turned out, like most of the reports) had Spanish authorities conducting strip-searches of females aboard American cruise ships in Havana harbor.

As the war for Cuban independence intensified, outrage over these alleged atrocities led the American public to demand US intervention. Eventually, President McKinley—who was reluctant to involve American troops—bowed to public pressure and sent the Maine to Havana for the protection of Americans (and their investments) in Cuba. When, on February 15, 1898, the Maine mysteriously exploded, the yellow journalists and their readers railed against "Spanish treachery." The explosion had probably been an accident, but no one was in the mood for an investigation into the precise facts. The nation clamored for war.

While on the Malecón in Havana, I heard another explanation for the cause of the explosion. I had taken a seat on the seawall opposite the Maine memorial. Waves pounded the rocks at the base of the wall. Small groups of family and friends strolled along the broad sidewalk. On the boulevard, Havana's sporadic traffic, a mix of 1950s-era Detroit cars—so-called "Yank Tanks"—and dilapidated Soviet vehicles, sputtered along at a slow crawl, while bicyclists labored in the heat. Down the street, the last rays of the sun glinted off the polarized glass windows of the US Interests Section building—the one well-maintained building in a long, deteriorated row, and yet somehow the gloomiest of the lot.

Again and again, gregarious *Habaneros* approached me, partly in hopes of cadging something from a well-to-do foreigner, but mostly in hopes of passing time in conversation—the activity that dominates and dictates Havana's languid pace. I asked my interlocutors about the

Maine and learned that the history texts in Cuba claim that the United States destroyed its own battleship in order to justify declaring war against Spain and establishing hegemony over Cuba. It was an unlikely theory. At the time, the United States did not have a particularly potent navy, and the sacrifice of a battleship on the eve of war would have been a foolish tactic. But implausible as it was, the explanation—reiterated by several Cubans I met—did indicate to me that Cubans saw the Spanish-American War in a different light. They were not so convinced that the Yankees had acted in a spirit of altruism. After hearing their conspiracy theories, I had to reconsider the words on the memorial; the phrase "imperialist voraciousness" now seemed more ambiguous than I had noticed upon first reading it.

McKinley finally obliged the clamoring public and declared war on April 11, 1898. At the time, the US Army stood at a mere twenty-five thousand soldiers, one-fifth the number of troops needed for war. The army struggled to find arms and equipment for the new forces, but it had no problem finding volunteers. Over a million men showed up at recruiting stations hoping to make the cut. Going to war was all the rage in the spring of 1898. Some men were indeed motivated by an altruistic desire to help the downtrodden Cubans in their drive for independence. Others were motivated by a sense of adventure and a shot at glory on the battlefield.

One of those eager to head into battle was the Assistant Secretary of the Navy, Theodore Roosevelt. Somewhat overweight, nearly forty years old, and lacking a military background, Roosevelt was hardly a qualified recruit. A wealthy scion, he had spent years in governmental positions awarded to him for loyal support of the Republican Party. He did, however, have a persistent urge to prove his manliness. When a stint as a cattle rancher in Dakota Territory didn't satisfy that urge, Roosevelt focused his attention on the political conflict with Spain. He longed for war and a chance to go to the frontlines where he might prove himself as a soldier. From his desk in Washington, Roosevelt became one of the loudest advocates for intervention in Cuba, calling it "righteous" and "advantageous to the honor and interests of the nation."

Once war was declared, Roosevelt used his Washington connections to obtain an army commission as a lieutenant colonel. He was given the task of organizing a volunteer cavalry regiment made up of men from the southwestern territories—cowpunchers, broncobusters, lawmen, American Indians, Indian fighters, gunfighters, gamblers, miners, and fur trappers. Roosevelt admired the "dauntless courage and boundless ambition" of these "wild, reckless" men. The ranks included such renowned westerners as Bucky O'Neill, "famous . . . for his feats of victorious warfare against the Apache," and Lieutenant Ballard, "who had broken up the Black Jack gang of ill-omened notoriety."

To this rugged crew, Roosevelt added some fifty men with backgrounds closer to his own: Ivy Leaguers from wealthy Eastern families. In citing their qualifications for active duty, Roosevelt touted their athletic accomplishments. Dudley Dean was "perhaps the best quarterback who ever played on a Harvard eleven." Bob Wrenn was "the champion tennis player of America." Other Easterners included "Waller, the high jumper; Craig Wadsworth, the steeplechase rider; Joe Stephens, the crack polo player; and Hamilton Fish, the ex-captain of the Columbia crew."

Bearing the august title of "First US Voluntary Cavalry Regiment," this disparate group gathered in San Antonio for training. With his inimitable sense of flair, Roosevelt provided the troops with a dapper uniform: slouch hats, brown duck trousers, leggings, boots, and blue flannel shirts accented with blue polka-dot bandannas knotted loosely around the neck. "They looked exactly as a body of cowboy cavalry should look," Roosevelt said.

Military fashion mattered a great deal to Roosevelt. He ordered his own lieutenant colonel's uniform from Brooks Brothers, and Marshall, his black manservant, kept Roosevelt's cordovan boots polished and shining like wet varnish. A silver regimental insignia pinned up the brim of Roosevelt's campaign hat. Twenty-four carat gold letters—"USV"—studded his stand-up collar.

Drawn to the lieutenant colonel's flair and the novelty of a regiment composed of cowboys and quarterbacks, the press corps immediately recognized that the First US Volunteer Cavalry was a source of great copy. Journalists filed daily reports on the regiment's training and repeated the latest Roosevelt quips. All they needed was a catchy, alliterative team name to seal the deal. First the journalists dubbed the regiment "Teddy's Terrors;" then "Teddy's Riotous Rounders;" then the name that stuck: "Roosevelt's Rough

Riders." In fact, Roosevelt was only second in command of the regiment. The actual commander was Leonard Wood. But to the press, Wood was leader in name and rank only. Roosevelt was the main man.

Roosevelt's audacity matched his flair. In his articles for *Scribner's Magazine* after the war, he boasted about sternly drilling the regiment on the fine points of military discipline. Yet Roosevelt himself was something of a loose cannon. He freely ignored orders and the chain of command whenever he wanted to do things his way. When the regiment was transferred to Tampa, the staging point for the invasion of Cuba, Roosevelt—a volunteer, mind you—took exception to the regular army's organization of the camp and reordered things as he saw fit. When the order was given to load the transport ships, Roosevelt champed at the slow pace of the loading; taking the initiative and defying army command, he commandeered a coal train at gunpoint in order to get his men to the quay faster. Later, fearing that the Rough Riders might get left behind, Roosevelt took possession of a troopship and boarded his men, thereby bumping a regiment of regulars that had been assigned space on the ship. In each instance, the press lauded his insubordination and cheered him on—a foreshadowing of events to come.

On June 20, 1898, thirty-two transport ships carrying the American expeditionary force arrived off the southeast coast of Cuba near Santiago, where the major land battles of the Spanish-American War subsequently took place. With sixteen thousand troops pressing up to the city's outskirts, and with an armada of American ships blockading the bay, Santiago was a city under siege in the summer of 1898.

One hundred years later, when I visited Santiago, a siege mentality persisted. City residences had gone several days without water. On the streets, people were engaged in an endless scramble for daily necessities, lining up outside shoe stores and bread stores, pushing to find out what hitherto unavailable item had suddenly, unexpectedly, gone on sale. Lines for city buses stretched three blocks and more. In the hotel restaurant, the waiter handed me a lengthy menu and left me to study it for fifteen minutes before he returned to inform me that the restaurant was out of everything except pork sandwiches and beer. To the people of Santiago, none of this was remarkable. The original American blockade in 1898 had lasted a mere two months; the current embargo was already in its thirty-seventh year.

To visit the sites of the war, I needed to hire a driver. The government-run tourist taxis, officially the only taxis available to foreigners, were charging implausibly high rates, so I walked over to the Parque Cespedes in the city center, where a number of men offered the services of their private cars. Some paid a monthly fee to operate with official approval. Others ran the risk of a fine if they were caught engaging in private enterprise.

The driver I chose, Rodolfo, fell in the latter category. Because carrying a foreigner enhanced his risk, he charged me a few dollars more than the licensed operators. But I liked his car—a huge 1954 Chrysler New Yorker in fine condition.

It certainly looked much safer than the rattletrap Soviet Ladas lined up along the plaza.

But before I could get in, Rodolfo signaled for me to wait. A policeman was approaching. It was all too obvious what was going on, but the policeman merely nodded, rapped his knuckles on the trunk of the Chrysler, and passed on by. He wasn't twenty feet past us when Rodolfo waved me into the car. As long as you were somewhat discreet, Rodolfo explained, the police weren't likely to bother you. But if you flouted the rules in front of them, they could come down hard on you. The fines could be severe—several months' wages.

I liked Rodolfo. He was a dapper man, dressed in a starched white *guayabera* shirt, his hair gone gray at the edges. He loved to talk. As we took the road east out of Santiago, headed for the beach town of Daiquirí, Rodolfo kept up a nonstop monologue. He was most pleased, he said, to meet someone from Miami. In the mid-1950s, he had attended the Miami Military Academy. He liked Miami so much—"a marvelous city"—and someday hoped to go back and see the school and the Dolly Madison Ice Cream Parlor that he used to frequent. When he described the school's location, I realized that it was not far from my house and that a Wal-Mart now occupied the site. I didn't have the heart to tell him that both the school and the ice cream parlor were long gone.

After the revolution, Rodolfo went to medical school and became a doctor, specializing in pediatrics. The health care system and education were the two great successes of the revolution, he said, and he was proud to have been a part of the success. But life was very difficult just now. As a doctor he made only twenty dollars a month, the same salary he had received for years. Prices, meanwhile, had risen dramatically. He needed to work as a taxi driver to supplement his salary. He was lucky he had this old car to use for generating income. His father had bought it before the revolution, and Rodolfo had inherited it from him. Under Castro's law, private property could not change hands except through inheritance. It was virtually impossible to acquire a house or a car, so you had to maintain what you had. The private property laws were, in his mind, the most onerous and asinine fact of life in contemporary Cuba.

After thirty kilometers of driving along the rolling bluffs above the sea, we came to Daiquirí, a small coastal town where the Rough Riders had landed in 1898. For them and the other American troops, it was a difficult landing. The transport ships couldn't get within a mile of the shore, and the surf was rough for the small lighters used to bring ashore 16,000 men and ten million pounds of rations, arms, and ammunition. Fortunately for the Americans, the Spanish Army did not show up in Daiquirí. Roosevelt guessed that a force of five hundred could have easily repelled the chaotic landing of such a large, clumsy operation.

On the day of my visit, the beach at Daiquirí was occupied by a contingent of Italian tourists, the women lying topless on the sand, the men in bright bikini briefs kicking a soccer ball and smoking cigarettes. A white-haired Cuban with a weathered face passed us, a fat cigar stuck in his mouth. He carried a tray of—what else?—daiquiris and mojitos down to the Italians. I walked over to a thatch-roofed souvenir shack to buy a bottle of water. The vendor, a young woman, urged me to buy a souvenir, and in fact she had a cassette of traditional *trova* music that looked interesting to me. Six dollars. Rodolfo was outraged—the same cassette was no more than three dollars in a bookstore in Santiago.

"It's true," the woman said. Behind her, a slouching security guard said, "Two dollars on the black market."

"So sell it to me for four dollars," I said.

"I can't," the woman said. "These things don't belong to me, they belong to Fidel."

"They belong to the people," the guard corrected her.

"It's the same damn thing," growled the ancient waiter returning with his empty tray. With his cigar and beard, he looked like an emaciated version of Fidel—a Fidel who hadn't eaten in a few weeks.

"It's not Fidel's fault," the guard said. "It's the Americans, they hate us." He looked at me. "Not you personally, of course."

What could I say? There was no point in denying the charge. Nearly forty years of an economic embargo designed to make people suffer was pretty good evidence of hatred, especially to those suffering from the embargo. Besides, the guard's comment made me think of something that Theodore Roosevelt had noted when he stood on this very beach one hundred years before me. It was here at Daiquirí that Roosevelt saw Cuban insurgents for the first time. He took one look and decided that they were "a crew of as utter tatterdemalions as human eyes ever looked on . . . It was evident, at a glance, that they would be of no use in serious fighting."

It was true that the Cuban insurgents didn't look good. They were emaciated, dressed in rags, and barefoot, having spent three years in the jungles and mountains, where they had survived for months at a time on green fruit, palm nuts, and snake meat. But Roosevelt's conclusion that the Cubans were "nearly useless" was unwarranted. For these "tatterdemalions" had managed in three years of jungle warfare to drive the Spanish Army into disarray. Constantly pestered by bands of guerrillas, the Spanish had lost their will to fight. Before the Yankees ever arrived, 100,000 Spanish soldiers had died and Spain had depleted its resources. Spain's dominion over the colony had all but dissipated.

Standing on the beach at Daiquirí, Roosevelt wondered why the Spanish Army had not repelled the landing. In keeping with American stereotypes about Spaniards, he put it down to neglect and laziness. He never thought to credit the "useless" Cubans, who had already taken and defended the beachhead so that the American troops could land. A year later, when Roosevelt wrote about the events in Cuba, he still slighted the Cubans. It was Spanish incompetence, he maintained, that left Daiquirí undefended. Not once in his memoirs of the war did he acknowledge the contributions of Cubans to what he considered a purely American victory.

Roosevelt's attitude toward the Cubans reflected official policy. America was in the war ostensibly to help the Cubans overthrow their oppressors. But once they arrived in Cuba, virtually every American—from the staff of generals down to the grunts in the trenches and the newspaper correspondents covering the war—showed nothing but disdain for the Cubans. The renowned novelist Stephen Crane, in Cuba to cover the war for Pulitzer's *World*, noted that "both officers and privates have the most lively contempt for the Cubans. They despise them."

The most salient example of American mistreatment involved the great Cuban general, Calixto García. For years, García had endured the harshest of conditions as he led the insurgents against a numerically superior and better equipped foe. Sheer will and strategic genius had enabled him to bring the Spanish Army to the point of capitulation. García's soldiers (along with the forces of Máximo Gómez operating in central Cuba) might well have been able to deliver the knockout blow themselves. They probably would have defeated Spain on their own if the Americans had simply sent arms and rations. Nevertheless, García welcomed the involvement of American forces—particularly the American Navy, which quickly bottled up the Spanish fleet in Santiago Bay—in the hopes that a quicker conclusion to the war would save lives.

So García, then seventy years old and in the last months of his life, marched four thousand men in five days across Cuba's highest mountains to reach the outskirts of Santiago in time to clear out any opposition to the American landing. Additionally, he deployed troops to strategic locations in order to prevent the Spanish from reinforcing Santiago. Far from the battles involving Americans, the Cuban guerrillas engaged in bitter clashes with large Spanish forces. Their efforts went unreported by the American correspondents, who for the most part clung close to Teddy Roosevelt during the campaign.

Despite these heroics, the American soldiers spurned the ill-equipped, starving, dark-skinned Cubans. The American commanders assigned Cubans to dig trenches and, since there was a shortage of mules, to carry supplies. Correspondents wrote that the Cubans were "worthless" and "a sorry disappointment." American history has accepted the assessment of the correspondents: For more than one hundred years, American textbooks have left the Cubans out of the picture.

As we drove from Daiquirí to Siboney, another beach town, I told Rodolfo about the comments of Roosevelt and the correspondents. He nodded. "It's one of the reasons our countries have bad relations," he said. "In the Cuban view, the Americans stole the victory from us. We call it *la fruta madura*, the ripe fruit. This means that Cuban independence was a piece of ripe fruit, plucked by the Americans after Cubans did all the cultivation."

In Siboney, a tour group of sunbathing Canadians cavorted on the beach. Castro once decried tourism as inimical to socialist principles; but in the 1990s, desperate for dollars, Cuba sought to recreate itself as a major tourist destination. Now millions of tourists were visiting Cuba each year, with the largest groups coming from Italy, Canada, and Spain. Knowing it must provide high-end amenities to attract tourists, the Cuban government was spending money on imported foods, construction equipment, fancy toiletries, and swimming pool chlorine, while Cubans stood in line for basics such as soap and underwear. Moreover, many hotels and beach resorts were closed to Cubans. The government apparently had no qualms over the irony of what amounted to a policy of apartheid in a socialist state committed to egalitarianism.

The sybaritic scene I found at Siboney was far different from the town's nightmarish appearance when the Americans occupied it in 1898. For it was here that the US Army established its field hospital. And it was here that American soldiers saw the grim reality of war—so different from their expectations when they had rushed to enlist. The hastily assembled troops were, in fact, ill equipped for war. The soldiers were issued wool uniforms—suitable for northern winters but not for the rainy season in the tropics. Many of the soldiers in the hospital tents at Siboney were suffering from dehydration and heat stroke. The rations were improperly canned, and some of the hospitalized soldiers were suffering from food poisoning.

When the battles began, hundreds of wounded were brought back to Siboney's beach to die or to wait for the surgeon's amputating saw. Where Canadian tourists now rubbed their limbs with tanning oil, empty ammunition boxes once stood, filled with amputated limbs. In 1898, the sandy soil was littered with bloody clothing and shoes cut from wounded flesh. Vultures circled overhead. Flies swarmed. And at night, land crabs emerged to pick at corpses and body parts. Those soldiers who were strong enough had to beat back the bold crabs that advanced on wounded soldiers too feeble to fend for themselves.

The scene was particularly nightmarish to the soldiers suffering the delirium of yellow fever or malaria. Three hundred seventy-nine men would die of combat wounds in Cuba; but more than five thousand succumbed to "yellow jack" or "the Cuban fever" as the troops called the disease. The dead were buried in the hills above Siboney, but no trace of their burial remains. Rodolfo and I asked a few people about the graves of American soldiers in the area. No one had a clue. One grizzled cane cutter, machete dangling from his waist, was bemused by my question. "No, no Yankee soldiers buried here," he said. "Perhaps the *señor* would do better to visit the Bay of Pigs to find American graves."

From Siboney, Rodolfo and I followed the road to Santiago. We passed a farmhouse where Castro, then a young rebel with a cause, had stayed on his way to attacking a barracks in Santiago, one of the first significant actions of the revolution. The road was lined with memorials to those who had died in that attack, but here, as at Siboney, all trace of the 1898 war had long since vanished. I tried to recognize the landmarks mentioned in contemporary accounts of the American invasion, but the jungle that then existed had given way to cultivation.

The Americans' first skirmish with the Spanish occurred three miles inland from the sea at a place called Las Guásimas. It was here on June 24 that the regular and volunteer cavalry, including the Rough Riders, attacked the enemy. After the skirmish resulted in a Spanish retreat, the correspondents—always following closely behind Roosevelt—lauded the heroic work of the Rough Riders, almost to the exclusion of other regiments, including regulars. Richard Harding Davis, a famous novelist and self-described "descriptive journalist," wrote a dramatic, colorful story with "TR" as the protagonist. Davis's later stories for the New York Herald expanded on the legend of Teddy Roosevelt and the Rough Riders. Most of the other journalists followed Davis's lead and glorified the Rough Riders in their dispatches.

But a few correspondents felt that Roosevelt had been a little bit too freewheeling in his exploits (these correspondents were subsequently snubbed and discredited by their colleagues and by Roosevelt himself). The contrarian interpretation of the skirmish claimed that at a critical point in the battle, Roosevelt had abandoned his assigned position and headed in the direction of the hottest firing. Unable to resist a chance to get in on the battle, Roosevelt had endangered the American line in his search for a "bully fight." Meanwhile, it was left to the regular cavalry, the First and Tenth Regiments, to turn the Spanish flank and save the troops that Roosevelt had left exposed.

When the stories came out in the main tabloids, however, this dereliction of duty was not mentioned. The newspapers unabashedly lionized the Rough Riders. Roosevelt and his men were simply too good a story. But there was something else that kept the correspondents and the public from praising those responsible for holding the line at Las Guásimas: That crucial action was the work of the Tenth Cavalry, and the Tenth was an all-black regiment, part of the officially segregated US forces. One Southern officer later said, "If it had not been for the Negro cavalry, the Rough Riders would have been exterminated. I am not a Negro lover . . . but the Negroes saved that fight." At the time, however, no newspaper wanted to report that the vaunted Rough Riders had been saved by black soldiers.

Cruising along in the '54 Chrysler, we passed some bluffs and entered a broad valley. The road turned to the west. "*Bueno*," Rodolfo said, "there's San Juan Hill." I scanned the far side of the valley and saw nothing but a few gentle undulations about three miles distant. After so much anticipation, I expected the famous hill to be grander and more imposing. I couldn't tell what exactly Rodolfo was pointing out.

"Where?" I asked.

"Straight ahead, where there's a Ferris wheel."

I studied the hazy ridgeline and spotted the wheel that now topped San Juan Hill.

"That's the 26 July Amusement Park," Rodolfo said. "Named for Fidel's attack on the Moncada barracks. It's most of the time closed now. Power problems."

The road brought us alongside the base of the several hills collectively known as the San Juan Heights. The Ferris wheel, on the far side of the ridge, fell from view, and looking up I could now see a few old cannon along a stone wall. Even with the cannon, the hill didn't look impressive, certainly not legendary.

Before ascending San Juan Hill, we detoured to the north side of the valley to visit the small town of El Caney, three miles from San Juan. The battles of July 1, 1898 began at dawn with an assault on a small hill on the outskirts of El Caney, where a few hundred Spanish soldiers manned a blockhouse. The American plan was to storm the blockhouse and thus prevent the Spanish troops stationed there from attacking the flank of US forces moving against the San Juan Heights. The American command misestimated the time needed for the seven thousand American troops to take El Caney. Instead of the planned two hours, the assault took eleven hours and the Americans suffered 450 casualties before the hill was won.

Some 1,200 Cuban reinforcements helped win the fight at El Caney, but in order to deflect criticism for their loss of time, the American command circulated reports that the Cubans had shirked their part of the fight—another instance in an already well-established pattern whereby the Americans blamed any mishaps on Cubans (while simultaneously refusing to give the Spanish any credit for staunch resistance). When battles went badly, Cubans were accused of funking the fight. When supplies failed to reach troops, Cubans were charged with thievery. The Americans seemed engaged in a deliberate effort to deny the contributions of Cubans to the cause. Because of that effort, to this day the Cuban insurgents have been virtually eliminated from the historical record.

The American record, that is. Here in El Caney the record was reversed. When Rodolfo and I walked around the battleground, now a small park, we found memorials dedicated to the Cuban soldiers who had fought for independence. There was no mention of American involvement.

Before we returned to San Juan, the Chrysler needed gasoline. On the way back into Santiago, we passed two filling stations, but Rodolfo eschewed these state-run stations. Too expensive, he said. One dollar a liter—nearly four dollars a gallon. Instead, he knew an attendant who would sell it to him for half-price. But when we reached the station, his acquaintance got jittery—the presence of a foreigner was liable to attract too much attention during the illicit deal.

"Don't worry about him," Rodolfo joked. "He's three-quarters Cuban by now."

"Then tell him to take off those sunglasses," the gasoline man said. "No Cuban can afford sunglasses like those."

To pull off the deal, we had to park around the corner from the station, where I wouldn't be so conspicuous. Rodolfo returned to the station for a large bucket of gas, which we then had to siphon into the tank—hurriedly, in case any government inspectors happened by on the lookout for instances of anti-socialist behavior.

"How can you get the gas for half-price?" I asked.

"Barter," Rodolfo said. "As a pediatrician, I have access to good quality milk at the hospital. I skim some, then trade it for necessities I don't have access to. The *gasolinero*, he has gasoline but no milk. You see how we are forced to live here."

The hunt for cheaper gasoline had delayed us more than an hour. Rodolfo needed to go to work and was running late. He would have to leave me, he said, at San Juan Hill. He apologized for abandoning me, and gave me his phone number. He hoped I could visit him before I left Santiago.

Rodolfo wasn't really abandoning me. Near the top of San Juan Hill was a hotel where I had reservations for the night. The tree-shrouded grounds of the "Villa San Juan" covered the north side of the hill: an older main building with a lobby and a ballroom, a newer complex housing guest rooms, a restaurant, and a pool. I checked in and was given a room that looked onto the rounded summit of San Juan Hill and a memorial park dedicated to the events of 1898.

I spent the next hour strolling around the park, looking at statues, reading the plaques, and trying to imagine what it had all looked like one hundred years before. One plaque directly addressed the question of the historical record: "In 1898 the victory was won through the decisive support given to the US Army by the Cuban Army of Liberation under the command of Calixto García, therefore this war must not be called the Spanish-American War but the Spanish-Cuban-American War."

But the Cuban insurgency was not the only group slighted in the story of San Juan Hill. From the beginning of the war, all of the attention was on Roosevelt and the Rough Riders. With report after report from the pens of famous journalists putting him at center stage, Roosevelt received much of the credit for the victory. But of course Teddy was not the only one on the field. Nor in fact was he even at the center of the action. From the memorial park atop San Juan Hill, I could look down on another, smaller hill about four hundred yards away. Called Kettle Hill, it was actually *this* knoll that Roosevelt and the Rough Riders had attacked in an action ancillary to and in support of the main charge up San Juan.

You would never know it from depictions of the charge, but the Rough Riders were not alone, even on the smaller Kettle Hill. Nor did they reach the top first. Soldiers from the Regular Ninth Cavalry beat Roosevelt up the hill. But the Ninth Regulars were black, and stories of their exploits did not sell newspapers. Consequently, they were all but excluded from descriptions of the battle. Roosevelt's own account ("a classic of elastic retrospect," one historian has called it) also fudged the facts. The future president wrote that the Rough Riders were the first to plant their guidons atop Kettle Hill, and technically he was correct: The guidon bearer for the black regiment was gunned down just as the Ninth reached the summit before the Rough Riders; therefore, the Ninth's flag did not get planted.

Meanwhile, at the main battle, the actual charge up San Juan Hill included white infantry and black cavalry, but no Rough Riders. Many accounts from the time credit a Lieutenant Ord of the Sixth Infantry with being the first American to crest San Juan Hill. With him was a Corporal Walker of the black cavalry. Ord was shot and killed atop the hill. Walker, who gunned down Ord's killer as the Spanish retreated, was the first to reach the top and live. Roosevelt, hunkered down on Kettle Hill four hundred yards away, was a spectator to the main charge. The Spanish Army had already fled when the Rough Riders ascended San Juan Hill.

After watching the assault, one white soldier wrote in his diary: "The charge up the hill by the colored regulars was the bravest charge since the charge of the light brigade." But Corporal Walker and the other black soldiers on San Juan Hill may very well have felt that charging up the hill was not nearly so difficult as what they had gone through just to get to Cuba. Before the war, they had been stationed as "buffalo soldiers" in the western states and territories. The War Department decided to send them to Cuba because blacks were supposed to have an innate ability to withstand jungle heat and tropical diseases. They were transferred to the Southern staging points at the very time when states like Louisiana were disenfranchising blacks through poll taxes and literacy tests. Lynchings were occurring at an average of two a week. As they traveled through the South, these soldiers—many on their way to die for their country—were not allowed into white-only waiting rooms. In Florida, while waiting to ship out, they were refused service at restaurants and barbershops.

Little had changed by the time they conquered San Juan Hill. Even after the battle, racial incidents occurred, one of which concerned Roosevelt. "None of the white regulars or Rough Riders showed the slightest sign of weakening," Roosevelt wrote a year after the war. "But under the strain the colored infantrymen began to get a little uneasy and drift to the rear. This I could not allow. So, I jumped up, drew my revolver, halted the retreating soldiers, and called out to them that I would shoot the first man who went to the rear." Roosevelt's account melodramatically distorted the truth. In fact, the black soldiers—professionals who knew their business—were under orders to retrieve entrenching equipment so that the troops could dig in. Roosevelt, an inexperienced amateur who had been given officer status, was corrected by professional officers. Yet in his written account, Roosevelt neglected to tell this part of the incident.

One of the officers correcting Roosevelt was Lieutenant John "Blackjack" Pershing of the Tenth Cavalry (the officers of black regiments were all white), who was adamant in his admiration for the black soldiers. So adamant, in fact, that among white officers Pershing had become derisively known as "Nigger Jack." Only later, when Pershing became a famous general in World War I, was the nickname softened to "Blackjack."

Other soldiers noted the valor of the black troops. Captured Spaniards spoke of their terror of the "smoked Yankees" who had relentlessly charged their lines. Some American soldiers were impressed, too. "We must never forget the colored troops," one said. "If it had not been for the Tenth Cavalry, there would not be a Rough Rider left today."

Yet the black soldiers were forgotten. They were unquestionably present, even prominent, in the battles; but after the fact they immediately began to fade from the picture. The journalists overlooked them. The famous illustrators erased them from the scene. For more than a century now, history textbooks have included only passing references to their exploits, if that. A 1997 "docudrama" on the Spanish-American War, following the pattern, gave only two African Americans speaking parts—a handful of lines that echoed the worst of the minstrel tradition. In the film's concluding panorama of the victorious troops atop San Juan, not a single black soldier was evident. A total whitewashing of history.

Leaving the memorial park, I stopped at the hotel's poolside bar for a beer. Like every Cuban I met, the waiter wanted to chat. Learning I was from America, he said, in heavy English, "I love the peoples but the government is bowl sheet."

There was another American at the bar, the only one I met during two weeks in Cuba. "What's up with him?" he said, pointing at the waiter.

"What do you mean?"

"All that about our government is BS. Think he's forced to say that?"

Trying to avoid being drawn into conversation, I shrugged. But the American was in a garrulous mood. "Almost nobody here speaks English," he complained. "After a while it gets to you."

He wanted to know what brought me to Cuba. Reluctantly, I said a few things about the Spanish-American War and the Rough Riders. He looked puzzled. "Rough Riders?"

"Yes. Teddy Roosevelt—San Juan Hill."

"Yeah, yeah, I know. It's just funny you said Rough Riders—here, look at this." He took something from his back pocket, a shiny foil packet, and tossed it on the bar. I picked it up. It was a condom. The brand name was "Rough Rider."

"How about that?" he said. "Ironical, huh? You know, I brought a whole box of those, 36 friggin' condoms and I've almost run out."

"Impressive."

"It's the *chicas* here. They're so hot. Cheap, too. I mean, the most beautiful girl you've seen in your life is yours for like twenty bucks. They say once you try black you never go back, and I'm starting to think there's something to that. I don't know if I want to go back."

"Back to what?"

"Bitchy American girls. Like my ex-wife, for one. Look, here you got beaches, black girls, rum. I'm telling you this place is a paradise."

I called for the check and tried to beat a hasty retreat. There was one more site I wanted to visit before it got too dark to take pictures. It was a mile's walk from the hotel, and I needed to get going. The American followed me out the door. "A walk sounds good," he said. "I could use a break from the action, if you know what I mean."

As luck would have it, I didn't need to devise some way of ditching him. At the front of the hotel, a group of *chicas* was waiting. They waved us over. "Oh, man, look at them," he said. "So sweet dressed like that. Maybe I'll take that break later. Damn, look at that one in the red. Hope they speak English. Come on, let's go get them."

I begged off. "Suit yourself," he said and fairly skipped over to the women.

I was headed for a tree in the nearby zoo, the tree where the Spanish Army had surrendered the city of Santiago to the Americans, about a mile from San Juan Hill. When I arrived, the zoo appeared abandoned. I passed cage after empty cage. A few caretakers stood here and there in the shade of overhanging trees, apparently with nothing to do. At the so-called "Peace Tree," I was alone except for an old man dozing on a bench. I walked around and around the massive trunk and examined the tablets bearing the names of the American dead, more than five thousand names all told.

The old man was watching me. When I passed by the bench, he spoke up. "Well, *amigo*, what do you think?"

"It's sad so many people died," I said. "But maybe it was for a worthy cause—the independence of Cuba."

The old man smiled sadly. "Then they died in vain. Independence was not the result of the Spanish-American War."

"You mean the Spanish-Cuban-American War," I said with a smile.

He shook his head and pointed at the tree. "No. By the time they got here, the Cubans had nothing to do with it."

It was true. When the Spanish surrendered on July 16, 1898, Cuban patriots such as Calixto García, who had spent decades fighting for independence, were rubbed from the picture just as cleanly as the African American soldiers had been. Not a single Cuban was invited to the ceremony of surrender. The American flag was raised over Santiago. For five years the United States would rule the island directly. After that, US Marines would freely intervene in Cuban affairs, and US corporations would buy up much of the island. For fifty-five years, Cuba's rulers would do Washington's bidding, until finally it was too much. The revolution turned the tables, and the island that he had treated like a colony suddenly became a very nasty thorn in Uncle Sam's side.

* * *

Night had fallen by the time I got back to the hotel. Before returning to my room, I went to the memorial park atop San Juan Hill one more time to sit alone in the darkness. I was thinking about the many misconceptions resulting from the Spanish-American War, and how the consequences of those misconceptions were still with us. A contemporary historian has made the point that the actual events of a war are sometimes not as important as the subsequent representation of those events; in other words, how we interpret what happened in a war is ultimately more important and of greater consequence than what actually happened.

Even as the sun set on July 1, 1898, and darkness covered the American troops entrenched on San Juan Hill, the story of the Spanish-American War was being interpreted and represented in a certain light and for a particular purpose. At the time, the war was seen as "an episode in the growth of free government" and "a step in the steady progress of the world towards universal liberty." In the century since, the war has been interpreted as the event that signaled the start of the American Century and put the United States on the path to becoming a superpower. It was, in short, a "splendid little war"—113 days in which the brash, upstart nation knocked off a tottering old world empire and established hegemony over the Western hemisphere. For most Americans, the consequences of the war were essentially and unequivocally good.

But in Cuba, the perspective was different. From where I sat on San Juan Hill, I looked over the dysfunctional amusement park toward Santiago—a city once captured by the American armed forces, now called the "Hero City" of the Cuban Revolution. Darkness hid the desperation of people struggling to survive in a land of chastened hopes. In the shadow of San Juan Hill, they stood in long lines, they hustled, they stole, they bartered, they turned tricks, they hid from the dreaded inspectors.

It was all part of the sad legacy of "a splendid little war" Americans had long since consigned to the history books.

A Bolero in Havana

Havana was easily the most affable and unpredictable place I had ever been. As I walked around the city, it seemed I was constantly falling into conversations—chance encounters that inevitably altered my plans and led me in unexpected directions.

Case in point: I was walking along the Malecón, the photogenic seaside boulevard that gives Havana much of its visual identity, when a peanut vendor intercepted my path. He greeted me like an old friend, calling me *compañero* and asking about my activities for the day. Shortly into my Havana visit I had learned to welcome these encounters. No need for the usual tourist leeriness: *Habaneros* are innately curious and outgoing, an attitude worth emulating. So I stopped to chat with the inquisitive vendor.

Pointing to the Riviera a block away I told him that I had just left my hotel, and that I was now on my way to the *Cementerio Colón* to see its famously ornate mausoleums and vaults. The peanut vendor approved of my intention to visit the cemetery (and advised me not to miss the firefighters' memorial therein), but he did not approve of the hotel. The Riviera was, in his view, much too expensive and not sufficiently Cuban. Before he continued on his way, the vendor gave me a packet of peanuts—a gift, he insisted, when I tried to pay. He also gave me a handwritten card bearing the address of a house with rooms to let—his parents' house. It was now legal, I had learned, for ordinary citizens to rent rooms to foreigners and to operate restaurants in their homes, an initiative the Cuban government had recently adopted to allow for modest private enterprise. The peanut vendor's parents were trying to make a little money by renting out a spare room. I would find it hospitable and comfortable, he said, and much cheaper than the Riviera.

It seemed like a pretty good idea—forgoing the tourist hotel for a private home. The peanut vendor was right about the Riviera: it was expensive, on par in fact with hotels in Miami Beach. I had wanted to stay there primarily because of the hotel's connection to pre-Revolutionary Havana—a period of glamor, intrigue, and vice, when mobsters ruled the city and Cuba advertised itself as "a tropical playground." Reading about the period in a couple of novels—Graham Greene's *Our Man in Havana* and Cabrera Infante's *Tres Triste Tigres*—had piqued my curiosity. All around the city you could find vestiges of this louche era—hotels, casinos, and nightclubs—some now shabby, some nearly pristine—that imbued Havana with retro allure. The Riviera was one of these vestiges. The mobster Meyer Lansky had built the swanky hotel in the late 1950s, just before the Revolution brought an end to the party. It had not been updated since then, and the musty but gleaming *tropical moderne* interior looked like a stage set for the Havana scenes in *The Godfather II*. Cool as this was, staying at the Riviera had its drawbacks, and the peanut vendor had pegged them exactly. Besides being expensive, the Riviera was also cut off from the city around it. Ordinary Cubans could not enter the hotel, and I was aware that staying there meant that I was getting a distorted picture of Cuba. So I decided to leave the Riviera in favor of rooming with the peanut vendor's parents. Better to stay with a family and learn more about daily life in Cuba.

The next morning, I gave the peanut vendor's card to one of the many taxi drivers waiting at the cabstand outside the hotel. He seemed dubious about the address. The driver frowned at the card and called a second driver over for a look. This *compañero* also frowned at the address. Soon, six or seven drivers got in on the discussion—a typical Havana confab with everyone talking at once. Eventually, the drivers agreed upon the likely location of the house and the best way to get there. I was waved into a taxi, and off we went, headed to visit the peanut vendor's parents at last. Or so I thought. Once we got underway, the driver asked me if I was already renting the room or just looking.

Just looking, I said. This revelation gave the driver his opening. He announced that he knew a better place—good family, nice house, great location, and (he added with an implied wink) a pretty daughter. Two daughters. By this point I had figured out that Havana was best experienced through a kind of acquiescence—just go along with whatever suggested itself and something unexpected and intriguing would soon manifest. In Cuba, it seemed, all my plans were fluid, changing moment to moment, such that I could not reliably predict where I would be in an hour's time or what

I would be doing or with whom. I started to insist on the original address then thought, why bother? After all, I owed no allegiance to the peanut vendor and had no reason to believe that his parents' house would be any better than the one now on offer.

I agreed to check out the place that the driver recommended, and the old taxi lumbered toward this new destination. But the spirit of randomness that sometimes presides in Havana would not let things resolve so neatly. Although the place looked agreeable enough, no rooms were available. The landlady suggested another house—her cousin or somebody—and off we went, only to get lost. Meanwhile, along the way the driver stopped to pick up a few additional passengers, and the four people now in the back seat, strangers to one another only moments before, immediately and eagerly entered into an animated conversation about how best to arrive at the notional address. Sitting up front, I tried to follow along, my Spanish no match for a full-blown Cuban charrette.

The talk was fast-paced, but the denouement was slow in coming. Eventually, one of the passengers, a middle-aged woman clutching a live chicken, realized that the *yanqui* was looking for a room. She had a bedroom available in her house, she said, and the *yanqui* was welcome to stay there if he so desired. I gladly accepted the offer, and off we went to the señora's house, the *yanqui* paying enough at the end to cover everybody's fare (though it was never clear to me where the others in the car were headed; they seemed all too content just to ride around to find out what would happen).

I now found myself in Miramar, a formerly elegant section of Havana where the houses were larger and the streets more tranquil than elsewhere in the city. The señora lived in a spacious three-story house; but only the first story belonged to her family. After the Revolution, most of the larger houses (formerly belonging to families that had since fled to Miami) were divided into flats and assigned to multiple families. The señora's family—five people in all—shared the flat, a tight squeeze. Even with so little space, they had partitioned the largest room in two, creating an extra room that they hoped to rent to foreigners. They had not yet filed the appropriate papers or paid for the license, which meant that I was technically an illegal guest. There were government spies on the block, the señora said, so if the matter came up, I was to say that I was visiting the family. Under no circumstances should I disclose that I was paying the family twenty dollars a night.

Because I was their first American boarder, I was treated as a great curiosity and received plenty of attention from the family, which consisted of the señora—her name was Esmeralda—her husband, two sons, and the wife of the eldest son. For two days, I was their chief entertainment, and our conversations went long into the night. During these conversations, my Spanish—competent in most situations—was put to the test. I generally had a hard time understanding Cuban Spanish (not at all like the Mexican and South American Spanish that I was accustomed to) unless people spoke slowly and deliberately—which almost never happens in Havana, for Cubans do not like to speak slowly. I was forced to concentrate, trying to catch a few key words that would allow me to guess at the gist of the conversation.

Our discussions ranged over a variety of topics, with money and baseball being the recurring themes. The family questioned me about life in the United States, about salaries for different occupations, about fashions, about the cost of various consumer items, and about the political opinions of Americans. Struggling to keep up, searching for the right Spanish words for my answers, I fielded their many questions (often asked simultaneously) and tried to feed their apparently genuine enthusiasm for learning about my daily life back home.

When they asked about my reasons for visiting Cuba, I told them about my interest in the pre-Revolutionary period—especially the famous nightclubs and casinos that had once made Havana a glamorous (and lurid) tourist destination. Hearing this, they all agreed that I should meet Lety and Orlando, the señora's aunt and uncle. Before the Revolution, these two had worked at some of the biggest nightclubs, Lety as a cocktail waitress and Orlando as a musician. They could tell me all about it. So the next day, I went with Esmeralda on an excursion to another part of the city to visit with her relations.

To get there, we had to take a bus. I offered to pay for a taxi, but Esmeralda said that the bus was a true Havana experience, a good way for me to learn how Cubans live. She was right.

A group of people had clustered on the sidewalk at the bus stop. Upon reaching the cluster, Esmeralda called out, "*Ultimo.*" A young man answered, "*Yo.*" Moments later, a new arrival called out *ultimo* and Esmeralda responded by saying *yo.* This was how Cubans determined the order for boarding a bus, Esmeralda explained. Rather than actually queuing, the people waiting on the bus formed an imaginary line according to temporal precedence. Upon arriving at the bus stop, you have to ask who is last in line (*ultimo*). That person responds (*yo*) and you know that you are to board the bus after the respondent. The next person to arrive at the bus stop follows the same procedure, and it is incumbent upon you to respond *yo* to the newcomer, who will follow you aboard the bus. And so on.

We waited about ten minutes, during which time some ten or twelve people arrived to engage in this call-and-response exercise. Then the bus came, and the boarding went smoothly, although there were no available seats. Somehow, we squeezed in among the other passengers standing in the aisle. The buses in Havana were rather odd looking. Called *camelos* because they have a hump in the middle, they were actually trailers attached to truck cabs. Despite the stuffy, crowded conditions and the heat inside the camel, the passengers seemed good-natured, even upbeat. They certainly kept up the chatter, which never really ceases in Havana. All around me, there were probably a good ten discussions going on simultaneously, rather lively discussions at that. On a couple of occasions, participants in different conversations appealed to me, as if seeking my insight on some matter that remained inscrutable to me. Clueless, I offered my assent to whatever was said, much to the passengers' satisfaction.

When we left the bus at last, we were in an outlying part of the city, a street of concrete-block houses reminiscent of a Florida bedroom community, circa 1950. There were small, fenced-in yards and carports—though few cars were in evidence. For the most part, hammocks and bicycles occupied the carports, with one exception: a mammoth rusted Chrysler from the 1950s. Its wheels missing, the car was propped on concrete blocks. It sat like a stalwart old gentleman in the shade ready to collar a passerby with stories of the good old days.

Esmeralda led me to a pink house, wherein we found precisely such a gentleman seated in a wicker rocking chair, a cane by his side. He was wearing a dapper *guayabera* shirt. An elderly woman sat on a couch whose cushions were protected with clear vinyl covers. Esmeralda introduced me to Orlando and Lety. In their late seventies now, they belonged to the last generation still alive that had grown to adulthood before the Revolution, a generation that dwindled by the day. They were a living connection to a bygone era.

Hard of hearing and apparently senile, Uncle Orlando sat grinning and disconnected throughout the ensuing conversation. In contrast, Aunt Lety was animated, energetic, and sharp. She was pleased that an American had come to her house. She had always liked Americans, she declared, and she didn't believe that America was really an enemy. Lety had a very good memory, and when Esmeralda explained that I was interested in learning about Havana nightlife in the 1950s, Lety launched into an animated discourse about how wonderful Cuba had been in those days. I caught only a small portion of her exuberant monologue, but I readily understood Lety's main point: In those days, Cuba was a paradise. Food was abundant, movie stars came to visit, and everyone was happy.

Lety waxed nostalgic while I sipped homemade lemonade and listened. A warm flower-scented breeze blew through the open windows and doorway. Now and then the old man coughed, shifted his weight, and kept on grinning bemusedly at the people in his parlor. My attention drifted toward a tabletop clock. Like the other furnishings in the room, it was old and well worn. It kept ticking, its pendulum swinging back and forth, but the hour and minute hands never moved. Our visit lasted hours, but the clock stayed stuck on two twenty-five.

At one point, Lety took out some old photographs to show me, photos of places where she and Orlando had worked— the Tropicana, with its lovely glass arches; the Montmartre with its streamlined art deco bar and stage; the Capri, where movie star George Raft had greeted patrons at the entrance to the casino; the Sans Souci with its exotic garden setting. Each photograph, Lety seemed to think, provided further evidence of a lost paradise. Studying a picture of herself in cocktail waitress attire, she fell silent, the first pause in her steady discourse. Tears came to her eyes. During the momentary silence, I heard a distant grumble of thunder. It was getting on toward late afternoon, when the heat of the tropical day would generate the inevitable daily rain shower.

The tabletop clock still marked two twenty-five.

Collecting herself, Lety flipped through some photos of a young Orlando dressed in Desi Arnaz–type outfits, posing with his band mates. He had been a trumpet player in various groups, including the big band of the Sans Souci stage show. He had played with all the great ones, Lety said. Beny Moré. Nat King Cole. Pérez Prado.

At that moment, the old man cackled something and then started singing. Lety laughed with pleasure. "Ah, he heard me say Beny Moré, *pobrecito*. He loves Beny Moré. All right, *papi*, we will listen to Beny Moré."

"Do you know Beny Moré?" Esmeralda asked me.

"Yes, I know the name."

"Ah, well, Beny Moré is the greatest Cuban of all," Lety said. "Not only the greatest Cuban singer, I tell you, but the greatest of all Cubans."

And with that declaration, she took out a record album and placed it on a creaky Soviet turntable. There was a crackle through the old speakers, then big band music and the silky romantic tenor of Beny Moré. It was one of the old songs, a bolero. The three Cubans in the room were instantly transported. They sang along, but softly, as though chary of competing with the greatest of singing voices. I watched and listened. This was soul music, I thought, the music of the Cuban soul.

Halfway through the third song, the thunder intensified. The day darkened considerably, and a strong wind picked up. Thunder boomed and lightning crackled. Then came the first splatter of rain on the tile roof, prelude to a hard tropical downpour. The room's single low-watt bulb struggled against the gloom. Beny Moré sang on; the rain and thunder seemed to blend in as backing instrumentation.

At the height of the storm, the electricity failed. The room went dim. Beny Moré was silenced. But after the briefest of pauses, the senile old man—in a quaking, tremulous voice— picked up where the song had left off. And he sang the rest of the song straight through, a voice in the shadows, the words of the old song fixed in his mind no matter how much else had vanished. Lety and Esmeralda joined him. It was extraordinary to hear, sitting in twilight while lightning flashes illuminated the three ghostly Cubans singing a cappella over the grumbling thunder: *Cómo fue, no sé decirte cómo fue . . .*

More than anything else I experienced in Havana, this one tableau stands out as emblematic somehow: a nostalgic, bittersweet song of the old days interrupted by a power failure; an aging, partly senile generation left to sing to themselves.

They sang and sang. Oh, how they sang—imperfectly, but with conviction, undeterred by whatever storms raged outside.

The Paradox of Diego de Landa

Yucatán is so rich in historical places it is easy to overlook sites that do not feature grand attractions. A place like Izamal, for example, with its large yellow sixteenth-century monastery and huge pyramid remnant, would be in most regions a principal tourist site. But in Yucatán, it goes almost unnoticed.

Maní is another relatively unknown and rarely visited place. Even though some of the greatest events in Yucatán's history occurred there, these days only a true wayfarer ever passes through. It isn't on a main road and guidebooks don't mention it. There isn't anything scenic or picturesque to contemplate. None of that mattered to me; I was keen to visit Maní, the place where, in 1562, the Spanish bishop Diego de Landa staged a great auto-da-fé and burned whatever Maya manuscripts he could discover—the place where Maya culture lost its literature.

The bus left me off at the village market. I asked a fruit vendor for directions to the church. "Do you want to buy my cherimoya?" she asked.

"No," I said. "I want to know where the church is."

She smiled at me from across a table full of green, scaly fruit, the winsome smile of a skilled vendor. "Have you ever tried cherimoya?" she asked.

I admitted that I hadn't.

"Then how do you know you don't want it?"

When I hesitated, she clucked, snatched a plump green bulb, and sliced it open to reveal the white pulp and black seeds. "My cherimoya is the best in all Mexico," she said.

I tasted the offered piece and nodded. It was very good.

She clucked again, quite pleased with herself, and said, "Now I will tell you how to arrive at the church."

Following her directions, a bag of cherimoya crooked in my arm, I walked along the dusty road toward the church. When the Spaniards arrived in Yucatán in 1519, Maní was the most important of some twenty city states. After twenty hard-fought years, the Maya finally capitulated to the Spaniards when the lord of Maní, Ah Kukum, surrendered to Francisco de Montejo and converted to Christianity. Using stones taken from destroyed Maya temples, the Spaniards then built a monastery in Maní to facilitate the mass conversion of the Maya people.

But the conversion was only superficial. Early in 1562, two Maya boys reported to the friars in Maní that they knew of idols and human skulls in caves outside the village. The surprised and alarmed friars collected the idols then brought some local people in for interrogation. The friars were even more surprised when the suspects openly admitted to praying to the idols for rain and good crops. All the indigenous people in the region, they said, did the same. With this news, the friars widened the investigation and brought in more Maya people for interrogation. Eventually, the town jail, the hospital, and several other buildings were filled with detainees.

At this point, the tortures began. First, the friars would tie the accused's wrists together then hoist him from the ground until he confessed his idolatry and told the friars where the idols were located. If the accused did not confess to a sufficient number of idols, heavy stones were fixed to his feet, and he was left to contemplate his insolence for a while. If the friars remained unsatisfied, they resorted to flogging and poured burning wax on the recalcitrant heathen. As the tortures continued, the friars added to a growing pile of idols in the patio outside the church.

The initial auto-da-fé was held in the atrium in front of the mission church. With ropes around their necks, the native penitents marched in, bearing the forbidden idols in their hands, and stood before the friars to celebrate Mass. On this occasion, the celebration concluded with a stern sermon and an admonitory lashing of the penitents.

When I arrived at this atrium, now a peaceful grassy plaza in front of an old, decrepit church, I found it difficult to believe that anything of great moment had happened at such a place. The day was completely still in the harsh sunlight of a Yucatán afternoon. The only sound came from inside the nearly ruined monastery—the shriek and shrill of children. I crossed the atrium and entered the building, passing from the hot glare to the mildewed dimness of the nave. Like other mission churches in Yucatán, San Miguel's church in Maní had a primitive, cave-like quality to it. The gloom of the interior contributed to the effect, as did the prevalent iconography depicted on the altars and *retablos*: Christ's gory passion, Our Lady of Sorrows, a saint with eerie bloodshot eyes, wooden sculptures of gaunt Franciscans, and everywhere clouds of severed heads supporting the unearthly feet of Virgins and maidens.

It was a relief to leave the dark nave by a side door for the open air of the cloister courtyard. Here I found a collection of bicycles. The children of the village had come to church this afternoon for catechism. The shouting I had heard from outside had died down and given way to murmured prayers. As I climbed a wide stone staircase to the monastery's second story, I thought about how proud—and self-satisfied—Diego de Landa would have felt to hear these pious voices, the voices of the descendants of the people he had tortured in the name of God. He would probably claim that this glorious result justified his harsh actions.

One of the more enigmatic figures in the history of the Conquest, Diego de Landa first came to Yucatán in 1549, at age twenty-five, in response to a call for Franciscans to assist in the work of Christianizing the New World. According to the historian Inga Clendinnen, Landa was a man of "endless volcanic energy, both physical and mental." Having learned to speak Mayan, he translated the catechism into the native language and revised the grammar that the friars had been using. Not content to remain at the tranquil surroundings of the monastery at Izamal, where the Maya people had been pacified, he ventured alone into the unknown heart of the peninsula to visit villages hostile to the Spanish. During these years of itinerant missionary work, Landa came to know the peninsula better than any European. He also achieved a remarkable intimacy with a people his compatriots considered sinister and volatile. Or so it would appear, judging from his *An Account of the Things of Yucatán*, written in Spain after Landa was forced to return to his homeland, a sort of exile from his chosen exile. The book, a precursor of latter-day ethnographies, includes a wealth of details on domestic life and the Maya worldview that could only be gathered by someone who had been accepted into that society. The single most telling sign of that acceptance was the Maya elders' revelation to the young friar of the secret, sacred books kept in the possession of the ruling lineages. It was an unusual action on the part of the guarded elders to defy tradition by taking the outsider into their confidence, one that can only suggest the intimacy Landa had attained with the Maya.

By 1561, he was made Provincial, the head of the order in Yucatán. A year later, the cache of idols was discovered and the troubles in Maní began. Several weeks after the first auto-da-fé, Landa arrived in the village to assume supervision of the inquisition. He set up his court under the trees outside the monastery, and there, for the next three months, Landa interrogated and tortured more than 4,500 Maya, including people whom he had befriended during his missionary days. At least 158 people died during the inquiries.

Upstairs, I wandered through the dusty cells where the monks had lived out their days in a hostile exile. Looking out a window on the north side of the monastery, I spotted a little arbor of banana and avocado trees. I imagined Landa holding court right there, in the tropical shade, under the glistening fruit trees. I imagined him contemplating the fruits of paradise dangling over his head as he awaited the arrival of another miserable backslider. There was, in the patio, a working *noria*, a mule-powered well with two large creaking gears for drawing up the buckets; the device looked ancient enough to have been functioning since Landa's day. I imagined the mules continuing on their endless rounds while the tortured humans dangled from the hoist a few feet away. And I imagined the buckets being hauled up, spilling cool water, so that the inquisitor might soothe his parched throat in between interrogations.

I continued through the cells until I entered a long room, some sort of gathering place. I was several steps in, the floor boards groaning, when I noticed a sign warning against entry: *Danger. Unstable floor.* The sign was positioned where it could not be read until the trespasser had passed well into the room. Gingerly, I backed out of this trap and tried a narrow stairway that led to the belfry, only to run into a padlocked screen that prevented passage onto the roof. I was disappointed: I remembered that the explorer John Lloyd Stephens had stepped out onto this roof more than 150 years before and beheld a "boundless view of the great region." I peered through the screen at the same view (though mine was somewhat more bounded)—toward the distant line of the Puuc Hills and the surrounding villages. I could see the first signs of a storm on the horizon.

Looking down on the grassy atrium fronting the church, I was again struck by the contrast between the place's present tranquility and its violent past. On July 12, 1562, this square was the scene of pomp and pageantry and persecution, a strange occasion that defies the imagination. Landa decided to stage a grand auto-da-fé of his own, a ceremony more elaborate and more terrible in its display of the Church's supremacy than previous purges in Yucatán.

Preparations for the great event required contributions from the entire community. Maya women dyed cloth for the making of painted banners. Others prepared yellow scapulars painted with bright red Saint Andrew's crosses—the *sanbenitos* that penitents would wear in the ceremony. The friars supervised the construction of crosses that were to be shrouded in black cloth. A large wooden platform was built in the square for the Spanish dignitaries in attendance.

On that July day in 1562, beneath a broiling Yucatán sun, the Franciscan friars of Maní processed into the plaza, bearing black-shrouded crosses. The friars intoned their litanies while those selected for penance followed in their yellow and red garments. A mounted guard rode behind, the Spanish soldiers dressed in armor despite the sweltering heat.

All around the atrium, thousands of Maya had been forcibly gathered to witness the macabre rituals. What went through the minds of the indigenous crowd that day, I wondered, as they gazed upon the colorful assembly of friars and penitents and upon the huge heaps of masks, wooden statues, pottery vessels, and jeweled human skulls—the idols that had so horrified the priests. They listened to Landa deliver a sermon in Mayan. They heard the proclamation of the sentences imposed on the confessed idolaters. They watched as their kinsmen, already debilitated from torture, were tied to posts and lashed, watched as blood added its rich hue to the spectrum of the day, watched as streaked backs burned in the hot sun and the stained stones of the plaza seethed while hordes of flies descended. And then, after the ceremonies, the sermons, and the punishments, they had to watch as Landa set fire to the heap of so-called idols the friars had collected from the Maya after the tortures—five thousand objects in all. Before the bonfire died down, Landa pitched in twenty-seven hieroglyphic rolls, the precious folding codices, made of beaten-bark paper and deerskin covers, that contained the sacred writing of the Maya. But to Landa, the books were satanic, not sacred, containing "nothing in which there was not to be seen superstition and lies of the devil." He thus consigned them to the flames. And with that fell move, Landa transformed his bonfire into a holocaust as costly as the fire that destroyed the Alexandria library.

There is no record of the Maya reaction to all this, other than Landa's own words. From his perspective on the viewing platform, Landa thought "they all showed much repentance and readiness to be good Christians." He did note, however, with some surprise, that "they regretted to an amazing degree" the burning of the codices, "which caused them great affliction." Landa recorded these observations in his remarkable *Relación de las cosas de Yucatán* ("An Account of the Things of Yucatán"), which he wrote in the mid-1560s in his home monastery in Toledo, Spain. After conflict with the Bishop of Yucatán over the treatment of the Maya, Landa returned to Spain to drum up support for his position (and to defend his actions at Maní before the Council of the

Indies). While in Toledo, he wrote the *Relación*, a short but informative disquisition that covers the geography of the peninsula, the cultural practices of the Yucatán Maya, and the history of the Spanish presence in the territory.

Ironies and paradoxes abound in Landa's story, the most obvious of which is that the man who worked so hard to destroy Maya culture was the same man who diligently recorded details of the culture and left the world such a wealth of information about it that one scholar has stated, "ninety-nine percent of what we today know of the Mayas, we know as the result either of what Landa has told us . . . or have learned in the use and study of what he told." And yet, Landa's book is so important to us largely because Landa himself destroyed the very texts that would have been an even greater source of information on Maya history and culture. At first glance, the enigmatic and contradictory Landa seems characteristically medieval—cruel, bigoted, dogmatic; a destroyer of things alien to his narrow-minded view of truth. At the same time, however, Landa was a model modern, the precursor of so many Europeans who followed him into "primitive" lands—all the scientists, anthropologists, ethnographers, colonists, writers, and naturalists, among others, who made exacting records of the cultures and environments that their own enterprise was in the process of making available and accessible for destruction.

In the few minutes I stared down at the atrium and the scene of the great auto-da-fé, the storm clouds had grown bigger and darker. Thunder rumbled and the wind picked up. The storm soon came upon Maní and unleashed a hard rain. Just another afternoon shower, typical of the region in the rainy season. In July, such storms could be expected daily; I wondered if a storm had come up on that July day in 1562. Did Landa, knowing the likelihood of rain, plan the event for the morning hours? Did they rush to get through the lengthy ceremony as the storm clouds began building on the horizon? And did the rain, when it came at last, quench the smoldering ashes of the pyre? Did the Maya watch the sky, hoping the rain god Chac would interrupt the event, or at the very least send cleansing rains to wash away the stains? Or did the storm clouds hold off that day, the sky remaining a clear, shimmering, empty, and remorseless blue, like the eyes of the Spaniard gazing upon the spectacle from the makeshift stage?

The rain kept me cloistered in the monastery for nearly an hour. I sat on a bench under the arcade of the interior courtyard and drifted in a light sleep while listening to the thunder, to the water running off the roof, and to the voices of local children reciting the catechism, the hard lessons repeated over and over until learned by rote.

The rain finally diminished to a drizzle, and I woke up to take my groggy leave of Maní. At the door to the church, a dwarf sidled from the shadows to intercept me. He dragged a malformed leg behind him, the worn leather of his boot scraping on the floor and echoing in the cavernous church. He came toward me and stared hard. With his large head and big round eyes, he looked like some cave creature emerging from the depths. But as usual, first impressions deceived. A soft, clear voice belied the dwarf's seemingly grotesque appearance.

"Do you like our old church?" he asked. He nodded when I told him I did. "Yes, it is an interesting place with an interesting history." He was, he told me, the doorman of the church and the custodian. He rattled a ring of keys on his belt as confirmation of his status. Did I see everything, he wanted to know? The well? The stone cross? The painting of Santa Lucia? In his opinion, the carving on the *retablos* here at Maní was the best in all of Mexico. It was a shame more people did not come to see it. More visitors might mean more money for the preservation of the church. "It's not in good condition," he said.

I told him I had come because of Maní's place in the history of Yucatán. I had come to see the scene of Landa's great auto-da-fé. But I wondered why there was no marker, nothing to commemorate that history.

The doorkeeper looked up at me with a sad, wry smile and shook his head.

"Ah, well, that is another matter. How do you say *odio* in your language?'

Hatred, I said.

"Well, you see," he said, "here there is much *odio* for Diego de Landa. No, there can be no memorial to Landa here in Maní."

Driving Lessons

For the first five months of the two years that I lived in Guatemala City, I relied on city buses for transportation. This was not a bad way to get around. Yes, the buses were crowded—people jammed the aisles and hung out doors—but I found it entertaining and educational to mingle with the throng. By riding those old diesel-spewing Bluebirds (usually school buses retired from service in the States), I experienced a side of Guatemalan society that I would have otherwise missed.

But eventually my inbred American need for convenience, comfort, and privacy took over. I bought a car. And with a car, I had to learn to drive Central American style. It took some time to get used to negotiating the madcap streets of Guatemala City, but with experience and an understanding of the conventions of the road, I eventually got the hang of it.

In Guatemala, traffic lanes are entirely notional. Many main thoroughfares do not even have painted lane lines. You simply create a space for yourself and charge into it, swerving only to avoid a pedestrian or a pothole. Guatemalans pack as many cars as possible on the road. Calzada Roosevelt, for example, is a boulevard wide enough for about three normal lanes going in one direction. Usually, however, cars are squeezed four or five across, and in major traffic jams six lanes are somehow created in the same space. You can literally reach out and touch a passenger in the car next to yours. Once I saw a truck driver shout to a smoker two cars over for a light. Not missing a beat, the smoker passed his lighter into the car beside him, from which it was handed up to the truck. The lighter then made the return journey.

Of course, most of the time traffic is flowing too rapidly for such pleasantries. Whole lanes shift, form, and split apart in seconds. A rusted Datsun passes you on the left, then darts across your path and that of two other cars—no signal—to make a wild right turn. A truck expels a cloud of diesel smoke that leaves you and everyone else flailing in a black haze. A bus with ten people hanging out the door cuts you off as it careens toward a bus stop; just as it screeches to a halt you realize it has no brake lights. In such conditions, you must not look down to change the radio station. It is a risk even to glance in the rearview mirror, and probably a waste of time to boot: Guatemalan drivers say that whatever is behind you doesn't matter anyway.

After a few weeks, I realized what contributes most to the chaos: the tremendous variety of vehicles and other means of transport competing for limited space at—and this is the decisive factor—wildly disparate speeds. You can be cruising along at a fine clip when suddenly the column of cars in front of you parts and you find yourself jamming the brake pedal to the floor to keep from slamming into a dump truck barely poking along, while on either side cars shriek past at perhaps one hundred kilometers an hour, barely a gap between them.

But the trucks are not the slowest things on the road. Bicycles, mule-drawn trash wagons, goats, cows, fruit carts, and pedestrians also clog up traffic. The pedestrians are the worst. Since Guatemala's driving code gives vehicles the right of way over people, pedestrians are forced to dart across four lanes in the face of oncoming traffic. Scores of people stand in the middle of the road, waiting to advance a few feet at a time. To a driver, these darting pedestrians turn each intersection into a fast-moving video game. Many pedestrians carry huge bundles on their heads or their backs, making the athleticism of the sprint all the more impressive. Age doesn't matter. Septuagenarians take up the challenge with aplomb, stepping in front of cement trucks as if they don't exist, ignoring the blaring horns.

Guatemalan drivers rely upon their horns a great deal, employing them freely and creatively in all traffic situations. The most accomplished—such as bus and taxi drivers— achieve a sort of virtuoso command of their instrument, using it to trumpet their anger, their bravado, their triumphs, even their nihilistic despair. In heavy traffic, you can hear an apparent cacophony come together in a symphonic statement on the stress and angst of modern urban life.

To get anywhere in the capital you need to master the horn. Once, I was stalled behind a particularly faint-hearted driver who was indecisive about entering the flow of traffic. My Guatemalan passenger shouted *Bocínele! Bocínele!*—Honk at him! Honk at him!—until I pressed the horn and squeaked out a tiny and ineffective complaint, immediately lost in the general din. My friend lost all patience, leaned over to the horn, and blasted out a series of staccato notes, an angry invective that perfectly imitated the cadence of a particularly vulgar Spanish insult. The startled driver shot forward into traffic, narrowly missing a speeding cab, which promptly and abusively sounded out its annoyance. *Así se bocina*, my friend said, his frustration satisfactorily vented. *That* is how one sounds the horn.

Obviously, the horn is a necessary piece of equipment, more important than a muffler, judging from the noise of Guatemalan traffic. When, at the end of my stay, I had my car for sale, I dutifully told prospective buyers that the radio did not work. Ignoring this, they would ask, "What about the horn?" A car-shopping Guatemalan always tests the horn the way an American kicks the tires.

Drivers also communicate their intentions with hand signals. To announce a last-second lane change, to make a wild, dangerous turn, or to create a lane where none exists, Guatemalans wave their arms out the window, flapping them as though they are trying to get the car to fly. This is an especially amusing exercise when passengers get involved, leaning out windows and waving frantically as the driver tries to nudge you off the road.

Accidents occur constantly. Every morning's newspaper features accounts of pedestrians run down, cars smashed, buses out of control. When the accident is particularly gruesome, the newspaper publishes photos of the mangled mess—horrific, bloody photos far worse than anything shown in American drivers' ed shock films. These photos fail, however, to instill fear in the minds of Guatemalans, who in comparison with *gringos* are exceptionally fatalistic and will undertake risky, implausible maneuvers with a shrug of the shoulders. I was especially surprised at their apathy toward—and sometimes disdain for—simple precautions. Seatbelts, for example, are not used. In fact, many cars do not even have them, seatbelts being a luxury item, according to the tax code, and therefore subject to higher import duties.

Most accidents are routine fender benders, and I was involved in several during my driving career in Guatemala. In such cases, both drivers jump out, glance at the damage, and agree that nothing serious has happened. They agree on this even if the damage is obvious because, above all else, the drivers wish to avoid involving the police. Once the police get in on it, a minor dent turns into a legalistic mess. Both cars are impounded pending further investigations. Days and probably weeks are spent filling out forms, petitioning bureaucrats, responding to inquiries and—who knows?—perhaps even standing trial if the assessed damages prove significant.

Avoiding the police is a constant concern for drivers in Guatemala. Traffic cops are stationed at many large intersections to serve as human traffic lights. For whatever reason or caprice, these cops might whistle at a car, directing it to the side of the road. Traffic cops do not have vehicles, so it would be simple enough to ignore the whistle and drive on. But this is not wise. Once your license number has been taken down and your file subsequently red-flagged, you are sure at some time in the near future to face a bureaucratic nightmare—forms, fines, more forms, legal fees, still more forms. That threat is powerful enough to encourage most drivers to stop and deal with the cops on the spot. In Guatemala, traffic cops are less intimidating than government bureaucrats.

But the police are formidable enough. Sometimes they employ roadblocks and randomly stop vehicles. Since they carry automatic weapons, you would do well to stop. The subsequent inspection is slow and tedious, but the outcome is relatively simple: pay *la mordida* ("a little bite"—idiomatic Spanish for a bribe) and you will be allowed to drive off.

The officer begins with a minute examination of your papers—license, identification, passport, auto registration, and so on. Usually some minor discrepancy manifests itself during this scrutiny, and that discrepancy becomes the basis for the charge against you. If by chance your papers are in perfect order, the officer will describe for you in elaborate and nonsensical detail the nature of your traffic violation. Whatever the charge, it always comes down to the final negotiations for *la mordida*. These negotiations must be conducted according to a prescribed etiquette.

As an opening volley, the officer shakes his head and says that, regretfully, this particular violation can only be resolved at the precinct station and that he will have to accompany you there—not that you are being arrested, oh no, it's just that, well, this case must be handled only so. For the driver, an appropriate response is to feign dismay, look at your watch, and fret over an important appointment that you must keep in a few minutes—very important, you insinuate with the air of a person of consequence.

The officer expresses his sorrow at this circumstance—it troubles his heart—and then after a few moments of silence during which the officer pretends to ponder the matter, he shakes his head again and says something about the violation—ambiguous as it is—being very serious.

Now comes time for your big line. As casually as you can, and yet with a note of plaintive despair in your voice, you say, "Isn't there any other way to take care of this?" The officer, taking his cue, sighs, rubs his chin, makes as if he's thinking really hard, and then with great panache says, "Well, since the *señor's* appointment is so important, perhaps he can give me the requisite money for the fine, and I will see to it that the paperwork is completed."

At this point, all that remains is the haggling. With some tenacity, you can cut the requested "fine" in half, but after such an ordeal most Americans, unaccustomed to bargaining, happily forgo a protracted argument over two or three dollars.

The first few times I was pulled over, I tried to play it cool, use superlative Spanish, let the police know that I knew the game and could play it with the best of them. Unfortunately, this strategy backfired. By showing them that I knew the game, I was inviting them to play it, and I always ended up paying a bribe, all the heftier because, as a *gringo*, I was no doubt *muy rico*.

Eventually I learned that it was much smarter to play dumb. Toward the end of my stay in Guatemala, my revised strategy involved butchering the language and responding to questions with wild non sequiturs. I mispronounced everything with the exception of *embajada* and *iglesia*. I made sure they heard "embassy" and "church" clearly, and for support I kept a Bible on the front seat, opening it up and pointing to certain verses. Even the most determinedly corrupt cops had no interest in dealing with a crazy foreigner or a religious fanatic, and after a couple of minutes of this they would give up and wave me through.

The police are impossible to avoid and so are flat tires, judging from the number of people changing tires roadside. Every street of consequence, and many of no consequence, has numerous little shops offering *servicio de pinchazo*, or flat tire repair. It is common to see an indigenous Guatemalan plugging up a tire while an elegant lady waits by her BMW, fanning herself. There are two reasons for the preponderance of flats: first, people tend to drive their tires until they are smooth as blotters; second, during rainy season literally tons of debris washes onto the roads—glass, nails, screws, shards of metal. The trick, as a friend told me, is to drive as much as possible in the middle of the road, avoiding the muck-filled margins. Of course, when all drivers are trying to do this, another dimension of intrigue is added to Guatemala's mean streets.

Deterioration also adds to the difficulty. Potholes, for example, can expand phenomenally in Guatemala City. I saw some potholes that an Olympic long jumper could not have leapt across. Every now and then, an unwary driver loses his front end to a pothole. The car, its front tires completely beneath the surface of the road and its punctured radiator or oil pan spraying, has to be lifted from the pothole by a gang of men. Someone sticks a tree branch in the pothole to indicate the danger until a few weeks later, when a road crew appears and places an orange sign—*Peligro!*—by what is now a ditch.

The roads in Guatemala City undergo daily visible change, continually eroding and transforming. Rains, heavy traffic, and inferior materials (often donated by wealthier nations who have no use for them) all contribute to the rapid dissolution of the roads.

With several hundred thousand vehicles operating in the capital, traffic would be bad enough on perfect roads. On deteriorated streets, traffic slows to an iguana's pace. The government occasionally attempts projects designed to alleviate congestion, but work on these projects is slow and uncertain. Funding can vanish, either because of prohibitive costs or corruption. Many a project is started and abandoned leaving behind a bigger mess and more congestion. Guatemalans themselves just shrug. What are you going to do?

After a while, I became tired of driving around Guatemala City. It wasn't that I couldn't handle the chaos, the confusion, or the stress. What finally got to me was an overwhelming sense of despair that gripped me whenever I drove anywhere. After running an errand downtown or driving to the shopping center, I would return exhausted and depressed. Driving around town, you can't help but see all that is wrong with the city and getting worse—an overtaxed infrastructure; lack of effective, purposeful government regulation (as every black cloud of exhaust from thousands of malfunctioning exhaust pipes reminds you); and worst of all, the jarring juxtaposition of great wealth and abject poverty, and the misery that the one inflicts on the other. It's not merely that you see all this—you can see it from a bus or a taxi just as well—but as a driver you *participate* in it in a way that you do not as a detached passenger. You participate in the congestion, in the pollution (the first thing you do when you bring an American car to Guatemala is remove the catalytic converter so that you can burn leaded gasoline, the only kind available), and in the disparity between rich and poor, as you—one of the *ricos*—spew your leaded exhaust on the subsistence vendors and the beggars who fill whatever space on the street that the vehicles leave unoccupied.

Maybe it was encountering these vendors and beggars that depressed me most of all. Walking around the city, I passed them all the time, but as a pedestrian I felt more ordinary, still a human being, with a little something in common with the vendor and even the beggar. A car on the other hand, is power. It enables you to lord it over those who stand, crawl, or sit, puny and powerless, in the streets, holding up bars of soap, bunches of bananas, or just a soiled, empty palm.

I found it hard to believe the number of people who made their living as subsistence vendors in the middle of traffic. Men, women, and children work every good-sized intersection in the city. For a *quetzal*—twenty cents—a boy will race over and drop fifteen or twenty bananas onto your seat. A couple of *quetzales* get you your choice of flower bouquets. Toilet paper, perfume, and chewing gum are among the items commonly for sale in the middle of the streets. The men, women, and children who sell them practice the most basic and brutal kind of capitalism—always on the brink of destitution, no future beyond whatever can be sold on a particular day, hostage to the whims of a market that has far more supply than demand.

But even these vendors are better off than the beggars, who have nothing to sell except whatever guilt and pity their wretchedness might wrench from passing drivers. Every kind of grotesquerie is on display along Guatemala's roadways—the maimed, the crippled, the deformed, the mad—all dependent for survival on your charity.

Would it be maudlin to say that my heart broke to see these people—the legless men sliding between cars on crude boards fitted with wheels, the barefoot mothers of five covered in dirt and insects, their scarified children in rags? Was it just a jejune exercise, a guilt-ridden reflex, that I always gave them whatever change I had? Or should I confess the truth: at times the beggars exasperated me. They were tiresome and annoying. I tried to time intersections so that I drove right through, preventing any confrontation. The presence of beggars raised moral questions too vexing to confront when I merely wanted to go to the supermarket. Driving around town led to introspection that was, frankly, more than I could bear.

Late at night, Guatemala's streets are haunted by children. They dart in and out of the eerie glow of your headlights cutting through the city's perpetual haze. Driving down the now empty boulevards through the windblown trash the street vendors have left behind, you see them huddled in doorways, the smaller ones wrapping themselves in newspaper blankets or curling like kittens in castoff cardboard boxes. The older ones sniff glue from plastic bags, seeking a buzz that will ward off hunger pangs and the chill of the night, or that will dull them to the beatings inflicted by the police—the kicks, the truncheon blows, the pistol-whippings.

Even past midnight, a solitary motorist is appealed to by scores of children—ten, seven, four years old. They emerge from the shadows of cypress and jacaranda trees to press up against any vehicle that stops. Dirty, barefoot, coughing—mucus drying on their cracked lips—they extend their hands, silently imploring the motorist for any spare change, even five *centavos*, enough to buy two tortillas. Their breath mists on the rolled-up windows of the car. Their fingerprints smudge the glass, an indelible mark that will not wash off even in the torrential rains of a tropical downpour.

Poetry in a Dangerous Time

P oetry surrounds you in Guatemala. There's the landscape with all its impossible variety bunched into a small part of the globe; there's the attire of the indigenous people, overwhelming the eye with the expressiveness of the spectrum; there are the sensual cries and whispers of the country's many languages; the constant presence of passion and cruelty. The sublime and terrible crowd into every tableau. Music and image permeate the place. Guatemala breathes poetry, Guatemala hums with poetry.

During the two years I lived in Guatemala, I heard it everywhere. Poets wrote columns for the daily newspaper. Poets read their works on national radio. Newscasters quoted poets. In the hallways of the university, students posted their occasional poems. When I was introduced as a literature professor and a writer, students and colleagues spontaneously began to recite for me entire poems by Neruda, Darío, and García Lorca.

On several occasions, I went to parties that culminated in recitations. After a long night of grilling meat, drinking toasts, dancing, and then singing along to the accompaniment of acoustic guitar, someone would begin reciting a poem. When the recitation was finished, everyone clapped, another round was poured, and someone else recited. Round after round it went, some poems drawing laughter, some provoking tears, all eliciting sighs of satisfaction. So profound was the Guatemalans' appreciation for poetry that I was prevailed upon to recite in English, even though few of the partygoers understood English. They wanted the music of language, the visceral feel of poetry, the sound more than the sense. They assumed that a professor of literature would have a great repertoire of memorized poems. Caught off guard on the first occasion, I was lucky to pull off paraphrases of Frost's "Stopping by Woods" and Robinson's "Richard Cory." After that, I set about memorizing some sonnets for future parties.

Perhaps the most amazing recitals I witnessed took place aboard city buses. The buses roared around Guatemala City's narrow, congested streets, spewing clouds of exhaust, with people jamming the aisles and doorways. You were lucky to get a seat, and if you did you were crammed with two other adults on a bench seat, along with a hen or two. Despite the inconveniences, riding on the city buses was enlightening and always entertaining. I learned more about Guatemala from those bus rides than I did anywhere else. Bus riding was particularly good for language learning. Sometimes you couldn't hear a thing because the bus lacked a muffler or the driver had a *merengue* station on high volume. But other times it was possible to carry on a conversation, or eavesdrop on someone else's.

And often enough, when the aisle was relatively free, a peripatetic vendor would board the bus and hawk his wares. These peddlers gave amazing performances. They would stand by the driver, call for attention, hold up their product (usually something health-related—a special herb or ointment, a newfangled toothbrush) and begin a long, well-rehearsed oration on the benefits and wonders of the product. Even as the bus bounced over potholes, swerved through traffic, or lunged around corners, the vendor maintained his balance and decorum with hardly a twitch, continuing with his speech in a rich, flowing, practiced voice. The Spanish was beautiful—clearly pronounced, rhetorically impressive, wonderful to listen to. I was entranced.

One day when I was riding the bus downtown, a man in an indigenous poncho boarded the bus and stood solemnly at the front of the aisle, one hand resting gently on the back of the first seat. Apparently the driver knew the man, for he turned off the radio in anticipation of his performance.

Without introduction, his eyes fixed in a histrionic gaze on the rear ceiling of the bus, the man began to recite poetry, half-speaking, half-chanting in a manner that for me suggested the kind of poet I had only read about—the troubadour, the mead-hall singer, the chanter of lays and epics. I listened intently. His practiced diction, his emotional intonation, his dramatic bearing all belied his appearance. He looked, in fact, like almost any beggar on the street in his odd hodgepodge of shoddy clothes, his laceless shoes of scuffed leather. But he was captivating. Everybody on the bus, even young children, seemed to pay attention as we careened through the capital's madcap streets—now screeching to a halt to let aboard new passengers, now accelerating around a corner, narrowly missing a donkey cart. Through it all the poetry man, this bard of the bus, concentrated on his art, raising his voice in drama, hushing it in grief.

I couldn't understand it all. What I did understand I suspected was not particularly great poetry; it sounded like patriotic and sentimental doggerel. But that was not the point. For me, the remarkable thing was that a busload of people sat quiet and even rapt as a man recited poetry for them. I could think of nothing like it in the States, except perhaps for the rappers on street corners and in subway stations of the inner city.

When he finished, no one applauded. A few people sighed, or nodded, and one old man, dapper in a three-piece suit of old-fashioned cut, dabbed at his eyes. Almost all of us dropped a few coins in the soiled palm of the poetry man as he passed down the aisle. At the next stop, he vanished out the door.

Guatemala's poetic ambiance fascinated me because I had come to the country to teach US literature—contemporary poetry being my particular interest—at the Universidad de San Carlos. My sojourn at the university as a Fulbright lecturer had been arranged by the United States Information Service office at the American Embassy, but there were logistical problems from the start. The embassy people brought me down in September, apparently unaware that the academic year in Guatemala runs from late January to early November, so that I was arriving just in time for the final weeks of the term. Because of my late arrival, I had very little to do other than visit some English language classes as a "distinguished visitor" (Guatemalans love titles and lavish epithets; even good friends called me *el doctor*). In these classes I answered questions about everything from North American weather to country music to vulgar idiomatic expressions used in Hollywood movies.

When the new year finally began, I was eager to meet my first class, "Contemporary American Literature." The students, advanced in the study of comparative literature, would read in English; but the class would be conducted in Spanish to facilitate conversation. I put together a small poetry collection of Robert Lowell, Elizabeth Bishop, Anne Sexton, Sylvia Plath, and more recent poets such as James Wright, William Stafford, Adrienne Rich, and Sharon Olds. For the most part, the classes went well, despite my inexact command of literary terminology. The students politely and discreetly corrected me after class when, for example, I used the word for "caricatures" instead of "characters." Discussion was lively and the students offered interesting and intelligent observations about the poetry, even when language and context proved difficult.

Several weeks into the course, I brought in some poems exemplifying the so-called confessional school of poetry. After reading them and clarifying some of the difficult passages, I spoke a bit about the origins of the confessional school, and some of the distinguishing characteristics of the poetry categorized as such. Just then, a young man made a comment that changed the direction the course had been taking. "It seems to me," he said, "that all the American poetry we are reading is just like this—confessional."

I was caught a little off guard—after all, the poems I had brought in thus far had represented a number of different schools and movements of contemporary American poetry, and my training made it difficult for me to see as "confessional," poets who I knew were "deep image" or "objectivist." Interested in his observation and a bit puzzled, I asked the student to elaborate. He pointed out that all the US poetry we had looked at was, though no doubt beautiful and powerful, essentially self-absorbed, even solipsistic. He wondered if contemporary American poets ever looked beyond themselves and their own limited landscape. Did any US poets engage with the world, especially in a political sense? Several students nodded in agreement as the young man spoke; I later learned that this question had been the concern of several after-class discussions in the cafeteria of the humanities building—the favored site for intellectual and political conversation. (The cafeteria itself revealed something of the students' concerns; one wall featured a mural, sponsored by the Association of Humanities Students—"the Revolutionary Student Vanguard"—that depicted a crowd led by a student raising his fist. The mural's epigraph suggested the nexus of poetry and politics: "We swear that freedom will push its naked flower through the violated sand.")

I understood the bent of the question. For almost half a century, Central America's most renowned poets had been activists and even martyrs: Otto René Castillo of Guatemala, who joined the guerrillas and died; Roque Dalton of El Salvador, who met a similar fate; and Ernesto Cardenal of

Nicaragua, a prominent figure in the Sandinista movement. For Central Americans, poetry and political activism were inextricable. I knew all too well that no US poet could match that level of commitment. I knew too that in poetry circles back in the States there had been a long-running debate about whether political content was even possible in poetry. I myself had sat in a poetry workshop as a student and listened to a renowned poet attack and dismiss the political poetry of Carolyn Forché, Robert Bly, Amiri Baraka, Denise Levertov, and others. The Guatemalan students' observations, incisive as they were, merited a thoughtful response.

To answer the students extemporaneously, I told them that US poets often debated this same question, with the anti-politics advocates tending to hold sway. I promised to bring in some examples of Vietnam protest poems, Forché's Salvador poems, and other works that meditated on social and political concerns (I had in mind, for example, C. K. Williams's "Tar"). I also suggested that even the most confessional poems could be read with political overtones, as many feminist critics were now pointing out, since these poems frequently addressed power structures such as patriarchy.

I was pleased with this disruption in the syllabus because I liked political poetry (or, the "poetry of witness," as it is sometimes called), but until then I had been reluctant to bring in overtly political work like Forché's. The embassy had cautioned me to avoid political issues, especially at San Carlos, which was regarded as a somewhat dangerous place for an American. In subsequent classes, however, I brought in a number of politically oriented poems and works by African American and US Latino poets. The class reacted with enthusiasm, but noted that even poems with an overt social "message" still seemed preoccupied with the poet as an individual—"Tar," in fact, illustrating just this point.

The campus of the national university certainly had a charged political atmosphere. Every building, virtually every wall, featured a large mural done by one of the many student organizations on campus. These murals depicted vivid scenes of revolutionary marches or dramatic and symbolic tableaus. My favorite was a grotesque CIA spider spinning a hemispheric web and devouring Latin American peasants. Rallies were held constantly in the courtyards of the building and in the main plaza outside the administration building. Fiery speeches by students and faculty addressed pressing national issues, and there were many pressing issues in a country that had experienced thirty years of civil war.

San Carlos was without question the most politicized place in the country, but the university had paid a horrible price for its political involvement. Students and faculty were often "disappeared," victims of Guatemala's nebulous death squads and other paramilitary groups. This repression was particularly bad in the early 1980s, when military dictatorships governed the country. In 1980 and 1981, some three hundred members of the San Carlos community were assassinated. One thousand more either disappeared or went into exile. Jeeps with darkened windows, the typical vehicle used in death squad actions, were often parked outside school buildings. In 1984, sixty-four students were disappeared or killed, and two economics professors were gunned down on their way to a rally. Students rubbed San Carlos decals off their cars and carried their IDs in their shoes—it was that dangerous to be identified as San Carlos students. But the worst came in 1985 when, on September 3, after several mass marches and demonstrations on the campus, troops invaded the university. Tanks rolled onto the campus, while soldiers ransacked files, broke up desks, spray painted over murals, and generally ran riot for four days. Three years later, when I arrived, piles of debris could still be seen. In the month of my arrival, thirteen students disappeared. Their tortured bodies were later found dumped in a roadside ditch outside the capital. The newspaper reported that they were murdered by *desconocidos*—"unknowns."

The biggest political event on campus was a weeklong, student-organized protest called the *huelga de dolores*, the "strike of sorrows." An annual event since the end of the nineteenth century, the *huelga* shut down classes for an entire week while students dressed in gowns and hoods blocked the entrances to the university. To get on campus, you had to purchase a pass that, placed on your windshield, demonstrated your support for the *huelga*. In return for a contribution, you received copies of student-produced literature—broadsides and lampoons full of political satire, usually based on clever word play, that criticized the government, the university administration, the United States, or whatever was the object of political scorn that season.

The weeklong protests ended with a parade. This was a raucous event of banners, floats, and chants—all mocking the hypocrisy of national institutions. The first *huelga* that I saw played on the theme of avocados, meant to draw attention to a remote village called El Aguacate—the Spanish word for avocado. It was in El Aguacate that, a few months previously, the army had massacred twenty people. During the parade, an effigy of the president was constantly pelted with the overripe fruit, so that afterwards the entire downtown was strewn with a green and black mess, as though a giant tank of guacamole had exploded. The satire was fun and funny. Both observers and students had a good time. Nevertheless, there was a bitter edge to the event that bespoke the anger and disillusionment these idealistic young people felt toward their country's traditional powers. Nor was the military much amused. One year, the military police attacked a group of students as they prepared a float. One student was killed. Fifteen later disappeared.

A few days before the *huelga*, as we were finishing the section on political poetry, I happened to mention to the class that a less canonical poetry had gained some attention in the United States. I described the poetry slams that I had seen in Chicago, and told the class that the political intentions of such events were as important as the poetic. Protest was often the principal motivation behind the poetry. I told the class that such events constituted a sort of poetry underground.

After class, Roderico—the young man who had first raised the issue of political poetry—stayed behind to ask me about the poetry slams. In Guatemala, too, he told me, there were similar events connected to the *huelga*—an open reading of political satires and protest poems by student poets. He wondered if I would care to attend. We made arrangements to meet on the evening of the reading at a bar called *Cofradia de Godot*, the "Brotherhood of Godot."

On the appointed evening, I made my way to the bar by bus. I was early, earlier than Roderico anyway, and for half an hour I sat uncomfortably alone, drinking a beer and wondering how many people in the place suspected me of being a CIA plant. Once Roderico arrived, however, all tension was relieved. A poet himself, he was well known in the underground literary scene. A crowd gathered around Roderico, and soon we were part of a long table of young people chatting and arguing about everything from politics to soccer. To one side, a man played guitar while a group around him sang the songs of Víctor Jara, the Chilean musician who had died during Pinochet's fascist takeover. Several joints were passed around. Empty bottles of beer and *aguardiente* littered the table. Someone was telling me that Fidel Castro had frequented this same bar during his brief time in Guatemala, long before the success of the Cuban Revolution.

Eventually, the reading began. Several poets recited in turn. The crowd was vociferous, responding to lines with cheers and cries of *presente*. I had a hard time following the poems, but I caught several words and phrases—*yanqui* and Reagan came up several times, along with puns on the Guatemalan president's name. It was, I thought, quite similar to American "slams," but I also felt there was something tangibly different in the mood of the event. I got the sense that we were looking over our shoulders; I at least was worried that security forces or paramilitary goons would burst through the door at any moment. I recalled a story about some *desconocidos*—the newspaper code word for death squads—who had invaded a nightclub and sprayed acid on the dancers. Surely this poetry reading was more seditious in the eyes of the authorities than disco dancing.

This furtiveness added a sense of urgency to the poetry. The slams I had seen in the States were counter-cultural, but not exactly seditious. Their tone was raucous and angry, with maybe a note of disillusionment; but at the same time, American slams involved a good deal of play-acting and posing. The Guatemalan reading was more urgent because of what was at stake—not just a sense of identity, but a question of life and death.

After a number of poets had read, the lights went out: presumably another power outage. At first, there were catcalls and hoots of laughter, but as things settled down to an eerie silence I felt the urgency intensify and a rush of fear passed through me and throughout the room. Roderico told me later that he understood my fear. It was in everybody's mind at that moment, he said, that perhaps the electricity had been cut for the *Godot* alone—a sign that a death squad was moving in. But the moment passed. Someone came in from outside and announced that the power was out all over that sector of the city. The guerrillas had dynamited another transformer. Immediately, the tension vanished. A cheer went up. The guerrillas had dynamited a transformer! Another blow to the military! *Que vivan los guerrilleros!* Candles were brought out and the poetry reading continued in the bronze glow of candlelight for another hour or so.

When the reading ended, it was too late for the buses, so Roderico offered me a ride home on his motor scooter. Outside, the wind rustled the trash in the gutter and turned the night chilly. I thought of the cold wind that harried a group of homeless people in the opening pages of *El Señor Presidente*, a novel by Guatemala's Nobel laureate, Miguel Ángel Asturias. The idea of bone-chilling cold in the tropics had seemed improbable to me before I had come to Guatemala; now I shivered as we rode through the unlit streets.

Normally, I would have been terrified to ride on a scooter through Guatemala's congested and crazy streets. But there was no traffic now. In the evening, Guatemala City shut down completely. The years of curfew were officially over, but the curfew mentality remained. Our trip was made eerier still by the power outage. We puttered through the darkened downtown and then out through the barrios where, in the hovels, cooking fires gave off ghostly flickers. As we neared my house, we passed a dark jeep parked for no apparent reason at an intersection. When we went past it, the jeep suddenly lit up the street with its bright beams, the engine roared on, the vehicle came up behind us and followed us for a few nerve-wracking blocks until we turned into the upscale neighborhood where I lived. Then it veered off in another direction. Even after Roderico had left me at my door, I continued to tremble.

It had been an insignificant moment; nothing had happened, nothing unusual for Guatemala anyway. But in those few minutes, riding through the darkened city, pursued by an ominous vehicle, I had a glimpse into what it was like to be a poet and an activist in Guatemala.

Coda: The Longest Road

for Ed Cloud, in memoriam

My most deeply rooted memories of the Christmas season are associated with the road. For me, winter vacation means a long journey westward across the varied terrains of the continental United States. Unbroken Midwestern fields, their dead stalks half buried in snow. Desolate vistas of the dry plains. Snow-filled crags in the southern Rockies. High deserts lying in cold contemplation, and warmer lowland deserts, blistering and shimmering below sea level. All leading at last to a magical glide into glittering Los Angeles, city of my Christmas reveries.

During my grade school years, my family lived cross-country from my parents' native Southern California. Every year, though there was too little money and not enough time, an inevitable longing overcame my parents as the holidays approached. It was Christmas time and they wanted nothing more than to be in California with their families. After a long night of hushed discussion, they gave in to desire, woke us children before dawn, loaded down the Chevy like it was a caravan camel, and off we went on a journey nearly as epic, wonderful, and uncertain as the magi's two thousand years before.

In those days, the way west followed Route 66. Beginning in Chicago, the great highway unraveled in quirky curves and twists and long straightaways all the way to California. There was nothing monotonous about it. Each mile revealed something unusual, something worthy of a postcard or a father's comment: "Hey, kids, will you look at that? Now there's something you don't see every day." It could be anything—a motor court of concrete teepees, a roadside attraction featuring rattlesnakes, or the world's largest totem pole. The endless wonders of Route 66 gave the highway a mythic stature no other American road can claim.

For me, a small boy, those long drives west had a profound influence on my later fondness for the American West. I recall sitting in the back seat wiping mist off the cold pane to stare at the landscape unfolding before me. Those were the days before interstate freeways turned travel into what is now an enervating repetition of identical interchanges— the same fast food franchises, the same hotel chains whether you are in Georgia or Minnesota. Back then, highway travel was charged with a kind of magic: each town held out the promise of something new, something different, and quite possibly something astonishing. For one thing, the old highways routed you right through every little town—right down Main Street, in fact, where the eccentricities of each isolated hamlet were displayed to the traveler. And since you were forced to slow down from sixty to twenty-five miles per hour (maybe even forced to sit for thirty seconds at the town's only stoplight), you got a glimpse of things strange and wonderful. Who knew what would come next: an Indian trading post perhaps, or a ghost town graveyard, or a couple of giant arrows stuck in the ground for no apparent reason.

Even the filling stations contributed to the fun. In those days, filling stations had first names—Bob's Standard, Hank's Esso, Gus's Last Chance Texaco, Gus himself waddling out to do the pumping. And they had architectural gimmicks like thirty-foot high statues of dinosaurs or lumberjacks or war-bonneted Indians. Some stations had sublime attractions inside, such as a box with a peephole and a sign: "LIVE! Baby Rattlers—see 'em for a quarter!" And when you paid and peeked, you saw only a pile of plastic baby toys, and then Old Gus came up behind you, chortling at his great joke and rewarding you with a stick of gum for being a good sport.

Of course, there were trials along the way: a snowstorm, for example, obliterating the road outside of Amarillo; or a tortuous night in a motel that abutted a Southern Pacific switching yard, all night long the trains banging, bumping, skirling. Then, too, there were the several occasions we ran out of gas in some hinterland, miles and miles beyond Gus's Last Chance Texaco. In the belief that in the next town gas would surely be cheaper than what the highway robbers in Hicksville were charging ("Thirty-eight cents a gallon, can you believe that?"), my father would drain the tank to just about the last drop—a constant torment to my mother— only to end up fuming at the price he was forced to pay in Podunk. If in fact we made it to Podunk. More than once, the rest of us sat stranded on the roadside, big trucks roaring by, and watched the disappearing speck of my father heading across Big Sky country or Lonesome Prairie country or High Chaparral country toward some outpost of civilization that may or may not exist on the horizon. But sure enough, an hour or two later he'd arrive riding shotgun in Gus's Last Chance Texaco tow-truck, jolly old Gus dispensing gas and giving sticks of gum to the good little buckaroos who'd been so tolerant of their father's foolhardiness.

Despite these occasional trials, I was mesmerized by the journey, and in my memory the ride out Route 66 remains a series of stirring sights: snow flurries whipping the wreaths and candy canes hung from lampposts in small Oklahoma towns; the neon lights of Tucumcari's motel strip, electric saguaros and bucking broncos ticking on and off in the desert night; the beautiful, mysterious sound of the word "Albuquerque" on signposts—then the city itself, with its chicken yards and adobe hovels, unlike anything I'd ever seen before; trading posts set against the red rock cliffs of Gallup; a chilly diner in Flagstaff on a day so frigid the food was cold before the waitress could serve it.

The critical point of the journey came somewhere in Arizona, the sun sinking low on our third or fourth day on the road. After whispered front-seat discussions, my parents would turn to us and ask if we wanted to stop at a motel or drive through the night to L. A. By then, our excitement was uncontainable. Bouncing on the seat, we chorused for California. My father—having already put in a six hundred-mile day—hunkered down for the final two-fifty. Despite the fervor inspired by imminent arrival, I eventually fell asleep in the backseat, knowing that come what may my father would get us to Los Angeles before dawn. Sometime in the middle of the night, I stirred momentarily when he cracked the window and warm desert air rushed in over my face. Then in the small hours, I found myself being lifted from the car, a perfume of citrus and oleander and eucalyptus filling my nostrils with the scent of California, the scent, for me, of Christmas.

Contrary to popular imagery, Christmas is, in my mind, a warm weather holiday. It suggests to me not snowmen or sleds or icicles, but cobwebbed orange groves, dewy palm fronds, and sand castles on the beach. It also suggests to me long family conversations that inevitably came around at some point or another to the topic of driving. Among my relatives, long-distance driving has always been the favorite topic of conversation. As a boy, I listened, enthralled, to the adults tell and tell again their sometimes humorous, sometimes hair-raising accounts of epic drives. There were stories of desert breakdowns, summit crossings in snowstorms, fogs so thick highways vanished. My father was particularly good at telling road stories. A born speaker and a trained lecturer, he could go on and on about cars and roads, reciting amazing tales of near catastrophes, enormous obstacles, and feats of endurance.

But my father's academic loquacity could always be quelled by the taciturn grunts of my blue-collar grandfather. "Huh, that's nothing," Grandpa blurted after my father or anyone else had gone on for a spell about some particularly trying circumstance. No one had driven more in a day than Grandpa had; no one had been through worse storms or bounced over worse roads or had to overcome more catastrophic vehicle failures than he. With one scoffing grunt, he would dismiss your great story, then launch into his own tall tale: "Shoot, that's nothing. Why, one time going up Grapevine Hill—" It was a source of amusement—and some frustration—to the rest of the family; no one could top the old man.

When I reached adulthood and had a family of my own, it was my turn to pack up the car and drive home for the holidays. My first few entries into the family travel log were none too impressive—humdrum one or two-day jaunts on perfectly smooth interstates, gas cheap and plentiful along the way, my late model car embarrassingly equipped with a stereo and cruise control. Hardly driving at all, my grandfather would say. "How was the trip?" he asked when I arrived. "Oh, just fine," I was forced to admit while he and my male relatives tried to conceal wry smirks. "No problems to speak of."

Then fate led me far from home, and I found myself living well beyond the pale (and the border for that matter) in Central America. December came around and the kids wanted desperately to visit Grandma and Grandpa in Ohio for Christmas. At first I rejected the idea; the airfare was just too exorbitant. But then one day as I stood in a Guatemalan market listening to a marimba band play "Silver Bells," a crazy notion crossed my mind. Why not drive? After all, a road connected Guatemala and Ohio—a rather long and uncertain road, to be sure, but if I made the drive, if I could actually pull it off, I would have the best driving story of them all. Five of us. Guatemala to Ohio. In a subcompact Dodge.

Not surprisingly, my family said I was crazy and tried to talk me out of it. But I was resolved, not only because I didn't have the money to fly, but also because I had a point to prove.

It took me five days to prove that point. First, twelve hours in ninety degree heat to cover two hundred miles and leave Guatemala. Then two days to cross Mexico, driving only in daylight because the lack of painted lines and guardrails made nighttime driving in Mexico perilous. We made the US border on the fourth day. The trip to this point had been arduous but not awful. We met with only minor difficulties: getting lost trying to follow the highway through a maze-like Mexican town, uncertainty over where to get gas or cash traveler's checks. But we had been out of touch for those four days, unaware of what was going on in the wider world. When we reached the border, without warning, we met with the unexpected: an epic arctic cold front that had been racing south as we pushed north. A "polar vortex," the radio weatherman called it. The temperature dropped steadily every mile we went. Corpus Christi registered fifteen degrees, the town's coldest reading ever. The next morning, an ice storm turned Houston's freeways into a long skating rink. Wind-driven snow forced us to go no more than thirty miles per hour all the way to Louisiana. But north of Baton Rouge, we drove out of the belt of Gulf Coast moisture. Up ahead, the road was free of ice, making the driving relatively easy despite the arctic blast, and so we kept going, afraid to stop for the night lest the car freeze up and refuse to start come morning.

Everywhere we went, the temperature dropped to all-time lows—zero in Jackson, minus five in Memphis, minus ten in Louisville. For the second straight night we pushed on without stopping, my wife and I taking turns, the kids huddled in the back seat, the contents of our suitcases piled on top of them for warmth.

Somewhere in Kentucky, about three AM, with the outside temperature far below zero, we reached the extreme. Even with the heater on full blast, frost covered every window in the car. Only a small band across the lower third of the windshield remained clear. Two feet from the vents, the heat completely dissipated. I chastised myself for attempting such a foolish stunt; with no other traffic on the freeway, the slightest car trouble would mean certain death. I noted the odometer reading each time we passed an exit so that when the inevitable breakdown occurred, I'd know how far back I'd have to go. Of course, the information was pointless—I'd probably freeze to death inside of a mile—but I felt better making preparations for the worst.

Now and then we passed a dark, deserted mall, and I saw parking lot lampposts decorated with the same candy canes and wreaths I'd seen in those small towns along Route 66 years before. On those Christmas drives of yore, the sight had seemed beautiful; now, at four in the morning, twenty below zero on I-65 in Kentucky, it all seemed sinister and ominous. I was certain we wouldn't make it.

But the car never quit. Darkness gave way to a bitter cold dawn, Kentucky yielded to Ohio, and we drove the final hundred miles into Columbus just in time for Christmas Eve. Basking in the warmth of my mother's kitchen, recounting my story to relatives, I began to appreciate the magnitude of the venture. Sixty straight hours of driving from Veracruz to Columbus. A temperature change of more than one hundred degrees in forty-eight hours. Courting disaster with every mile. Truly it was a tale that couldn't be beat.

Later, I found my grandfather alone in the darkened living room. He stood by the window, Christmas tree lights silhouetting his diminished, aging frame. Outside, a light snow eddied in the arctic wind. He let a few minutes go by, watching as the evening went dark. Finally, he asked his question:

"So tell me, how far'd you drive, son?"

"About four thousand miles."

He was quiet again and I waited. Then he scoffed.

"Is that all?" he said at last. "Shoot, I thought you said you drove a long ways."

I felt a surge of annoyance, an urgent need to protest his obstinacy. I hadn't expected accolades from him. I had just wanted him to acknowledge my accomplishment. I had wanted to share with him the rigors of the journey. Yet he had rebuffed me in his usual gruff fashion. Grandpa, I wanted to say, don't you know what I went through during those four thousand miles?

But the anger passed when I saw his weathered face in the Christmas-light glow, the wrinkles so like the lines of a road map. I saw in those lines that Grandpa did share the journey. He had been there and back, many times over. He knew all about those four thousand miles and thousands beyond that.

I put my hand on his shoulder. "Merry Christmas, Grandpa," I said. And together we stood at the cold pane, watching the snow swirl down.

About the Author

Stephen Benz is the author of two books of travel essays: *Guatemalan Journey* and *Green Dreams*. He lives in Albuquerque, New Mexico and teaches at the University of New Mexico.

Books from Etruscan Press

Etruscan Press Is Proud of Support Received From

Wilkes University

Youngstown State University

The Raymond John Wean Foundation

The Ohio Arts Council

The Stephen & Jeryl Oristaglio Foundation

The Nathalie & James Andrews Foundation

The National Endowment for the Arts

The Ruth H. Beecher Foundation

The Bates-Manzano Fund

The New Mexico Community Foundation

Founded in 2001 with a generous grant from the Oristaglio Foundation, Etruscan Press is a nonprofit cooperative of poets and writers working to produce and promote books that nurture the dialogue among genres, achieve a distinctive voice, and reshape the literary and cultural histories of which we are a part.

etruscan press

www.etruscanpress.org

Etruscan Press books may be ordered from

Consortium Book Sales and Distribution

800.283.3572

www.cbsd.com

Etruscan Press is a 501(c)(3) nonprofit organization.
Contributions to Etruscan Press are tax deductible
as allowed under applicable law.
For more information, a prospectus,
or to order one of our titles,
contact us at books@etruscanpress.org.